THE GREEK–TURKISH]
AND NATO

THE GREEK–TURKISH RELATIONSHIP AND NATO

FOTIOS MOUSTAKIS

Britannia Royal Naval College, Dartmouth

FRANK CASS
LONDON • PORTLAND, OR

First published in 2003 in Great Britain by
FRANK CASS PUBLISHERS
Crown House, 47 Chase Side, Southgate
London N14 5BP

and in the United States of America by
FRANK CASS PUBLISHERS
c/o ISBS, 920 NE 58th Avenue, Suite 300
Portland, OR 97213-3786

Website: www.frankcass.com

British Library Cataloguing in Publication Data

Moustakis, Fotios
    The Greek–Turkish relationship and NATO
    1. North Atlantic Treaty Organization 2. Greece – Foreign
    relations – 1974 – 3. Turkey – Foreign relations – 1980 –
    4. Greece – Foreign relations – Turkey 5. Turkey – Foreign
    relations – Greece 6. Greece – Military policy 7. Turkey –
    Military policy
    I. Title
    327.4'950561

ISBN 0-7146-5436-1 (cloth)
ISBN 0-7146-8357-4 (paper)

Library of Congress Cataloging-in-Publication Data

Moustakis, Fotios, 1970–
    The Greek–Turkish relationship and NATO/Fotios Moustakis.
        p. cm.
    Includes bibliographical references and index.
    ISBN 0-7146-5436-1 (cloth)
    1. North Atlantic Treaty Organization. 2. Greece–Military relations–
    Turkey. 3. Turkey–Military relations–Greece. 4.National security–
    Mediterranean Region.   I. Title.
    UA646.5.G8M68 2003
    355'.031'0949509561–dc21   2003043985

Typeset in New Baskerville 10.9 pt/12 pt by Cambridge Photosetting Services,
Cambridge
Printed in Great Britain by MPG Books Ltd, Victoria Square, Bodmin, Cornwall

Contents

Foreword

The second echelon NATO enlargement 'big bang' variant, announced at the NATO Prague Summit of November 2002, integrates seven new candidate countries into this transatlantic security organisation and raises a number of practical questions whose answers will shape NATO's future. Will there be a 'division of labour' and costs between European and US NATO member states? Can the capabilities gap and even the gulf in 'strategic cultures' on both sides of the Atlantic be bridged? Will the new members continue the process of democratic security building, or will the lack of progress of the first echelon (Czech Republic, Hungary and Poland) be repeated? How effectively will new and existing member states respond to the increased emphasis placed on civil-security sector reform – a process that had largely been overlooked prior to the events of 11 September 2001? Which states realistically have the possibility for third echelon membership and what new roles might PfP states usefully adopt?

Clearly the decision when to enlarge and which states to integrate is and has always been primarily a political decision – as first echelon post-Cold War enlargement as much as the Cold War inclusion of Greece and Turkey into the alliance demonstrated. This book analyses the relationship between these longstanding existing NATO member states – in terms of demoncratic peace theory elaborated in the 1990s and Karl Deutsch's concept of a pluralistic security community, first articulated in the 1950s. NATO argues that there are five basic criteria for membership – a consolidated democracy, the observance of human rights, a viable market economy, democratic civil-military relations and a co-operative foreign policy. But this raises the question: how can NATO be described as a security community with a membership that consists of these mutually antagonistic states, one of which is best described as a 'managed' or 'illiberal democracy'?

Within this detailed study Fotios Moustakis suggests that the Greek–Turkish dyad has constructed what might be termed a hybrid community in south-east Europe. This is an aberrant or partial security community, and its existence has important implications for second echelon NATO member states in this region. More importantly, as NATO reaches out to integrate the third echelon, in particular Croatia, Bosnia-Herzegovina, Serbia and Macedonia, different variants of this hybrid model are likely to present themselves and require equally elaborate responses from NATO.

Thus, this book is both topical and timely and provides an underlying context with which the reader can examine the current nature and future direction and viability of NATO over the medium to long term. It allows us to step back from the hoopla and euphoria of the 2002 Prague Summit to consider larger and more abstract existential, theoretical and conceptual issues that will shape NATO, its ability to define its role, duties and missions. The underlying integrity of the NATO strategic doctrine – whether it be the one elaborated in Washington in April 1999 or the one that will likely be articulated at the accession conference – is challenged by the analysis and arguments of this research book.

Graeme Herd
Professor of Civil–Military Relations, George C. Marshall Center
for European Security Studies

January 2003

List of Figures

List of Abbreviations

ACCS	Air Command and Control System
ACE	Allied Command Europe
AFSOUTH	Allied Forces Southern Europe
AMF	ACE Mobile Force
ANAP	Motherland Party
APC	Armoured Personnel Carrier
ATACMS	Advanced/Army Tactical Missile System
ATAF	Allied Tactical Air Force
BASIC	British American Information Council
BBC	British Broadcasting Corporation
BISA	British International Studies Association
BSC	Balkan Security Council
BSECZ	Black Sea Economic Co-operation Zone
C3	Command, Control and Communication
CSBMS	Confidence and Security Building Measures
CFE	Conventional Forces in Europe
CFSP	Common Foreign and Security Policy
CHP	Republican People's Party
CIA	Central Intelligence Agency
CINCSOUTH	Commander in Chief Allied Forces Southern Europe
CJTF	Combined Common Joint Task Forces
COMLANDSOUTH	Commander Allied Land Forces Southern Europe
CSCE	Conference on Security and Co-operation in Europe
DP	Democratic Party
DPC	Defence Planning Committee
DPQ	Defence Planning Questionnaire
EC	European Community
ELIAMEP	Hellenic Foundation for European and Foreign Policy

EMF	European Monetary Fund
EOKA	National Organisation of Cypriot Fighters (after 1960 revived as ACKA-B)
EU	European Union
FIR	Flight Information Region
FRY	Federation of Yugoslavia
FYROM	Former Yugoslav Republic of Macedonia
GAP	South East Anatolian Project
GDP	Gross Domestic Product
GNA	Grand National Assembly
GSEE	Greek Trade Union Federation
HP	Populist Party
ICAO	International Civil Aviation Organisation
ICJ	International Court of Justice
IDIS	Institute of International Relations Athens
IFOR	Implementation Force
IMF	International Monetary Fund
KFOR	International Security Force in Kosovo
KKE	Communist Party of Greece
KYSEA	Government Council for Foreign Affairs and Defence
LOROP	Long-Range Oblique Photography Systems
LOS	Law of the Sea
LOSC	Law of the Sea Convention
MAP	Membership Action Plan
MCM	Mine Countermeasures
MDP	National Democracy Party
MIT	Turkish Secret Service
MPA	Maritime Patrol Aircraft
MPFSEE	Multinational Peace Force in South Eastern Europe
NAC	North Atlantic Council
NACC	North Atlantic Co-operation Council
NADGE	NATO Air Defence Ground Environment
NATO	North Atlantic Treaty Organisation
ND	New Democracy
NOTAM	Notice to Airmen
NSB	National Security Board
NSC	National Security Council
OSCE	Organisation for Security and Co-operation in Europe
OYAK	Armed Forces Mutual Fund
PASOK	Panhellenic Socialist Party
PDD	Presidential Decision Directive

PfP	Partnership for Peace
PKK	Kurdistan Workers' Party
PSC	Pluralistic Security Community
PSC	Principal Subordinate Commander
RAND	Research and Development
RC	Regional Command
RPP	Republican People's Party
SACEUR	Supreme Allied Commander Europe
SC	Strategic Command
SECI	Southeast European Co-operative Initiative
SFOR	Stabilisation Force
SIPRI	Stockholm International Peace Research Institute
STANAVFORMED	Standing Naval Force, Mediterranean
TLE	Treaty Limited Equipment
UN	United Nations
UNCLOS III	Third United Nations Convention on the Law of the Sea
UNFICYP	United Nations Peacekeeping Force in Cyprus
UNPREDEP	United Nations Preventive Deployment Force
UNTAES	United Nations Transitional Administration in Eastern Slavonia
US	United States
USSR	Union of Soviet Socialists Republics
WEU	Western European Union
WTO	Warsaw Treaty Organisation

Acknowledgements

I would like to express my deep gratitude to Professor Michael Sheehan in the Department of Politics and International Relations at the University of Aberdeen, for his constructive guidance and invaluable support in providing me with critical commentaries on the security challenges and problems in the eastern Mediterranean. Without his contribution this book would not be possible.

I would also like to express my deep gratitude to Professor Dr Graeme Herd, at the George C. Marshall European Center for Security Studies, for his immense help in providing me with constructive comments with regards to the heterogeneous nature of the eastern Mediterranean region.

I would like to thank all the military officers and academics of the Balkan region who provided me with invaluable information and general help with regards to the security problems of the Balkan region.

I wish to express my sincere gratitude to my friends, Tracey German, Sang Gap Lee and George Tsiboukis, for their general help during the research. My special thanks to Dr Bianca Piachaud for proof-reading my draft, and being a pillar of strength during my research. Without her support, advice and kindness the outcome of this book would be different.

Finally, I would like to extend my deep gratitude to my family, without whose financial support and belief in me this work would have not taken place. I dedicate this book to them.

Fotios Moustakis
2003

Introduction

The aim of this book is to identify and examine the realities behind the lack of normal friendly relations between the two allies Greece and Turkey within NATO. To this end, the work will be focused on the area in which Greek and Turkish foreign, security and defence policies meet and interact. It will deal with civil–military relations in the decision-making concerning the international situation and policy of the countries of Greece and Turkey.

Despite numerous security studies which explore the causes and disputes of this relationship and offer suggestions for resolving Greek–Turkish bilateral problems, the current work will try for the first time to elucidate the reasons for the aberrant character of the eastern Mediterranean within the NATO structure using Karl Deutsch's work on security community. In 1957 Deutsch evolved the concept of 'pluralistic security community' along with 'amalgamated security community'. He suggested three requirements as the conditions for the emergence of a pluralistic security community: i) compatibility of major values; ii) mutual responsiveness; and iii) mutual predictability. The notion of security community developed in his work has had a lasting influence in international relations theory but most importantly, it has been characteristic of all NATO member states in the post-Cold War era.

In the Cold War the NATO alliance claimed to represent a mixture of security community and military alliance. In the post-Cold War era in a series of public declarations and statements – the Rome Security Concept of 1991, Mediterranean Dialogue of 1994 and Washington Security Concept of 1999 – NATO claimed to represent a security community.

Contrary to traditional security approaches to Greek–Turkish relations (which also will be applied) the current work *inter alia* identifies and develops a theory which portrays the current *status quo* in the sub-region of the eastern Mediterranean in the post-Cold War period. Although the eastern Mediterranean region has been investigated thoroughly during the Cold War and the post-Cold War period, no one has approached this topic using the PSC[1] theory with special emphasis on Greece and Turkey. This theory is particularly applicable to the eastern Mediterranean since NATO has evolved in the post-Cold War era into a security community[2] (see Chapter 4). Potential NATO members must adopt the following principles:

- an established democracy
- respect for human rights
- a market-based economy
- armed forces must be under civilian control
- good relations with neighbouring states.[3]

This demonstrates that NATO is not merely a military alliance, but has evolved to become a pluralistic security community.[4] Since 1991 and the end of the Cold War, EU and NATO expansion plans have been premised on the assumption that western Europe constitutes a 'security community' in which the possibility of war between its members has been reduced to zero. Thus, states which are admitted to the two bodies would find themselves in, and contribute to, the expanded European security community.

Security community theory embraces the work of Deutsch et al. in the 1950s through to Adler and Barnett in the 1990s. Closely associated with it in the European context is the concept of democratic peace. This was first promulgated by Kant, and was taken up in the early 1980s in the work of Michael Doyle. It formed a central part of the strategic view of the Clinton administration.

However, the assumptions underlying both the 'security community' and the 'democratic peace' do not hold true for all of the NATO members. The crucial aberrant case is the ongoing Greek–Turkish confrontation. This has proved resistant to the security community developments seen elsewhere in the NATO area.

Thus, the foremost objective of this study is to explore the reasons why the notion of the security community and more specifically the PSC does not yet exist in the southern flank of NATO. In order to achieve its objective, the study will address the following questions:

- How important is the eastern Mediterranean region for western interests?
- How were Greek–Turkish foreign and security policies formulated before and after the Cold War?
- How did their bilateral relations influence the effectiveness of the NATO organisation?
- Does the reality of a PSC exist in the southern flank of NATO?

- Do Greece and Turkey fulfil the first criterion of the PSC theory, i.e. compatibility of major values?
- What kind of conflict-resolution mechanisms can NATO apply in the eastern Mediterranean in order to eliminate the possibility of an intra-alliance conflict?

So far most of the academics and analysts specialised in the security studies of the Balkan region have approached the bilateral problems of Greece and Turkey from a realist perspective. Academics such as Aybet, Bahcheli, Karpat, Sezer, Hale, Karaosmanoglou, Kuniholm, Mango, Stearns, Brown, Fuller, MacDonald, Wilson, Larrabee, Lesser, Veremis, Coufoudakis, Couloumbis, Papacosmas and Rossides have investigated Greek and Turkish bilateral issues. Their views, together with the main body of academic work that has been conducted in relation to the eastern Mediterranean will be quoted in this work. However, the secondary sources will be employed to identify and present the Greek–Turkish differences and to complement my argument. The study will also focus more on the political than the technical aspects of the cases and their results.

My hypothesis is based on the fact that Greece and Turkey (even though they are members of a wider security community in the post-Cold War era) have not so far been able to accommodate/resolve their differences, in relation to the Aegean Sea and Cyprus. The results will conclude that Turkey has not fully met the criteria of a PSC and as a result a *Hybrid Region* has been developed in the eastern Mediterranean (the *Hybrid Region* portrays the current *status quo* in the eastern Mediterranean, see Chapter 4).[5]

METHODOLOGY

For the purpose of this research the following two methods will be employed:

1. historical analysis
2. case study method.

Since these two methods will be used interchangeably, it is necessary to assess their relevance with regards to social sciences, and in particular to this thesis.

Historical analysis/research

A possible confusing feature of historical research is that in most cases it does not involve direct observation of, or the collection of data concerning, the phenomena under study, since it draws on reliable evidence from previous recorded observations and data. There is a possible exception to this where an elderly person who experienced, witnessed or was involved in some way in the phenomenon of interest, may be interviewed in order to collect data directly, but this represents a minority of historical research data, and one that may not be very reliable. In this sense, the function of historical research is to systematically and objectively locate, evaluate and synthesise the available evidence.

Historical research data is always inadequate and requires some degree of reconstruction on the part of the researcher in order to fill in the gaps and to suggest a systematic account given the evidence and its reliability. Although historical analysis defines its specific topics of interest (e.g. a biography of Albert Einstein) it tends to include social, geographic, cultural, economic, political, legal, and psychological aspects of the topic. In this sense it is multi-disciplinary and multidimensional.

As indicated earlier, historical analysis attempts to test the truthfulness of observations made by others by the examination and/or re-examination of existing evidence. Additionally, new evidence may become available which questions or modifies previous accounts and systems of understanding. In the evaluation of evidence the researcher may formulate hypotheses about the phenomena of interest and subject these to test and modification.

Within historical research there are two general sources of data, primary and secondary. Primary sources are those items which are original to the problem or topic and which have a direct physical relationship to the events being reconstructed (e.g. weapons, manuscripts, archives, laws, reports, newspapers). Secondary sources are those that do not have a direct physical relationship to the event being studied. Historical analysis typically involves two stages:

1. Appraisal of the authenticity of sources. This stage seeks to evaluate the validity and reliability of the evidence.
2. Appraisal of the meaning/importance of the source. After establishing the validity and reliability of the source, the researcher must evaluate the content of the source in terms of its importance and implications for current views and understanding about the topic.[6]

Arbnor and Andersson have sought to place historical analysis in a theoretical context. Historical analysis is not just a simple retrospective study but a reflection of the view that history is always present and that new history is always in the process of being created from current social, political and economic reality. History can be viewed as a means of interpreting both the present and the future – 'a hermeneutic bridge'.[7] The purpose of systematic historical analysis is not, however, to derive some form of 'historical truth' but rather to reflect historical diversity as a stimulus to action. With reference to the points mentioned earlier, the case in support of historical analysis in social sciences may be summarised in the following manner:

- History is a diagnostic instrument that helps us to put a problem in its context and environment. It supplies a thread and helps us to create order among a mass of data; it provides patterns. No two sets of circumstances are ever entirely identical although there is often a general pattern that recurs frequently.
- It helps us to avoid reinventing the wheel.
- History does not provide solutions but a thought process, and we have to realise this and accept ambiguity and complexity.
- History can help us to change things before we have to, which is actually the basic purpose of strategic thinking: foresee changes, act before they hit us, and prepare to benefit from the new situation.

Case study method

The use of the case study for research purposes has become increasingly widespread in social science. Books dealing with political sciences and other social sciences related modules often utilise the case study approach as an effective research tool. Although case studies vary in character, there are essentially two types that are of particular interest. The first attempts to derive general conclusions from a limited number of cases, while the second seeks to arrive at specific conclusions regarding a single case. Yet despite these variations, both forms are capable of producing results of general interest.

Yin provides a comprehensive definition of the case study as a possible approach to research. The author states that the case study inquiry

- copes with the technically distinctive situation in which there will be many more variables of interest other than data points, and as a result
- relies on multiple sources of evidence, with data needing to achieve coverage in a triangulation[8] fashion, and as another result
- benefits from the prior development of theoretical propositions to guide data collection and analysis.[9]

In other words, the case study as a research strategy comprises an all-encompassing method – with the logic of design incorporating specific approaches to data collection and data analysis. Therefore according to Stoecker, the case study is neither a data collection tactic nor a design feature alone, but a comprehensive research strategy.[10]

Yin distinguishes between three types of uses of case study research. These refer to case studies being used for exploratory, descriptive and explanatory purposes. When assessing the general applicability of the case study method, Yin argues that the case study is the preferred strategy when 'how' or 'why' questions are being posed, when the investigator has little or no control over events, and when the focus is on a contemporary phenomenon within some real-life context.[11] Therefore, if the research questions are mainly 'what' orientated, it is a justifiable rationale for conducting an exploratory study – the goal here being to develop pertinent hypotheses and propositions for further inquiry.[12] Conversely, if the questions are 'how' and 'why' in nature, a more explanatory study is required because such questions deal with operational links that need to be traced over time, rather than mere frequencies of incidence.[13]

Assuming then that 'how' and 'why' questions are to be the focus of the study, Yin points out that a further distinguishing feature of the case study method is the extent of the investigator's control over and access to behavioural events. In this instance, the case study is the preferred mode when examining contemporary events, but only when the relevant behaviours cannot be manipulated. Therefore although the case study relies on the same techniques as a historical analysis, it adds two sources of evidence not usually included in the historian's repertoire: direct observation and systematic interviewing. Thus, the case study's unique strength is its ability to deal with a wide variety of evidence such as news reports, official documents, remarks in context, personal writings and literary works and so forth which is more than what is available in a historical study.

Gummesson cites that one of the greatest advantages of case study research is that it provides the opportunity for a holistic view of a process. The detailed observations entailed in the case study method enable the researcher to study many different aspects, examine them in relation to one another, and to view the process within its total environment.[14] Accordingly, case study research presents a greater opportunity than other available methods for obtaining a holistic view of a specific research project. Since considerable effort is required to construct a case study of this nature, it is therefore possible to carry out perhaps one, or a very limited number of case studies in a particular research project.

Although the use of case studies as an analytical tool has received growing recognition in both Europe and the US, a frequent criticism levelled against this technique is that it is inferior to methods that are based on random statistical samples of a large number of observations. Hagg et al. summarise the criticisms of the case study as a scientific method under the following three headings:

1. Case studies lack statistical validity.
2. Case studies can be used to generate hypotheses but not to test them.
3. Generalisations cannot be made on the basis of case studies.[15]

Hamel et al. also note that the case study has been faulted for another vital aspect:

> For its lack in the collection, construction and analysis of the empirical materials that give rise to the study. This lack of rigor is linked to the problem of bias. Such bias is introduced by the subjectivity of the researcher, as well as by the field informants on whom the researcher relies to get an understanding of the case under investigation.[16]

APPLICATION OF CASE STUDY METHOD/ HISTORICAL ANALYSIS IN THE BOOK

For the purpose of this book a combination of historical and case study methods was utilised. Given the objectives of the research, it was felt that these two methods were the most appropriate analytical tools. Chapters 1–3 applied the case study method. These case studies provided a descriptive, explanatory and exploratory analysis. However, this method was not used in isolation but instead incorporated a historical analysis approach in order to examine the objective of this study. The research adopts a methodology of comparative study (Chapters 2, 3) in order to identify, examine and understand security relations between Greece and Turkey, and how these relations have been formulated within the NATO structure. Since these chapters are focused on the chronological examination of each case, they assign many parts to the historical approach on the cases and to the analysis of the present security situation and issues in the eastern Mediterranean.

In the case of Chapter 4 an explanatory case study of Greece and Turkey was employed in order to validate the *Hybrid Region*. Here too, a historical analysis was presented.

Moreover, in terms of methodology, a variety of sources of information were used. A series of interviews were conducted during the

1996–9 period with the current and former Greek military as well as Greek, Turkish and other European academics specialising in Balkan security issues. Due to the sensitivity of the topic most of them asked me to ensure their anonymity. Other primary sources utilised, included governmental documents, NATO documents and reports, conference papers and newspapers. The extensive secondary scholarly literature as well as relevant data was examined. These methods were chosen to provide a maximum overall view of the subject. Analysis attempted to allow for the element of bias present in some of the sources.

CHAPTER OUTLINE

The contents of each chapter and the outline of the book will be discussed as follows. The first chapter provides an overview on the importance of southern-eastern Europe and the sub-region of the eastern Mediterranean for western interests with main reference for NATO.

The second chapter contain an analysis concerning Greek security challenges and the Greek–NATO relationship during the Cold and the post-Cold War period and within the Greek–Turkish bilateral framework.

The third chapter explicates Turkish security challenges and the Turkish–NATO relationship during the Cold War and post-Cold War period under the prism of Greek–Turkish relations.

The fourth chapter is aimed at developing and testing the concept of PSC explicated by Deutsch and his associates in the 1950s, in the eastern Mediterranean. Ultimately, the purpose of this chapter is to argue that a flawed development of a PSC in the eastern Mediterranean has led to lack of solidarity, stability, unity and co-operation among the two southern NATO members.

The fifth chapter attempts to introduce a series of mechanisms which would facilitate the prevention of an intra-alliance conflict in the eastern Mediterranean. Even though there have been various proposals on measures to build a security regime in the eastern Mediterranean, no real mechanisms for conflict resolution yet exist in the region. The emergence of the *Hybrid Region* in the eastern Mediterranean hinders any plausibility of interdependence between these two NATO members and as a result encourages Greece and Turkey to compete strategically and economically. This is followed by the conclusion which incorporates a short overview of the findings.

NOTES

1. For the purpose of this book security community and pluralistic security community will be used interchangeably.
2. 'The Atlantic Alliance continues to provide residual defence insurance, the means for proactive security policy on behalf of its members, and the foundation of a pluralistic security community in which war among its members has all but been abolished', see P.H. Gordon, 'Recasting the Atlantic Alliance', in P.H.Gordon (ed.), *NATO's Transformation: The Changing Shape of the Atlantic Alliance* (London: Rowman & Littlefield Publishers, 1997) p.24.
3. G. Evans and J. Newham, *Penguin Dictionary of International Relations* (London: Penguin Books, 1998) p.353.
4. See also the NATO Washington Declaration signed on 23 and 24 April 1999, paragraph 3, 'We will contribute to building a stronger and broader Euro-Atlantic community of democracies – a community where human rights and fundamental freedoms are upheld...where war becomes unthinkable'.
5. The *Hybrid Region* is not a complete pluralistic security community nor a traditional antagonistic situation. It entails elements of both.
6. See Barry P. Bright, 'Introduction to Research Methods in Postgraduate Thesis and Dissertations', *Newland Paper*, 18 (University of Hull, 1991) p.76.
7. Evert Gummesson, *Qualitative Methods in Management Research* (California: Sage Publications, 1991) p.87.
8. Triangulation itself is not a specific method but is rather a technique involving the use of several methods. Its main purpose is checking the internal consistency and reliability of research findings and their validity.
9. Robert Yin, *Case Study Research: Design and Methods* (California: Sage Publications, 1994) p.13.
10. ibid., p.13.
11. ibid., p.1.
12. ibid., p.5.
13. ibid., p.6.
14. 'See Gummesson, *Qualitative Methods*, p.76.
15. Hagg et al. '*Case Studies in Social Science Research*', Working Paper No. 78–16 (Brussels: European Institute for Advanced Studies in Management, 1978) pp.7–13.
16. J. Hamel et al., *Case Study Methods* (California: Sage Publications, 1993) p.23.

1

South-eastern Europe: a Region of Challenges and Opportunities

[NATO's] main security front has swung away from
Central Europe to its Southern Flank
*(US Secretary of Defence
Seville, 29–30 September 1994)*

In this chapter an overview will be conducted on the sub-region of the eastern Mediterranean for western interests and more specifically for the NATO alliance. A brief analysis will also be presented of the Balkan region in order to reveal the factual characteristics of the whole Balkan region. This is done because the Balkan–eastern Mediterranean zone is the geo-strategic context in which Greek–Turkish interaction takes place.

The important changes that have occurred within the last twelve years in Europe such as the fall of communism, the disintegration of the Soviet Union, the wars in Bosnia and Kosovo and the associated new security challenges, have led to the essential question as to what will the future of security in Europe look like and what role should NATO play, as the most important military structure in Europe? Most of the debate has been focused on the new role of NATO and the implications of the expansion eastwards. It is believed by many international analysts that the expansion of NATO is of the utmost importance towards consolidation of European security.[1] Undoubtedly, every post-war period is by definition a period of many instabilities and much unpredictability. So it was after the First World War, so it was after the Second World War, and so it is after the Cold War. It is commonly believed that until 1989, east–west relations were marked by a certain stability, even if one artificially imposed in the former socialist countries and at the international level. The dramatic changes in the east and the disruption of the equilibrium of the world balance of power have led to a new international security environment. Currently an unstable period has been replaced by a 'stable instability' period.[2]

In this context, the question of the interest of NATO members in the continued existence of NATO and in the workability of the alliance is embedded in a fundamentally changed context. What practical benefit does NATO have if, in the absence of a clear military enemy and direct threat, it no longer assumes a meaningful security task at a time when risks and crises erupt in eastern Europe and in the Mediterranean region with accompanying destructive effects on a large scale?[3]

During the Cold War, eastern Mediterranean[4] security issues were defined largely as a function of the Soviet threat in the overall east–west confrontation and competition. Greece and Turkey were important because they helped control Soviet access to, and influence in, the Aegean, the Balkans and the Middle East. With the demise of the Cold War, however, the locus of risk has moved to the southern flank of NATO. The Bosnian and Kosovo experiences have shown how crises on the periphery of the NATO organisation can spill over and affect important alliance interests as well as how difficult it is for the US to remain aloof from a conflict in which the interests of its key allies are at stake.[5]

Undoubtedly, the current era is characterised by the attempt to replace Cold War confrontation based on the balance of power – two blocks facing each other across the east–west divide – with an international system of stability, peace and co-operation through interlocking, complementary institutions. Within this context NATO is attempting to enhance security, a belief based on its success over the forty years of Cold War and partly because of a potential regional conflict that could threaten the stability of Europe and the Transatlantic alliance. NATO'S response to change has been a dramatic revision of its traditional strategy, from the single pillar of collective defence of NATO territory to a military mechanism capable of supporting multiple objectives.[6]

The southern region and especially the eastern Mediterranean will be at the forefront of many discussions within the NATO organisation due to various important reasons. The end of the Cold War and the erosion of the post-Second World War alliance system which defined east–west competition for four decades have forced nations to explore new frameworks to address emerging security requirements. The Mediterranean countries are among those in search of new relationships and alignments, but while that task is being addressed by virtually all states, an acute sense of urgency is attached to the search among Mediterranean nations.[7]

The demise of the east–west competition has shifted attention toward dormant, but simmering inter and intra-state rivalries which could present security threats affecting entire regions.[8] The strife in the former Yugoslav space and the continuous tension and antagonism between Greece and Turkey are obvious examples. With this shift in attention will also come a slow but certain transformation in regional political-military balances as new security challenges surface.[9]

With the decline in relevance of the superpower nuclear balance as a barometer of the global strategic climate, the state of the superpower nuclear balance has also become less relevant to the security of allies who benefited from what it was known as the 'delicate balance of terror'.[10]

The Mediterranean nations are exploring the new security environment of the post-Cold War era and assessing the instruments available to secure their vital interests in a region which NATO and the west had generally regarded as a peripheral strategic theatre.

In view of these challenges and risks the importance of the eastern Mediterranean for NATO is evident. Its military significance has been outlined and extended by the establishment of a southern European command headquartered in Naples – one of the three major commands directly subordinate to SACEUR – and by the US Sixth Fleet headquartered in Gaeta.[11] An article in *NATO Review* clarifies also the significant role the Mediterranean now plays for the alliance. The article states that 'the Mediterranean could emerge as Europe's new front line as the West confronts the strategic challenges of the post-Cold War era'.[12] The authors emphasise how the interaction of demographic, political, economic, technological and military cross-currents destabilises the region. The NATO Secretary General stated in a speech on 25 November 1996:

> This is what we mean when we speak about building a new European security architecture; building a set of political relationships where each state feels secure and at ease. This – not the antagonism of the past – is the context in which NATO's approach to the Mediterranean must be viewed. NATO must look to the South, as well as it must look to the East.[13]

During the Cold War political realities made the Northern Tier the focus of confrontation, but now that region is of lesser immediate concern. The southern region, although critical to re-supply and sustainment during the Cold War, was widely regarded as a secondary priority. Now the southern region has replaced the central region as the cutting edge of alliance concerns for stability.[14] To this end a RAND report argued that

> During the Cold War, the attention of Western policymakers was focused primarily on the Central Front. The Mediterranean was

regarded as of secondary importance. However, in recent years – and especially since the end of the Cold War – the Mediterranean has assumed new importance as a focal point of Western concern.[15]

If one wants to assess the importance of the eastern Mediterranean for the alliance various important factors have to be taken into account.

THE IMPORTANCE OF THE EASTERN MEDITERRANEAN: FACTUAL REALITIES

The eastern Mediterranean, enclosed by the three continents of Europe, Asia and Africa, extends from the Straits of Sicily in the west to the coasts of Cyprus, Turkey, Lebanon, Syria, Israel and Egypt in the east. It contains the Adriatic, the Ionian and Aegean Seas and the south-eastern Mediterranean basin. It connects three continents and twelve nations with a population of more than 200 million people.

Since ancient times the eastern Mediterranean has been the scene of conflicting interests. Cretan, Phoenician, Carthaginian, Hellenic and Roman fleets mastered the sea successively and secured their power and prosperity. It has been either a familiar route of trade and culture, or a fault line between hostile states and civilisations. Seldom have nations won a war in the eastern Mediterranean without control of the sea and many nations have lost wars when its use was denied to them. It should be remembered that Athens, a sea power, was in the end defeated by Sparta, a land power, when the latter finally mastered the sea and learned to use its advantage.[16]

The Cold War witnessed east and west striving to control the great waterways separating and uniting Europe and Africa, the Middle East and Asia, through a balance of power and antagonistic alliances (NATO, Warsaw Pact).

Daily, up to 2,000 merchant ships follow trade routes in the Mediterranean. Over 90 per cent of the Greek and Turkish trade and 70 per cent of Italian trade is carried aboard these ships. All Middle East oil imports for Greece and Italy and nearly half of those for France, Germany and Spain move via these routes.[17] The role of Mediterranean-supply shipping routes is therefore vital for the economic development and thus the progress of European and other countries. It allows the transfer and exchange of goods and the supply of oil and other raw materials. At least 40 per cent of the oil for European countries is routed through the eastern Mediterranean. It is also vital for non-Mediterranean countries. Bulgarian, Romanian and 40 per cent of the Russian import–export trade is routed through the

Dardanelles, the Aegean Sea and the Mediterranean. Undoubtedly, these countries are heavily reliant on the Mediterranean for their commerce.[18] A study by Richard Whitman reveals that the

> Mediterranean countries provide 24% of the total European Union (EU) member state energy imports, 32% of the imports of natural gas, and 27% of oil imports. However, there is a disproportion between the EU member states who are reliant upon the producers of the southern and eastern Mediterranean; Spain, France, Italy, Greece and Portugal derive 24% of their oil supplies from the region; Spain, France, Italy, Portugal and Greece derive 42% of their gas supplies from the region. Europe is linked to the supply from the region via the Transmed pipeline carrying Algerian gas to Italy, via Tunisia, and to the Maghreb–Europe pipeline to carry Algerian gas, via Morocco, to Spain and Porgugal. An electricity interconnection has also been on stream between Morocco and Spain since 1995.[19]

Furthermore, the Suez Canal had been perceived to be important enough for at least two major European countries to react militarily to its takeover by Egypt in 1956.[20] With regard to the Middle East, the Gulf War (1990–1) between the Allies and Iraq provides a good example of military intervention resulting from the need to secure vital sources of oil. US President George Bush admitted that this was the reason behind the military action in the early days of the Gulf crisis.

Taking all these factors into account, a significant reason that necessitated NATO to extend its assistance to the eastern Mediterranean during the 1950s (Greece and Turkey) was the economic importance of this region. Taken by itself, the western industrial world's, particularly NATO's heavy reliance on the petroleum of North Africa and the Middle East, has placed the Mediterranean in a new economic and strategic light. Strategic stockpiles in the region are practically non-existent, and many of the littoral nations have marginal international monetary reserves. Ironically, the largest oil-producing countries that do have comfortable reserves, such as Algeria and Libya, require constant supplies of food and goods to keep their 'made in Europe' infrastructure functioning.

Furthermore, the eastern Mediterranean is a common link connecting the countries of the area and functions as a route for economic and cultural exchanges. The activities of fishing, passenger and tourist shipping are enormous and critical for the economies of most of the Mediterranean countries. All of these activities could be limited or stopped if terrorist acts or sabotage or the threat of a regional conflict were to be allowed to rise. In times of tension and crisis the security of the sea lines of communications in the eastern Mediterranean would be essential for the successful concentration of oil stocks and strategic reserves in the European countries of NATO.[21]

It is instructive to mention that according to NATO and US war plans the eastern Mediterranean/Middle Eastern region was of 'critical and fundamental' strategic importance in the event of war with the Soviet Union[22]. Its oil reserves, considered vital for the west in the early stage of a conflict, could not under any circumstances be allowed to fall into unfriendly hands. It was estimated that 84 per cent of the Soviet oil refinery capacity could be hit by US bombers operating out of the Cairo–Suez area. More importantly when Britain was forced out of its Cairo–Suez canal base under the terms of the 1954 Anglo-Egyptian Agreement, the Cyprus base assumed for Britain a conventional and strategic role. On the conventional level it safeguarded British and western interests, namely the uninterrupted flow of oil to Britain and Europe by the safest and cheapest route. The Cyprus base also provided conventional support to NATO's southern flank. On the strategic level, the Akrotiri air base provided British and US bombers with a platform from which to attack, with nuclear weapons if necessary, the southern industrialised and oil producing regions of the Soviet Union.[23]

During the Cold War period the Mediterranean region was always perceived in the context of the east–west military competition in Europe. NATO's main objective was to use the Mediterranean as a strategic link in order to facilitate forward defence in key areas of threat around the southern region (e.g. in north-east Italy, Thrace and eastern Turkey, where the terrain itself favours forward defence). Uninterrupted access in the Mediterranean region would also allow for operations designed to influence the outcome of conflict in central Europe, including the attack of targets within the Soviet Union via the Black Sea. At the same time the existence of key 'choke' points in the Aegean, at Sicily, Malta and Crete, as well as at Gibraltar, Suez and the Turkish Straits, was considered by NATO to be a formidable barrier to any Soviet attempt to challenge the *status quo* in the Mediterranean.[24]

Furthermore, there are some other important factors which should also be taken into consideration regarding the sea control in the eastern Mediterranean area:

- The whole basin is open to all aspects of maritime warfare, and the fact that every part of it is within the range of land-based MPA and strike air forces is very significant.
- The length of westbound and eastbound routes along the

northern African coast exposes shipping to continuous detection and possible attack by air, surface and sub-surface units.

- It includes deep oceanic areas where nuclear submarines with long-range missiles could operate. As a result bathythermographic conditions in the area make submarine detection a difficult task.[25]

- It is a relatively restricted area for surveillance and the collection of information about the presence, movement and new developments of naval and merchant shipping of countries considered to be potential aggressors.

- Mobility for ground forces is extremely difficult in this area. Because of the fragmented terrain of the allied nations in this area, the sea provides the means by which their land forces can be mutually supported.[26]

By stating these factors one can clearly recognise the importance of the eastern Mediterranean region for the alliance, and therefore stress the imperative necessity for a deeper understanding and involvement into the challenges and risks which are daunting in that region.

THE GREEK ISLANDS AND THEIR IMPORTANCE FOR THE ALLIANCE

One other factor which has to be taken into account with regards to the defence of the eastern Mediterranean is the key role that the Aegean Sea and especially the Greek islands play in the defence of the Southern Tier of the alliance. The Aegean Sea is a semi-enclosed sea, containing a great number (approximately 3,000) Greek islands and islets. Merchant shipping and naval units operating in the Aegean have to pass successively through narrow shipping passages (less than 15 nautical miles wide) which are formed between the islands and the mainland. These passages of the Aegean, together with the Greek islands and the passages which are formed east and west of Crete, allow for defence in depth between the Dardanelles and Crete. The Greek naval and air forces can easily control the sea lines of communications through the narrow passages; first of all by

- Radar installations for sea surveillance on the islands with C3 installations providing a real-time picture of the area.
- Fast patrol boats with guided missiles which undertake the task of shadowing and marking the potential opponent. The protected bays and coasts provide excellent waiting positions for this task.

- Surface-to-surface missile launching systems on the islands contribute to the neutralisation of the potential aggressor.
- Mine barriers can impose damage to surface ships and submarines that try to pass through the island complex. Moreover, MCM units can operate from nearby bases, located all around the Aegean to keep the Greek ports and Aegean choke points open for the use of allied ships.
- Helicopters based on the islands contribute to the overall operations. The Greek airfields and landing facilities provide bases for maritime patrol aircraft which, together with the port facilities offered to the naval forces, constitute an ideal complex by which maritime operations in the Aegean Sea can be effectively supported. It is also worth mentioning that if carriers were deployed in the Aegean to support the land battle in depth, they would use the close proximity of Greek islands as a well-protected haven.[27]

Here, the importance of Crete for the NATO alliance can also be outlined. Crete is at the centre of the eastern Mediterranean and it is the fifth-largest island in the Mediterranean. It is almost equidistant from Sicily and Suez and relatively close to the northern coast of Africa. Its geographical position and its air and naval bases provide for effective sea control and protection of sea lines of communication which connect the Suez Canal with the Dardanelles and the ports of the eastern Mediterranean with Gibraltar. Due to its geographical position Crete can be used: i) for air and naval base operations in the eastern Mediterranean basin and especially for opposing the threat from the south; ii) as an MPA air base for the effective surveillance of the whole eastern Mediterranean area; iii) it has good self-defence capabilities due to the rugged geography of its territory which facilitates resistance and opposition to any amphibious or air-landing operation. Due to its position, Crete has assumed a great strategic significance for NATO, more particularly for the southern region, as a main maritime base. It is generally believed that whoever controls Crete can easily gain sea control of the eastern Mediterranean.[28]

The strategic importance of Crete was also proved during the 1991 Gulf War by the facilities provided to allied forces. More specifically around 220 allied ships received port facilities, fuel, ammunition and other logistic support from Souda naval base; more than 2,000 allied transport, reconnaissance and other types of aircraft used Souda air base. Despite the demise of the Soviet Union the key role that the Greek islands can play for NATO and especially for the Southern Tier will always be present and undeniably important due to their geo-strategic location.

DEALING WITH THE CHALLENGES

For the first time in history, the international community and the NATO alliance are in a position to build peace and stability, to unite the Southern Region, by co-operation and dialogue through complementary international organisations such as the US as opposed to competing power blocs or hegemonic empire. This opportunity was discussed at the January 1994 NATO Summit, where Heads of State encouraged all efforts to strengthen regional stability in the Mediterranean basin. At the June 1994 Istanbul meeting of the NAC, Foreign Ministers went further by requesting the Council in Permanent Session 'to examine possible proposals by its members with a view to contributing to the strengthening of regional stability'.[29]

A similar view was expressed by US Secretary of Defence William Perry who also called for an intensification of alliance efforts in this area on 5 February 1995 at the Munich Conference on Security Policy:

> While we must focus on Russia and the East, real immediate challenges to NATO Allies have been mounting in the South ... To date, NATO has not effectively faced these challenges.[30]

The challenges which he described were the growth of instability and extremism in North Africa and elsewhere, the instability in Bosnia, the tension between Greece and Turkey, terrorism and proliferation:

> We must all come to grips with the threats to our interests posed by the growth of instability and extremism in North Africa and elsewhere. This is not just a Southern European problem.

He also noted that some allies were reluctant to divert increasingly scarce resources; others were reluctant to get the alliance involved in non-traditional military threats. Secretary Perry urged that future ministerial meetings consider at least three questions:

1. How should NATO engage the 'responsible states' of North Africa in a 'security dialogue and relationship', including the extension of existing bilateral contacts between North African countries and NATO nations?
2. How should NATO give special emphasis to proliferation in the Southern Region, as well as globally?
3. How can NATO continue to be used to build trust and improve relations in the Aegean region[31]?

It is the latter question which constitutes a serious problem within the NATO alliance and tends to develop a serious test for the credibility of NATO in the post-Cold War era. Even though there have been various approaches with regards to the other two questions[32] there has been no serious research to unravel the real reasons behind the persistent instability in the eastern Mediterranean region.

After so many years, the Mediterranean sector of NATO still lacks coherence. Since the collapse of the Soviet Union the danger of a major conflict has emerged between two NATO members, Greece and Turkey. These two countries continue their debilitating struggle focused on Cyprus and over a cluster of disputes, including territorial waters, and airspace over the Aegean (see following chapters). As a result the security and integrity of the alliance has been weakened and above all they have reduced regional military co-operation within the NATO structure in the eastern Mediterranean.

In the post-Cold War environment, NATO's role has been re-examined. The new NATO strategy is based on multi-faceted threats such as the Gulf War and Yugoslavia, international terrorism, mobility and crisis management rather than deterrence. Moreover, NATO's primary role will be the management of peace and stability. This is a role that NATO has not exercised in the past. According to NATO officials, in the future the military will most likely play a more non-provocative role in crisis management, such as the forward basing of defensive measures and intelligence which will be a very important factor. NATO diplomats and academics argued that the Yugoslav war and more recently the Kosovo crisis highlighted a dilemma for the US-led alliance. Officials are keenly aware that their military machine, honed for more than forty years to face the Soviet military threat, will appear useless unless it can be used to help manage crises (for example, the Aegean Crisis over Imia/Kardak between Greece and Turkey) in an unstable world.[33] According to M. Legge, who was responsible for drawing up NATO's new strategy doctrine, failure to extend the boundaries of possible action 'at least through Europe would put NATO's credibility at risk in public opinion and undermine support for the Alliance in the United States'[34].

Undoubtedly, post-Cold War events have revealed that NATO must be able to respond rapidly and flexibly to a wide variety of contingencies. In particular, the tragic events in what used to be Yugoslavia underscore the urgency of being prepared to undertake new peacekeeping missions. The changes in the former communist Balkan countries and especially the crises in the Balkans have strengthened the influence and presence of all western powers and their organisations (NATO, EU) in this region. The position of the US in the Mediterranean, with its strategy of 'extended defence' remains, irrespective of the disappearance of the other superpower. The disappearance of former differences in bloc positions of Balkan states and the present orientation of most of them to co-operation with NATO, makes it possible for NATO to reconsider its position and role in south-east Europe.

THE BALKAN REGION: PAST AND PRESENT

One cannot analyse the importance of the eastern Mediterranean without referring to the Balkan region. Given the current facts one can point out that at the beginning of the twentieth century the security situation in the Balkans was marked by the disintegration of the Turkish Empire, with the major European powers and the tiny Balkan states vying for its legacy. At the end of the twentieth century the security situation in the Balkans was marked by the disintegration of Yugoslavia with the former republics clashing over its legacy and the major powers over new spheres of influence in the region.

In between these events there stretched one whole century in which the powder keg became a metaphor for the Balkans, for the confrontations between the major European and world powers over spheres of interest and the wars between the Balkan states for disputed territories and the realisation of conflicting national programmes.[35] Neither several Balkan wars, including the latest one in the territory of Yugoslavia, nor the two world wars have led to pacification on Balkan soil.[36] On the contrary, they have provided strong evidence that there is a very long road to peace and stability in the Balkan region and perhaps this is the best opportunity for NATO to play a catalyst role in the whole region.

Of course there are several reasons which contributed to the creation of the Balkans as a 'powerful generator of instability in Europe'[37] such as the geo-strategic and geo-political significance of the region for the big powers. The geo-strategic importance of the Balkans is based on the following facts:

- The Balkan area lies astride important land routes between Europe and the Middle East.
- The Balkan peninsula's material and more recently ecological resources are far from negligible.
- The Balkan territory, between the Danube river, the Black Sea and the Mediterranean represents a significant factor in the European and global strategy of the major powers.

The Balkans had the greatest geo-political significance in the early decades of this century when the major European countries contended over the legacy of the Turkish Empire and the spheres of influence in the Balkans. At the time, the Balkans represented a significant element in the European balance of power and in their efforts to gain a certain advantage in the First World War which was in the offing.

In the Second World War, the geo-strategic significance of the Balkans declined from the standpoint of Germany's main thrusts of expansion and also the strategic preoccupation of the big allied powers. Although after the Second World War the so-called Iron Curtain cut the Balkans in two, decisions about the development and outcome of the Cold War were taken far from the Balkans, especially in central Europe.[38] Neither bloc would give up on the Balkans even though they did not look upon them as a region of essential importance for the fate of peace.[39]

This decline in the geo-strategic significance of the Balkans would have continued after the eastern bloc had fallen apart and bipolarism come to an end, even if a crisis had not emerged in the Balkans against the background of the break-up of the Yugoslav federation especially because the Balkan area had increasingly lagged behind the tempo of European integration. The Balkans are now in the lime-light due to the following reasons:

- The crisis in the area of former Yugoslavia reflects negatively on the process of European integration and the establishment of the new world order.
- The crisis in the area of former Yugoslavia has in some respects confirmed that the big European and world powers share common interests, but has also highlighted their differences of approach and interests, based on old historical and geo-strategic beliefs.
- Rightly or wrongly, attempts to settle the crisis on the territory of the Yugoslav space were seen as putting to the test the ability of the European and international community to control crises in the post-Cold War period.

It is for these reasons that in the twenty-first century the Balkans remains an area of concern for Europe and the US so long as crises in this region continue to be unresolved.

THE BALKANS AND THE POSSIBILITY OF A SECURITY SYSTEM

No comprehensive security system has ever existed in the Balkans. The Balkan Pact, concluded by Yugoslavia, Romania, Greece and Turkey in 1934, was the closest thing to such a comprehensive Balkan regional security system. Although the Balkan Pact was established as a mechanism for mutual co-operation among the Balkan countries, it represented a political barrier under the patronage of France and Great Britain to the influence of Germany and Italy, and to countries within their zone of influence such as Bulgaria. However, on the eve of the Second World War efforts were made to draw Bulgaria into the Balkan Pact. Had these efforts succeeded, there would perhaps have been something close to a comprehensive regional security system in the Balkans.

After the Second World War, the Balkan countries came under different regional security systems, NATO and the Warsaw Pact. The only regional, though partial, system of security was the Balkan alliance of Yugoslavia, Greece and Turkey, established by the Ankara agreement of 1953, which was short-lived.

In view of the Balkans' historical legacy of persistent conflict and the new antagonisms that surfaced with the disintegration of Yugoslavia, peace and stability in the Balkans might be achieved only through a comprehensive Balkan regional system of security.

A comprehensive regional system in the Balkans should be viewed as a kind of a pact or alliance of all the Balkan countries which might be linked with NATO or the CSCE or included in regional agreements envisaged in Chapter 8 of the UN Charter. There are two roads to such a Balkan regional security system.

One road would imply a prior resolution of territorial and ethnic problems which are the 'apple of discord' among the Balkan countries. The other road would call for the creation of such a political atmosphere in relations among the Balkans countries as would make it possible by establishing a joint security system to sweep away or peacefully resolve their disputes over territorial and ethnic questions and thereby secure peace and stability in the region.

The former road appears more promising because the removal of the sources of conflict would establish a firmer foundation for a regional security system. Regrettably, it should be kept in mind that throughout this century neither the wars that have swept the Balkans nor the periods of peace such as the period of bipolarism have seen the elimination of major policy conflicts.

To all intents and purposes, this means that there remains the second road, that of fostering a political climate which would help to set up a comprehensive regional system in the Balkans despite unresolved territorial and ethnic disputes. Its establishment would mean that the Balkan countries would no longer take up arms against each other but would settle their disputes by peaceful means. In that case, conditions would be created to settle disputed questions concerning territory and ethnic minorities and, what is more important, conditions would be created to come to a common realisation that in the last analysis such questions cannot be solved on the basis of any Balkan country's maximalist programmes, but only if they were recognised and accepted as a historical and geo-political reality.[40]

Involvement of all Balkan countries[41] in the process of NATO enlargement would be a major contribution towards achieving this goal. To justify this standpoint one should bear in mind NATO's and the UN's conflict prevention and peacekeeping missions in the area today. The first is the IFOR for Bosnia which was later transformed into the SFOR, without which the peace in Bosnia–Herzegovina and the implementation of the Dayton Peace Accords would have been impossible.[42] Another is the UNTAES on which the future of eastern Slavonia and of Serb–Croatian relations as a whole depends. The third is the UNPREDEP in the Former Yugoslav Republic of Macedonia (FYROM) which, despite the small number of troops it has, has played a very important role in preventing an expansion of the Yugoslav crisis. More recently NATO launched 'Operation Allied Force' against the Yugoslav forces in Kosovo which resulted in the eventual deployment of the KFOR.[43]

Two Balkan states, Greece and Turkey, are NATO members and others which were in the Warsaw Pact are members of the Council for Co-operation with NATO. This road is likely to be taken by the states emerging on the territory of former Yugoslavia. However, at least one open question remains: will NATO want to embrace the Balkan states outside of its original activity?

THE ROLE OF THE SOUTH-EAST EUROPEAN CO-OPERATIVE INITIATIVE (SECI)

The disappearance of bipolarity brought new alignments in the Balkan region on the side of the US: in the first place, among the former republics of the Yugoslav Federation (Slovenia, Croatia, the Moslem– Croatian Federation in Bosnia and Former Republic of Macedonia), then Albania, Romania and Bulgaria. All of these countries see their future within western European integration and seek to ensure their own security by linking up with NATO through the 'Partnership for Peace' programme and possibly, full-fledged

NATO membership.[44] However, NATO has thus far opened its doors for only three of the central European countries (Poland, Hungary and the Czech Republic), while the other candidate countries have to be satisfied with 'Partnership for Peace'. The reason behind this can be traced to the beginning of the 1990s where European and US analysts placed the Balkan countries at the bottom of the list of candidates for joining European and NATO integration processes, not just because of their economic underdevelopment and the shortcomings of their social and political structures, but on account of their alleged cultural incompatibility with western European societies.[45]

Therefore, the current US administration in order to show its interest in the region, has chosen to form the so-called SECI, which foresees the establishment of a regional organisation of eleven countries (Albania, Bosnia–Herzegovina, Bulgaria, Croatia, Greece, Hungary, FYROM, Moldavia, Romania, Slovenia and Yugoslavia) with an aggregate population close to 150 million.[46] As there is very little that could be common to such a heterogeneous group of countries, the US idea is to have co-operation focus on infrastructure and environmental problems in the area (fields in which their common interests are the least controversial), and be based on self-help, though the west would promote joint projects through the World Bank, the IMF and other financial institutions.[47] Under these circumstances during the first meeting of this group on 5–6 December 1996 in Geneva, Croatia and Slovenia withheld their signatures fearing that SECI might lessen their chances of becoming part of the central EU integration process.

Due to the political geography of SECI (SECI encompasses territories between Russia, western Europe, the Mediterranean and the Middle East), this ambitious plan is likely to be seen as a utopia due to the considerable investments which will be necessary for their infrastructure and economic development to become compatible so that the region could function as a trade bloc. Moreover, the differences (especially when dealing with security concerns) had become apparent at the Ministerial Meeting of the Balkan Countries at Thessaloniki in June 1997 where they were all agreed that the 'Partnership for Peace' programme and NATO could reduce the tensions and create conditions for the political solution of open ethnic and territorial disputes.[48] Creation of a regional security system might help to alleviate some of the most visible security threats and threat perceptions. In that respect, the presence of NATO in the Balkans can be constructive as was stated in the Thessaloniki Declaration:

The Ministers stress the important role of NATO for peace and stability in Europe and consider that the accession to NATO of the South-East European States which have applied for membership to that organisation would contribute to the enhancement of its role.[49]

However, post Cold War Greek–Turkish rivalry continues to produce instability in the Balkan region and as a result diminishes any chance of a comprehensive Balkan regional security system. Being by far the most powerful military nations in southern Europe, a potential war between Greece and Turkey within the NATO organisation would devastate the Balkan region and jeopardise the very existence of NATO due to the countries' membership in the alliance.

The next two chapters will look at the issues that divide Greece and Turkey in terms of security relations and membership of NATO. They will also examine the strategic importance of these two countries and their contributions to the NATO alliance.

NOTES

1. See R. Asmus, R.L. Kugler and F.S. Larrabee, 'NATO Expansion: The Next Steps', *Survival*, 37, 1 (1995) pp.7–33. See also Simon Lunn, 'NATO in Evolution: The Challenges for 1994', *Brassey's Defence Yearbook* (London: Royal United Services Institute, 1995) p.116. See also Richard L. Kugler, 'NATO Military Strategy for the post-Cold War era: Issues and Options', *RAND Report* (1992). See also Karl Kaizer, '*Reforming NATO*', *Foreign Policy*, 103 (1996) pp.129–43; Javier Solana, 'The Washington Summit: NATO Steps Boldly into the 21st Century', *NATO Review*, 47, 1, (1998) pp.3–6. See also Philip Zelikow, 'The Masque of Institutions', *Survival*, 38, 1, Spring (1996) pp.6–18 and Tom Dodd, 'NATO Enlargement', *Research Paper*, *97/51* (London: International Affairs and Defence Section, House of Commons, 8 May 1997).

2. The majority of the former communist states have embarked on a vigorous attempt to democratise their political systems and liberalise their economies. However, many political, economic and societal problems still exist and it will take some time until they can successfully be tackled.

3. The Mediterranean region is made up of many sub-regions, each with unique concerns, and interests. The eastern Mediterranean is one of these sub-regions. As a whole, according to M. Nimetz 'the region is, and historically always has been, a dynamic one through which commerce moves, people travel, and civilisations exchange knowledge, ideas, technologies, and values. When the Mediterranean region has had relative security, the world as a whole has benefited. As a result, the interests of the United States and the European Union are profoundly affected by the security of the Mediterranean', Matthew Nimetz, 'Mediterranean Security After the Cold War', *Mediterranean Quarterly*, 8, 2 (1997) p.27.

4. For the purpose of this book the term 'eastern Mediterranean' will consist of Greece, Turkey and Cyprus.

5. R.D. Asmus, F. Stephen Larrabee and I.O. Lesser, 'Mediterranean Security: New Challenges, New Tasks', *NATO Review*, 44, 3, (1996) p.28.

6. See *NATO Review*, May 1995 and January 1996. For further study see also Paul Cornish, 'European Security: the end of architecture and the New NATO', *International Affairs*, 74, 4 (1996) pp.751–70.

7. The terms 'Mediterranean nations', 'Mediterranean region' and 'Mediterranean Sea' will be used in this book to include all states within the eastern Mediterranean and the region bordering it. Sources of instability that can be identified encompass poor economic performance, control of key energy supplies, demographic change and population movements, Islamic fundamentalism, terrorism, drugs trafficking, proliferation of conventional and unconventional weapons.

8. R. Aliboni, G. Joffe and T. Niblock (eds), *Security Challenges in the Mediterranean* (London: Frank Cass, 1996) p.161.

9. For more details see A. Cottey, 'Western Interests in the Balkan Wars', *Brassey's Defence Yearbook*, (London: Royal United Services Institute, 1994).

10. NATO had adopted a conciliatory policy with regards to Russia. As a result, NATO has agreed to the reorganisation of the flank zones in the CFE agreement in order to pacify Russian concerns along its southern border. At the same time NATO instituted the 1997 Founding Act on Mutual Relations, Co-operation and Security between NATO and the Russian Federation – a policy which represents a sharp departure from the politics of the Cold War. The document established a permanent institutional framework for a security partnership between NATO and Russia. The Founding Act provided Russia with a voice but not a veto in NATO discussions on all non-Article Five tasks including peacekeeping missions. This unprecedented co-operation was institutionalised by twice-yearly meetings under the auspices of the Permanent Joint Council where they would discuss 'issues of common interest related to the security in the Euro-Atlantic area', see Tom Dodd, 'NATO's New Directions', *House of Commons Research Paper*, 98/52 (1998) p.21. See also *SIPRI Yearbook 1998: Armaments, Disarmament and International Security* (Stockholm International Peace Research Institute: Oxford University Press, 1998) pp.142–5. See also Marshall I. Sergeyev, 'We Are Not Adversaries, We Are Partners', *NATO Review*, 6, 1 (1998) p.17.

11. L.S. Kaplan, R.W. Clawson and R. Luranghi, *NATO and the Mediterranean* (Wilmington, Delaware: Scholarly Resources, 1985) p.3.

12. See R. Asmus, F. Stephen Larrabee & I.O. Lesser, 'Mediterranean Security: New Challenges, New Tasks', *NATO Review*, 44, 3 (1996) p.25.

13. See Admiral T. Lopez, 'AFSOUTH – Focus on the Southern Europe', *NATO Sixteen Nations*, 1 (1997) p.57.

14. See Nicola de Santis, 'The Future of NATO's Mediterranean Initiative', *NATO Review*, 1 1998) p.32.

15. F. Stephen Larrabee et al., 'NATO's Mediterranean Initiative', *RAND Report* (1998), p.1. See also Z. Khalizad and Ian O. Lesser (eds), 'Sources of Conflict in the 21st Century: Regional Futures and US Strategy', *RAND Report* (1998) pp.239–40. Ian O. Lesser argues that the 'Mediterranean is the front line in relation to many of the most pressing security and security-related issues facing Europe', see Ian Lesser, 'Mediterranean Security: New Perspectives and Implications for U.S. Policy', *RAND Report* (1993).

16. Many Greek military analysts argue that Turkish claims over the Greek islands and islets coincided with the building of a strong Turkish navy.

17. See *NATO Sixteen Nations*, 1 (1997) p.58.

18. See Vice Admiral E. Lagaras, 'Sea Control of the Eastern Mediterranean: The Role of the Greek Islands', *NATO Sixteen Nations*, 1 (1992) p.3.

19. See Richard G. Whitman, 'Securing Europe's Southern Flank? A Comparison of NATO, EU and WEU Policies and Objectives', *NATO Report* (1999) pp.25–6. See also 'The Mediterranean Region in 2020 and its Role in the European Energy Network', *Commission of the European Communities*, MEMO/95/52.

20. E.R. Grilli, *The Southern Policies of the EC: Keeping the Mediterranean Safe for Europe* (Cambridge: Cambridge University Press, 1993) p.180.

21. 'The focus of Mediterranean security policy from 1945 through 1990 may have been on keeping the Soviets out, because of the USSR's goals and the nature of its system, but this

was just a fleeting manifestation of the long-term goal of the West…to establish and maintain in the Mediterranean region a secure environment for the movement of people, goods and ideas', M. Nimetz, 'Mediterranean Security', p.27.

22. See Melvyn P. Leffler, *A Preponderance of Power* (Stanford, California: Stanford University Press, 1967) p.110.
23. See Marios Evriviades, 'Power Competition in the eastern Mediterranean: An Historical Perspective and Future Prospects', in A. Theophanous and Van Coufoudakis (eds), *Security and Co-operation in the eastern Mediterranean* (Nicosia: Intercollege, 1997) p.57. See also Philip Windsor, 'NATO and the Cyprus Crisis', *Adelphi Paper*, 14 (1964) p.6.
24. See Ian O. Lesser, 'Mediterranean Security: New Perspectives and Implications for U.S. Policy', *Rand Report* (1993) pp.5–6. See also Jonathan T. Howe, 'Link or Barrier – Defense of the Mediterranean', *NATO's Sixteen Nations*, April (1990).
25. In 1963 the Americans deployed in the eastern Mediterranean the Polaris submarine-launched ballistic missiles. The Polaris missile and its various versions, including the Poseidon gave the US navy deployed in the eastern Mediterranean the capability to attack, for the first time, the industrial heartland of the Soviet Union, such as the vital installation at the Baku oil fields and major population centres south of Moscow.
26. See *NATO Sixteen Nations*, 1 (1992) pp.36–7.
27. For the important role of the Hellenic navy in the eastern Mediterranean see Vice Admiral H.N. Stagas, 'The Hellenic Navy's Role in Mediterranean Security', *NATO's Sixteen Nations*, 1 (1994) pp.32–4. For the role of the Turkish navy in the Mediterranean and the Black Sea respectively see Admiral I. Tinaz, 'Maritime Security in a New Environment: The Role of the Turkish Navy', *NATO's Sixteen Nations*, 1 (1992) pp.65–8, and Admiral V. Bayazit, Black Sea and Mediterranean Challenges for the Turkish Navy', *NATO's Sixteen Nations*, 1 (1994) pp.67–73.
28. This opinion was expressed by A. Hitler during the Second World War.
29. See Rodrigo de Rato, 'Co-operation and Security in the Mediterranean, North Atlantic Assembly, Political Committee', *Report* October (1995), p.5.
30. ibid.
31. ibid.
32. For further study see Aliboni, *Security Challenges*. See *also North Atlantic Assembly Reports* (1995).
33. *The Guardian*, 10 January 1992.
34. *The Financial Times*, 21 February 1992.
35. For an excellent study of the Balkan region and the influence of the major European powers see Misha Glenny, *The Balkans 1804–1999*, (London: Granta Publications, 1999).
36. However, the period of Soviet domination during the Cold War era did pacify the region.
37. Interview with Professor P. Simic, Director of the Institute of International Politics and Economics, Belgrade, during a Corfu International Conference about Conflict Resolution, in summer 1997.
38. Most of the International Analysts including organisations like NATO and the EU have focused their research about potential enlargement in central Europe.
39. 'During the Cold War, the balance of the Balkans was regulated within the broader European balance under the "2+2+2" formula. Namely, two of the six Balkan states were members of NATO (Greece and Turkey), two were members of the Warsaw Treaty (Romania and Bulgaria), Yugoslavia was non-aligned from the mid-1950s, whilst Albania was in self-imposed isolation from the end of the 1950s. Although not a single ethnic or territorial problem that was prevalent in the Balkans was resolved in the course of this Cold War period, the region was calm because the bipolar division helped suppress the many local disputes that were threatening to burst'. Interview with P. Simic, Corfu, 1997.
40. Effectively this would create a Balkan 'Security System' based on Deutsch's work. For a view about the stabilisation of the Balkan region see B. Blagoev, 'Two Models for Stabilisation of the Balkans and South-Eastern Europe', *Balkan Forum*, 2, 5 (1997) pp.49–63.

41. See R. Vukadinovic, 'South-Eastern Europe: Instabilities and Linking Strategies', *Conference Paper*, Corfu (1997). See also Lev Vorohkov, 'The Challenges of NATO Enlargement', *Balkan Forum*, 2, 5 (1997) pp.5–39.

42. For the role of the SFOR see NATO fact sheets, 1 October 1999, *www.nato.int/sfor.*

43. See NATO basic documents, *www.nato.int/kosovo/docu/a990609a.htm.*

44. Romania acceded to the 'Partnership for Peace' programme on 26 January, Bulgaria did so on 14 February and Albania on 23 February 1994. Slovenia joined the programme on 30 March, FYROM did so on 15 November 1995. For further study see *NATO Review* (March, 1996), *NATO Review* (May, 1995), *Brassey's Defence Yearbook* (1994).

45. On this point, see W. Wessels, 'Deepening Versus Widening? Debate on the Shape of EC-Europe in the Nineties', in W. Wessels and C. Engel (eds), *The European Union in the 1990's Ever Closer and Larger?* (Bonn: Europa Union Verlag, 1993). See also *To Vima*, Greek daily newspaper, articles about NATO and the Balkans, 30 March 1997, 13 April 1997.

46. (SECI), US Department of State, 28/5/96.

47. P. Simic, 'NATO and the Balkans', *Conference Paper,* Corfu (1997).

48. For further study see *To Vima*, Greek newspaper, 6 July 1997.

49. See *Thessaloniki Declaration on Good-Neighbourly Relations, Stability, Security and Co-operation in the Balkans*, Thessaloniki, 10 June 1997.

2

Greek Security Challenges and its Relationship with NATO

One of the chief axes[1] which determines the strategic position of Greece within the current international system is the southern flank of NATO. This axis constitutes the foundation upon which Greek strategic thinking is formulated and Greek policy options are developed. This region is currently in a state of fluctuation, as the post-Cold War order is undergoing fundamental changes and long-established structures and regimes are rendered obsolete.[2] The rapid reduction in tensions in east–west relations has been accompanied by the resurfacing and exacerbation of local and regional conflicts that were dormant during most of the post-war period due to the strategic overlay centred by the bipolar security system.[3] These regional tensions have affected the southern flank of NATO and especially Greece and Turkey. Despite the demise of the Soviet Union and the collapse of communism, NATO has found itself in the invidious position of having Greece and Turkey, the two main participants on its southern flank, in dispute with one another over the Aegean and over Cyprus.

Therefore, this chapter will assesses NATO's role in Greece and how this partnership developed during the Cold and post-Cold War period. In order to examine NATO's role in Greece, it would be appropriate to analyse the relations of Greece with Turkey and to place them within a historical context. From this, it can be seen that Greece's role within NATO has been determined by its problems and disputes with Turkey.

HISTORICAL MORPHOLOGY OF GREECE

Greece is a small country of ten million inhabitants strategically located around the north-eastern margin of the Mediterranean Sea. Emerging from its struggle against the Ottoman Empire during the 1820s, Greece found itself trapped into a dependency upon foreign

powers and a passive role in international affairs. Since the aim of the
revolutionaries of 1821 was restoration of the grandeur of Byzantium,
the puny Kingdom of Greece that emerged in 1830 was no more than
a sad caricature of what had been aspired to. It was sovereign only in
name, for the three 'Protecting Powers' – France, Russia and Great
Britain – claimed and exercised authority within the new state. When
the Great Powers disagreed, in pursuit of their own interests, they
exerted influence upon supporters within Greece to forward their
respective policies.[4] This situation reinforced and embittered the
factionalism that became characteristic of Greek public life. Nevertheless, the Greek leaders continued to strive for the liberation of
Greeks still living within the borders of the Ottoman Empire, but the
resources of the newly established kingdom of Greece were patently
insufficient to overthrow the Turks without help. Therefore, support
from the Great Powers was necessary. A policy of currying favour with
one Great Power alienated the others, and the disaffected Great
Powers were in a position to stir up powerful political rivals to the
existing government in Greece almost at will. Effective government
and successful irredentist policy against the Ottoman Empire were
impossible in such a situation. Greece's attempt to assert its own
policy, independent of Great Power approval, was denied by them
and customarily met firm opposition.[5]

However, the desire of the Greeks to establish Greater Greece
(Megali Idea) could not be abandoned. After all it was the *raison d'être*
of the kingdom. Twice the complex working of European diplomacy
allowed Greeks to acquire additional territory, largely at the expense
of the Turkish Empire. In 1864, Great Britain transferred the Ionian
islands to Greece and in 1881 the Turks were forced to cede Thessaly
to compensate Greece for the emergence of the state of Bulgaria after
the Congress of Berlin.[6] However, in 1897, when the Greeks tried to
follow an irredentist foreign policy against the Ottoman Empire they
had to turn to the Protecting Powers (France and Great Britain) in
order to avoid a humiliating defeat.

The emergence of Elefterios Venizelos on the political scene in
Greece, during the Balkan Wars of 1912–13, was catalytic for the
future of Greece. Under Venizelos, the Greeks formed the Balkan
League with Serbia, Bulgaria and Montenegro to fight against the
Turks. When Greece acquired southern Epirus and Macedonia, its
territory increased by about 70 per cent and its population grew from
2.8 million to 4.8 million.[7]

The First World War brought about a national schism of major
dimensions in Greek politics, because the leaders could not decide
whether to fight in the war or remain neutral. On the one hand,
Venizelos and his Liberal Party favoured and pressed participation on

the side of the Entente (France, Great Britain, Russia, US) and on the other hand, King Constantine was sympathetic to the Central Powers (he was married to Kaiser William II's sister) and advocated neutrality. Despite this political split Greece finally entered into the war when Anglo-French pressure forced Constantine to leave Greece. For his loyalty and 'good behaviour', Venizelos received promises of territorial gains from the victorious allies. But the political divisions within Greece, and subsequently between Greece's patrons, Britain and France, led Greece to a catastrophic and humiliating military defeat in 1922 by the Turks, known in Greece as the Great Debacle.[8]

Despite the defeat of Greece in Asia Minor by the Turks, in July 1923 the Treaty of Lausanne laid the foundations for peaceful relations between Greece and Turkey for many years to come. Venizelos and Ismet Inonou, Turkey's representative at Lausanne, agreed to a very complex compulsory exchange of populations in most major areas except Constantinople (Istanbul), Imvros and Tenedos, western Thrace and Cyprus (then under British rule) in order to reduce tensions and make each nation more homogeneous. Turkey also received eastern Thrace, Imvros, Tenedos and Smyrna, but Greece kept western Thrace and had its sovereignty recognised in Mytilini, Chios and Samos. The treaty also revoked the special guarantee that Britain, France and Russia were to protect Greece, preventing those three powers from using the guarantee as a pretext for interference.[9]

Exhausted by many years of war, both countries turned their attention to internal developments, particularly to the problems associated with economic and political reconstruction. On the political scene in Greece, rival political and military elites sought to capitalise on the rancorous spirit which the defeat of 1922 left behind. Nevertheless by the end of the 1920s the worst of the crisis had passed. Venizelos was restored to power and in a dramatic turnaround from previous patterns, he and Turkey's leader Kemal Ataturk established an unprecedented co-operation between these two countries. In their efforts to secure joint interests and stability in the Balkan region, they developed a Balkan Pact, which also included Yugoslavia and Romania. Their aim was to prevent any involvement from the major powers, but this policy was never likely to succeed against determined outside interference. Therefore, regional commitments were abandoned the moment the Axis allies advanced toward the Balkan region and collapsed after war broke out in September 1939.[10]

The end of the Second World War found Greece devastated from the Axis occupation and presented with the additional burden of facing the growing strength of an indigenous communist movement, backed by the dominating presence of Soviet forces in eastern Europe and the support of neighbouring countries such as Yugoslavia.[11]

Shortly after Greece's liberation indirect Soviet support for the Greek communists, supplemented by direct assistance from Yugoslav Marshal Josip Tito, was attempted in Greece where guerrilla warfare developed.[12] By early 1947 Great Britain, due to its limited resources, realised that it could not sustain its former hegemonic role in Greek affairs[13] and asked for the assistance of the US. The expansionist policy of Stalin which was accompanied by the establishment of communist regimes in Poland, East Germany, Romania, Hungary, Bulgaria, Albania and Czechoslovakia aroused profound anxiety in Washington. In March 1947, when Great Britain declared itself unable to continue support of Greece, President Truman instituted his policy of aid for Greece and Turkey and thereby committing the US to preventing further communist expansion.[14] Greece and Turkey were the first two countries to benefit from the 1947 Truman Doctrine, in the form of direct US financial and political support for the struggle against communist subversion and Soviet pressure.[15] The Cold War commenced, and for Greece the reality was that the US undertook the hegemonic role, formerly assumed by Great Britain, in Greek affairs. Coincident with extensive military and economic aid, which contributed to the crushing of the communist guerrilla insurgency in 1949, came increased US involvement in Greek affairs.[16] Former Prime Minister Alexandros Papagos' aphorism that 'we exist not only thanks to our own decision, but because the Americans exist' expresses Greek dependence on the US at the time. In return for US aid received in a time of desperate need, the Greek political elite provided significant services to the US. Greek foreign policy in the late 1940s, 1950s and early 1960s became little more than a reflection of US views.[17]

GREECE'S ENTRY INTO NATO

The urgency of civil war related problems and the inability of a divided and paralysed government to handle the domestic situation effectively disposed Greek politicians to allow the US an implied role in Greek internal affairs even if this was a natural affront to national sovereignty. Committed Greek anti-communists exploited this situation and pressed for US involvement and NATO membership as a more permanent guarantee of its national security against the communist threat from the north. After vigorous efforts from the US administration the Congress convinced its public to assist Greece due to the imminent Soviet threat which was not limited to Greece but would have serious implications for Turkish and west European security.[18] The Truman Doctrine was officially announced on 12

March 1947 and the Marshall Plan was proclaimed in June 1947. Greece's total share of the plan was 1.7 billion dollars in economic aid (loans and grants) and 1.3 billion dollars in military aid between 1947 and the 1960s.[19] Between 1946 and 1987, military and economic assistance totalled more than $13 billion to Turkey and $9 billion to Greece. Of these amounts, military aid accounted for $9 billion to Turkey and $5 billion to Greece.[20]

The fear of communist danger forced Greece and Turkey to come even closer than had been the case in the 1930s. Both countries tried to raise the question of being accepted by the Atlantic alliance in 1950. In their efforts to convince the alliance they despatched combat forces to South Korea. They were acting as members of the UN, but their motive was clearly to overcome objections to their entry into NATO. As long as Greece was in the throes of a communist rebellion, Britain and several other NATO members opposed admission for fear that they might be drawn into an unwanted conflict. Only the US and Italy openly favoured the entry of Greece and Turkey into the alliance. British objections were finally removed when efforts to forge a Middle East Command linking Egypt with NATO failed and the Egyptians demanded instead the evacuation of the British forces from the Suez Canal. The assassination of pro-British King Abdullah in Jordan, the Anglo-Iranian dispute over the nationalisation of the oil industry, and the Arab–Israeli dispute, finally convinced Britain and the other NATO members (mainly Denmark, Norway and the Benelux countries) that other steps should be taken to shore up the western position in the eastern Mediterranean. On 22 October 1951, a protocol was signed for the admission of Greece and Turkey. The process was completed on 18 February 1952, when the two countries officially became NATO members. The southern flank was further cemented by a treaty of friendship and co-operation between Greece, Turkey and Yugoslavia. A formal treaty of alliance was signed in August 1954.[21]

In the Cold War climate of the early 1950s, co-operation within NATO to face the Soviet threat seemed reasonable for Greece, but other security factors came to determine her foreign and domestic policy. It was widely expected that Greece would concentrate mainly on economic and political reconstruction, but this was not the case due to the emergence of bilateral differences with Turkey which surfaced to torment the relationship of Greece with NATO. While other NATO members focused on pursuing a strong commitment to collective defence during the Cold War era, Greece and Turkey shifted their attention to divisive regional issues. In order to understand the deterioration of NATO–Greek relations, it is necessary to look at the real and perceived factors that aggravated them.

CYPRUS DISPUTE

Cyprus drove a wedge between the new allies almost as soon as they had become NATO members. Cypriot efforts to achieve unification with Greece, sparked murderous anti-Greek riots in Turkey in 1955 which caused Greece to withdraw from NATO exercises for the first time. The Cyprus dispute is essential in understanding the progressive deterioration in Greek–Turkish relations, and the problems that were caused in the alliance. The issue of self-determination and union (enosis) of Cyprus to Greece was first raised by Greece at the UN General Assembly in 1954. Britain decided to introduce Turkey into the matter, to provide a counterweight to Greek demands. The Turkish government assumed responsibility for the welfare of the Turkish Cypriots and eventually tried to promote and safeguard Turkish–Cypriot affairs.[22] So an anti-colonial struggle gradually developed into a confrontation between Greece and Turkey.

The Cyprus dispute reflected a dilemma confronting successive Greek governments – the choice between strategic interests and the demands of public opinion and national aspirations. Successive administrations opted for the former, protected by secret diplomacy. This choice was the result of the political repercussions of the Cyprus problem on Greek political stability and relations with NATO and Turkey. The fact that Greece adopted NATO's suggestions for resolving the dispute led to inevitable clashes between Athens and Nicosia, culminating on 15 July 1974. The Greek-sponsored coup against the government of Cyprus triggered the Turkish invasion of the island five days later.

Turkey's leaders proved receptive to the idea of a solution to the Cyprus problem based on their minimum goals of a revised London and Zurich constitutional framework, which they pursued in the Cyprus intercommunal talks (1968–74). However, their main goal was the partition of Cyprus through a Greek–Turkish agreement. Turkey was aware of the weak bargaining position of the Greek dictators (1967–74). The latter were isolated at home and abroad, and their support of the destabilisation of the Cypriot government in turn weakened President Makarios's bargaining position even further, *vis-à-vis* the Turkish–Cypriots. As a Turkish diplomat stressed:

> The Greeks committed the unbelievably stupid move of appointing Sampson, giving us the opportunity to solve our problems once and for all. Unlike 1964 and 1967, the United States leverage on us in 1974 was minimal. We should no longer be scared off by threats of the Soviet bogeyman.[23]

After all, it had been Soviet[24] and US action that stopped the Turkish invasion threats and the bombing of Cyprus in 1964. Moreover, during the 1967 crisis on Cyprus, Greece met the terms of the Turkish ultimatum by withdrawing from Cyprus all the troops it had stationed since 1964.[25] Under these circumstances the invasion was seen as likely, though not inevitable.[26]

The entire history of post–1975 intercommunal talks was summarised in a memorandum conveyed by Greek–Cypriot Foreign Minister Rolandis to UN Secretary General Dr Waldheim in 1979. According to the Rolandis document, each time the Greek–Cypriots had made moves to accommodate a Turkish position, the Turkish side had taken a step back. First from 'federation' to 'federation by evolution' and then to proposals for the effective creation of two states.[27] It was widely believed among Greek leaders that NATO bore a great responsibility for the invasion and in general for the whole dispute.[28] One cannot neglect the fact that there was a unique situation in Cyprus because: i) a NATO member, using NATO weapons, took 35,000 of its forces out of the NATO structure in order to occupy part of another democratic European country; ii) Turkey effectively colonised another member of the western community. It was the first time in post-war European history that colonisation, invasion and occupation of a western European country by another had occurred. Turkey's aggressive attitude resulted in the occupation of 37 per cent of Cyprus, 52 per cent of the island's coastline, 70 per cent of its natural resources and 65 per cent of its tourist infrastructure.[29]

In assessing the US and NATO role in the Cyprus affair, Dr Sakellarides, a former US State Department official, best summarises the Greeks' perceptions of what was seen to be a tragedy:

> American or world public opinion cannot be deceived by the United States' specious arguments that the Turkish aggression was made to prevent its annexation by Greece. What the world saw was an act of brutal aggression aiming at the destruction of the overwhelming Greek majority of Cyprus.[30]

US Senator Kennedy concurred:

> The Turkish invasion turned the island into a shambles. In political terms, it violated the integrity of an independent state; in economic terms, it shattered the island's flourishing economy; and in human terms, it brought personal tragedy to thousands of families and turned half of the population into refugees, detainees, or beleaguered people caught behind the cease-fire lines.[31]

It is believed that the passive US attitude towards Cyprus can be explained by the fact that the US concern was not the rights or wrongs of either side or the fate of the two communities on the island, but rather a way to limit the potential damage to NATO and to the US strategic position in the Mediterranean.[32]

On 28 August 1974 Constanine Karamanlis, Prime Minister of Greece following the restoration of democracy, decided to withdraw Greece from the military arm of NATO as a protest against what Greeks saw as the US government's indifference to the Turkish invasion of Cyprus. The possibility of war against Turkey was not feasible due to the fact that the army was ill-prepared to confront a Turkish attack. His decision was also based on the belief that Turkey, a NATO member, had disregarded international agreements and remained a threat to Greek national sovereignty. By October 1975, however, Karamanlis contemplated the possibility to return Greece's armed forces to the NATO military command. Karamanlis's concern that Turkey would further advance its claims in the Aegean, with Greece's absence from the military command, was the main reason behind his decision to reconsider previous actions.

The restoration of democratic government in 1974 by Karamanlis was a major turning point in the political history of Greece. Karamanlis's foreign policy was characterised by diversification and a multi-faceted approach. He attempted successfully to expand Greek foreign policy options and reduce the heavy reliance on the US. In particular the May 1979 agreement securing the country's entry into the EU marked the beginning of a new era. Greece was accepted as an equal political and economic partner among the European states. EU membership in the 1981–2000 period has also served Greece both as diplomatic lever and as restraining mechanism. Greece's EU membership has convinced Turkey that its European future can only be achieved through abandonment of *casus belli* declarations and full normalisation of relations with Greece. At the same time, the EU has acted as a restraining mechanism. As a leading Greek academic argues:

> Greece has found itself, like Odysseus, tied to a European Union mast permitting it to resist the tempting siren songs of atavistic nationalism and irredentism. Without that mast, the Greek ship of state would have veered off course into a rough-and-tumble of the Balkan vortex, becoming a part of the problem.[33]

The Cyprus imbroglio has festered for some three decades but it also furnished the occasion for challenge on another front: the Aegean Sea. Those issues have even more serious ramifications than the Cyprus dispute. They directly affect the sovereignty and vital interests of both countries and the solidarity of NATO. For Greece, the Cyprus crisis was the catalyst in Greek foreign and defence policy after 1974. A threat from the Warsaw Pact was no longer perceived as the primary security consideration and disillusionment with the US and NATO contributed to a reconsideration of Greece's defence orientation.[34] To this end 'In the regional setting, Karamanlis operated on the premise that the primary and immediate threat to Greece was posed by the revisionist policies of fellow-NATO ally Turkey'.[35] The Greek government felt that Ankara rapidly escalated the 1974 crisis by challenging the *status quo* in the Aegean and thus turned the original dispute into a complex, multi-faceted problem.

THE AEGEAN DISPUTE: GREEK VIEWS AND THEORIES

Besides the Cyprus issue, four other critical issues have given rise to serious tension between Greece and Turkey and have influenced the effectiveness of NATO in the eastern Mediterranean: i) delimitation of the continental shelf; ii) Aegean territorial waters; iii) the alloca-tion of operational responsibility of the Aegean and its air space within the framework of NATO; iv) Turkey's claims concerning the demilitarisation of the islands of the Aegean. The Greek perspective is outlined as follows, drawing on interviews and analysis from Greek military officials and leading academics.

The problem of the continental shelf came to the forefront for the first time on 1 November 1973. On that date, the Turkish government published in the official *Turkish Official Gazette* a map that arbitrarily designated areas of the Aegean – including Greek areas – where the government of Ankara had issued a licence permitting research activities on the part of the Turkish Petroleum Company.[36] The subsequent tension reached crisis level in 1974 and again in 1976, when the Turkish oceanographic research vessels *Candari* and *Hora* sailed into the Aegean for the purpose of carrying out research activities on the seabed just outside the territorial waters of the Greek islands.

With respect to the delimitation of the continental shelf, the following differences exist between Greece and Turkey. The Greek position is that customary international law, as accepted by both the 1958 Convention on the Continental Shelf and its successor, the UN Convention on the Law of the Sea (LOS) in 1982, allows exploration and exploitation rights over the Greek continental shelf up to one hundred miles from its coastal and islands' baselines.

Turkey asserts that the difference to be settled concerns the partition of the entire Aegean continental shelf, and claims that it should acquire areas of continental shelf west of the Greek islands up to the middle of the Aegean. It also asserts that much of the Aegean seabed is in fact a prolongation of the Anatolian land mass.[37] Because Turkey itself wishes to exploit the seabed though, it has not questioned the sovereign and exclusive right of a coastal state to explore and exploit the natural resources of its continental shelf. By this logic, Turkey does not accept that the Greek islands are entitled to a continental shelf therefore. It felt it was within its rights not only because of the proximity of the Greek islands to the Turkish coast, but also because otherwise, by the Greek formula, nearly 97 per cent of the Aegean seabed beyond Turkish territorial waters would be Greek.

Throughout this period and until 1989, bilateral negotiations, and ICJ proceedings, produced no result. In November 1976, experts from Greece and Turkey agreed at a Berne meeting to establish a code of behaviour to govern future negotiations on the continental shelf. They also undertook to abstain from any initiative or act that would prejudice negotiations.[38]

Subsequent meetings provided few results. Fundamentally, Athens and Ankara remain concerned about sovereignty questions. Turkish insistence on a demarcation line for the continental shelf midway between the Greek and the Turkish mainlands intensifies Greek fears.[39] Athens sees this demarcation line as a direct threat to the sovereignty of the many Greek islands lying east of it. Turkey would have justification for establishing an economic zone with installations and then a security zone in the seas around these islands. The Greek government holds that these islands form a political continuum with the Greek mainland and that with increased regional penetration, the Turks would be able to interfere with Greek internal sea and air communications. The islands would then become threatened enclaves whose sovereignty would be menaced. This Greek archipelago, with its 400,000 inhabitants, is politically and economically linked with the mainland.

THE AEGEAN TERRITORIAL SEA

The most important and potentially divisive disagreement over the Aegean concerns Greece's territorial sea. Since 1936 Greece has claimed a six-nautical-mile territorial sea. Turkey's claim in the Aegean is identical, but it extends to twelve nautical miles off both its Black Sea and Mediterranean coasts.[40] Current claims have three high-seas corridors across the Aegean that permit Turkish vessels departing east-coast ports, such as Ismir and Kusadasi, to reach the Mediterranean without having to transit Greek waters.

Until UNCLOS III, which concluded in 1972, the issue of the breadth of territorial seas in the Aegean had caused little friction due to the fact that Greece and Turkey's opposing six-mile limits had proven workable. However, UNCLOS III was convened in great part to resolve the issue of territorial sea breadth, resolution having proven elusive at the two previous conferences on the law of the sea, in 1958 and 1960.[41] It explicitly recognised that every coastal state has the right of territorial waters to an outer limit of twelve nautical miles. Given the configuration of the Greek islands in the Aegean and the fact that islands are generally deemed to have territorial seas of their own, extension of the territorial limit would increase the Greek portion of the Aegean to 63.9 per cent and Turkey would only have 10 per cent.[42] High seas would shrink from 56 per cent to 26.1 per cent, and all ships leaving Turkish–Aegean ports for the Mediterranean would have to pass through Greek waters. Turkey believes that the right of innocent or transit passage is an inadequate guarantee and that it is too vulnerable to total enclosure.[43]

THE ATHENS FLIGHT INFORMATION REGION (FIR)

By refusing to accept an extension of Greece's territorial waters, Turkey points out that the existing six-mile limit should set the standard for Greek air space, which since 1932 has extended four miles beyond the limit of Greek territorial waters. In 1952 and 1958 the International Civil Aviation Organisation (ICAO) designated the Athens FIR to coincide with the sea and air boundaries, separating Greece from Turkey. A demarcation line divided the Athens and Istanbul FIR along a line roughly equal to the outer edge of the Turkish territorial sea. Greece thus had the responsibility for civilian and military air traffic over almost all of the Aegean. To have placed the FIR line farther to the west would have required Greek aircraft to pass through a Turkish control zone on flight to and from Greek islands in the eastern Aegean.

This agreement worked well for more than two decades, but it was first challenged by the Turks immediately following their invasion of Cyprus. In August 1974, Turkey arbitrarily issued NOTAM 714 by which it unilaterally extended its area of responsibility up to the middle of the Aegean, within the Athens FIR. Greece responded quickly on 7 August with NOTAM 1018, denying the validity of the Turkish act as contrary to existing practices. This was followed by the Greek NOTAM 1157 on 13 September, declaring Aegean air space a danger zone.[44]

Finally in 1980, Ankara withdrew NOTAM 714, when it realised that it was prejudicial to its interests and especially to the tourist industry.[45] One should also bear in mind, that during that time NATO, Greece and Turkey were negotiating the return of Greece to the alliance, and the issue of the NOTAMs pervaded those talks, with revocation consistently cited by NATO as one of the prerequisites to agreement.[46] Nevertheless, Turkey continues to violate the Athens FIR with its military aircraft under the pretext that the Chicago Convention does not concern military aircraft.

FORTIFICATION OF THE EAST AEGEAN ISLANDS

Another issue that can be characterised as extremely important for Greek–Turkish relations is the question of the fortification of the east Aegean islands. Turkey has invoked the relevant provisions of the Lausanne Treaty and Convention (1923) as well as the Paris Treaty (1947) even though Turkey never became party to this treaty due to its neutral status during the Second World War. Turkey has used it to protest against the fortification and militarisation of the east Aegean islands.

Contrary to Turkey's assertions, the militarisation of the islands of the eastern Aegean falls into three distinct categories: i) the right to install military forces on the islands of Limnos and Samothrace has been established by the Treaty of Montreaux of 1936, and has repeatedly been recognised by Turkey;[47] ii) concerning Lesvos, Chios, Samos and Ikaria, the Treaty of Lausanne imposed partial demilitarisation of these islands and not total demilitarisation as Turkey claims.[48] On the contrary, the treaty foresees the presence of some military forces, and Greece does indeed maintain a military presence on these islands in light of the need to protect its eastern frontier; iii) for the same reasons, Greece maintains in the Dodecanese a certain number of National Guard units which have been registered within the framework of the Treaty for Conventional Forces in Europe.

Apart from the aforementioned, Article 51 of the UN Charter declares that every country has the inalienable right of the legitimate defence of her territory. According to Greek academics and to most of the Senior Military Officers the exercise of this right is particularly applicable and necessary in the case of Greece, given: i) the Turkish invasion of Cyprus in 1974; ii) the formation by Turkey of the 4th Army Group of the Aegean, which is stationed exactly opposite the Greek islands, and is equipped with the largest fleet of landing craft in the Mediterranean;[49] iii) the fact that Ankara is not a party to the Treaty of Paris, and therefore does not have standing to complain of any violation.[50]

GREECE AND NATO: ICY RELATIONS DURING THE COLD WAR PERIOD

All of these problems between Greece and Turkey have influenced their role in NATO and their relations with the US. After 1974 it became clear among elites and publics in all three countries – especially in Greece – that the role of US influence in the region was beginning to recede. The Turkish military action in Cyprus served as a crude reminder that the US was no longer in a position (or no longer willing) to stop Greek–Turkish disputes in Cyprus or elsewhere from turning into actual and costly military conflict. On the other side, given the prominent role (politically and militarily) of the US in NATO and given the continuing dependence of both Turkey and Greece on the US for the upkeep and improvement of their defence establishments, both Greece and Turkey have been competing for US attention and have sought to enlist the US in a role of peacemaker, arbiter or just plain balancer.[51]

As a result of the Turkish invasion of Cyprus, Greece withdrew its military from NATO commands. Moreover, she also terminated the recently acquired home-porting rights of the US Sixth Fleet and denied the US the use of the naval base at Eleusis. It was also announced that NATO and US bases in the country would be placed under Greek authorities. Greek–US relations deteriorated further with the murder of the CIA station chief in Athens, Richard Welch by the 17 November terrorist organisation.[52] Then in February 1975 Congress imposed an arms embargo on Turkey for having violated the terms of the Foreign Assistance Act by using US arms and equipment to invade Cyprus. Ankara retaliated in July by suspending all military arrangements with the US and halting the activities of almost all US bases in Turkey.[53]

This situation provided NATO and the US with a serious dilemma regarding the making of choices in the troubled eastern Mediterranean region. The dilemma can be simply stated as follows: what does NATO do when two member states, whose strategic value is interdependent, enter into a situation of conflict that is hard to reconcile? If NATO (and the US) abstains from involvement, it may be considered to be impotent, indifferent, or implicitly supportive of the stronger party in the conflict.[54] If, on the other hand, NATO assumes an activist stance in an attempt to mediate Greek–Turkish disputes, it risks arousing the displeasure of one or even both of its members. Since the early 1950s the US and NATO have considered both Greece and Turkey as being strategically vital.

The 1981 electoral victory of Andreas Papandreou and PASOK brought scepticism among the NATO officials over Greece's future within the alliance. Despite Papandreou's electoral campaign pledges that Greece would withdraw from NATO altogether, once he was in power, he adopted the Karamanlis multidimensional foreign policy.[55] This meant that Greece would continue cultivating the climate of détente and co-operation with its northern neighbours and the Soviet Union, while seeking more improvement in the already good relations that Greece maintained with the states of the Arab world – especially with the oil-producing states.[56] *Vis-à-vis* western multilateral organisations to which Greece belonged, especially the European Community and NATO, Papandreou adopted a position that could be summarised as ideologically reluctant, but substantial active participation in these organisations. He explained this retreat from pre-election promises by stating that although PASOK's long-range vision was a Europe free of Cold War entanglements and military alliances, the realities of the situation in the short run dictated that Greece should operate cautiously and prudently to avert foreign adventures that might result in great national damage.[57] Since Papandreou perceived Turkey as the primary threat to Greek security, he decided to reformulate Greek defence policy.[58]

On the NATO level, Papandreou informed the first NATO DPC that Greece would observe its obligations in terms of force commitments and the supply of early warning information, but that full participation would require a guarantee of the country's eastern frontier against aggressive acts from Turkey. Despite the threat posed by Turkey, the alliance refused to provide any guarantees for the protection of Greek sovereignty and territorial integrity.[59]

Greece refused to participate in NATO exercises in the Aegean and requested, without success, that the alliance should train in the international waters and air space of that sea. To reinforce its objections, Athens refused the use of NATO infrastructure facilities to forces involved in exercises to which Greece was not a party. At issue was the island of Lemnos which Greece wanted to include in NADGE and exercise scenarios. The fortification of Lemnos by Greece based on the 1936 Montreaux Convention has been objected to by Turkey which claims that Greece violated the 1923 Treaty of Lausanne. In an attempt to overcome the Lemnos deadlock, Papandreou tried a roundabout approach at the end of 1984. Greece officially notified its allies of its forces on the island in the DPQ and asked that they be placed under NATO command, but failed to override Turkey's veto.[60]

Despite Papandreou's strong declaratory positions prior to the 1981 elections, the Socialist government pursued a rational policy with regards to the allocation of forces, aligned to the demands and needs of NATO's military doctrine. Admiral Lee Beggett, Jr

(CINCSOUTH) in an interview with the Turkish daily *Cumhuriyet* (17 June 1985) argued that the 1000-km borderline with Albania, Yugoslavia and Bulgaria was well covered by the Greek First Army Corps (Albania), the Second Corps and half of the Third (Yugoslavia) and the other half of the Third Corps, with the entire Fourth (Bulgaria). Furthermore, the Third and the Fourth Corps were well manned in peacetime and they were characterised as highly flexible in case of emergency. Most of the Greek armed forces were concentrated in the regions which were perceived as possible routes of attack (Vardar-Axios river and Nestos-Evros river).[61]

The electoral victory of Papandreou and the return of Greece into the military structure of NATO did not change the political landscape in the eastern Mediterranean with regards to the relations of Greece with NATO and Turkey. Eventually, things got worse when tension between Greece and Turkey almost spilled over into hostilities in March 1987 in a flare-up over oil exploration outside territorial waters. The situation was sufficiently grave that NATO permanent representatives convened an emergency session to call for non-recourse to force. A process of rapprochement was initiated by Prime Ministers Papandreou and Ozal and culminated in several meetings between them during an economic symposium in Davos, Switzerland at the end of January 1988. The two men tried to create a climate of confidence through subsidiary measures. However, the 'spirit of Davos' did not last and probably could not last for the simple reason that the real problems were not handled or solved, but were simply avoided.

All of these factors made Greek politicians from Karamanlis (1974) to Papandreou (1981) pursue a continuous and coherent defence policy. Even though their foreign policies differed, their main concern was the danger from the 'east'. In reality there is no significant difference between the process of Greek foreign and defence policy-making. Although defence is relatively constant, while foreign policy more evidently reflects the ideological inclinations of the party in power, the source is identical in both instances. As was the case under Karamanlis, Papandreou as Prime Minister was the major initiator of defence policy, aided by his ministers, the Chief of the Defence Staff and certain personal advisors. Greece's problems with Turkey, rather than the obligations towards the Atlantic alliance of which it is part, have since 1974 become the main point of Greece's security concerns. According to all Greek politicians the 'threat' within the alliance constitutes the most serious constraint on Greek foreign and defence policy, and as long as it persists the role of Greece within NATO will be problematic.

GREECE IN THE POST-COLD WAR ERA

Henry Kissinger said in 1965, that

> Of course no alliance can perfectly reconcile the objectives of all its
> members. But the minimum condition for effectiveness is that the
> requirements of the alliance [should] not clash with the deepest
> aspirations of one or more of the partners.[62]

However, this minimum condition has not been met on NATO's
south-eastern flank. The alliance has tended in the past to look the
other way and not to take any serious initiatives to resolve underlying
Greek–Turkish issues.[63]

It is widely believed in both countries that NATO is not impartial.
Each is convinced that the alliance tilts in favour of the other. The
Greeks believe that strategic considerations – *realpolitik* – invariably
give Turkey more weight in NATO councils because of its larger
population, troop strength and border with Russia and the vital US
interests in the Middle East. The Turks, on the other hand, believe
that the weight of their membership is limited by its purely strategic
character, and that NATO favours Greece for historic, cultural and
religious reasons. In other words, both Ankara and Athens consider
that NATO undervalues their membership, albeit for different
reasons. Paradoxically, NATO's neutral policy, while intended to
project the alliance's impartiality and encourage both countries to
settle their own disputes, appears to have had the opposite effect.
Ankara and Athens logically surmise that the south-eastern flank is
considered low priority and this gives them little reason to place
NATO priorities before their own.[64]

Until recently, NATO did not have a coherent post-Cold War
Mediterranean policy as such, although it did commit itself decisively
in peace-enforcement operations in former Yugoslavia. The first indi-
cation of the alliance's interest in the Mediterranean as a whole began
with the January 1994 Summit, which noted in its final communiqué
that 'security in Europe is greatly affected by security in the Mediterranean'.[65] The remarks of the US Deputy Assistant Secretary of
Defence for European and NATO Affairs, Joseph Kruzel, on 27
February at AFSOUTH outline the security challenges of NATO in
the Mediterranean:

> Today the real threat to European Security comes not from the
> northern region, where much of the Alliance's attention is now
> focused, but in the south, where existing conflicts and potential for
> catastrophe are pervasive.... For NATO, the Mediterranean, rather

than the Elbe, has become the front line for a variety of security issues ranging from the spread of extremism and uncontrolled migration to the proliferation of weapons of mass destruction ...[66]

While most of these challenges have been addressed by NATO (including the Bosnian conflict and Kosovo crisis), the tension in the eastern Mediterranean between Greece and Turkey has not been addressed adequately by the alliance.

For most European countries, the collapse of the Soviet Union triggered a profound change in security policies. Greece has been an exception to this pattern. The end of the WTO and the collapse of Yugoslavia were important, but the end of the Soviet Union made little difference because Greek security considerations are dominated by the relationship with Turkey.

As a result, the first priority of foreign policy since 1974 has been the consolidation of democracy and the quest for a strategy of economic convergence with more advanced EU partners, designed to safeguard Greece's European privilege. In their efforts to secure full economic and political integration in the post-Maastricht Europe, Greek policy-makers, whether from the ranks of ND (in government between 1990 and 1993) or the Socialist Party (PASOK) (in government since 1993) have opted for a Euro-Atlantic stance (akin to the Portuguese and Italian models). In other words they can pursue political and economic integration through the EU and simultaneously rely chiefly on NATO for the provision of collective defence and collective security values.[67]

The second priority in Greek foreign policy objectives is the maintenance of a sufficient state of military balance in the Greek–Turkish nexus of relations. The US has also acknowledged the necessity of a military equilibrium.[68] Since 1974 (following the Turkish invasion and continuing occupation of northern Cyprus) all Greece's political parties have considered Turkey as posing a major threat to Greece's territorial integrity in the Aegean and western Thrace. NATO has not provided a mechanism for intra-NATO dispute settlement and this fact led successive Greek governments to pursue a military balance of forces (mainly in the air and sea) with Turkey.

GREEK FOREIGN POLICY UNDER THE CONSERVATIVE PARTY

After winning the election of 1989, ND's main objective was to declare Greece's association with the western institutions. The main consideration of the Conservative government with regards to foreign policy was: i) the evolving shape of the European Community which would determine Greece's economic future; ii) the forms of western collective defence and security co-operation, which would assure Greece's security.[69] Greece, along with other southern EC members, favours an acceleration of the community's political union through a 'deepening' of its institutions.[70]

The Maastricht Treaty on European Union, which was ratified in December 1991, was greeted with satisfaction in Athens. At the same time Greece was also accepted to become a member of WEU. However, the EC's decision that Article 5 of the modified Treaty of Brussels – which provides a security guarantee in case of attack on members – should not be applied between member states of NATO and WEU[71] caused considerable irritation in Athens and diminished the importance of WEU membership from Greece's perspective.[72] The decision of WEU to invalidate Article 5 in case of a Greek–Turkish conflict renewed Greek interest in NATO and the US. Most of the political parties in Greece (excluding the Greek communists) realised that NATO poses the most credible deterrent against threats to Greece's security.[73]

During the period of 1991–3, Prime Minister Mitsotakis improved relations with the US and he also become the first Greek Prime Minister to visit Washington since 1964. Greece's positive stance during the Gulf War (naval support, use of air space and bases) strengthened the Greek–US relationship. Despite US criticism of the Greek policy toward the Muslim minority and the Slavic-speaking Greeks in Greek Thrace,[74] which caused irritation in Athens, the realisation that there is no substitute for a security relationship with the US and NATO, proved to be an imperative factor for the formulation of Greek foreign policy.[75]

GREEK FOREIGN PRIORITIES UNDER THE SIMITIS GOVERNMENT

After PASOK's impressive victory in the October 1993 election, Papandreou and the Socialist Party came to power. During the 1993 election economic issues largely dominated the electoral campaign and in general terms foreign policy played a minor role.

There was no remarkable change in foreign policy, yet today's Socialist Party scarcely resembles that of the 1980s, imprinted on the western consciousness as a period of fiery, leftist–nationalist rhetoric and awkwardly controversial positions on a raft of east–west and third world issues, long personified by Andreas Papandreou, PASOK'S founder and leader until his death in June 1996.[76]

Papandreou's successor, Premier Costas Simitis, shifted from nationalist populism to European pragmatism.[77] His start though was inauspicious. An argument with Turkey over the ownership of the Imia/Kardac islets in the Aegean broke out within days of his appointment. Simitis sensibly let the Americans prod him into compromise, which his political enemies derided as a humiliating climbdown.[78]

Under Simitis, co-operation, pragmatism and taking a leading role in the troubled Balkans has been the preferred approach. A hopeful sign for future relations with Turkey came in July 1997 at the Madrid NATO Summit as the Greek and Turkish leaders, with the support of the US and NATO General Secretary J. Solana, made a pledge to respect each other's rights and avoid the use of force against one another in the future. Many difficult problems remain unresolved for Greece in the Balkans, in the Aegean and in Cyprus, and a new realism in Greece's foreign policy under the Simitis government suggests that Greece will pursue a constructive foreign policy.[79] However, according to some scholars, the widespread belief that Simitis's foreign policy has steered Greece away from a nationalist foreign policy to a modernist/Europeanist direction is premature and simplistic.[80] Simitis has stated that

> a national strategy must be simultaneously a Balkan strategy … our aims for the creation of peace, for the continuous improvement of the international economic conditions which determine domestic condition … for a strong Greece, are inextricably bound with the process of European Integration.[81]

This policy can be challenged due to the fact that Greek foreign policy in the Balkan region aims towards countering Turkey's expansionism and influence, and in this sense the elements of continuity with Andreas Papandreou's nationalism remain considerable. At the same time Simitis's attempt to reinstate Greece's westernist diplomatic tradition can be associated with the liberalism of Karamanlis. Therefore, Simitis's foreign policy can be characterised as a dualistic one, combining nationalist and westernist elements with the aim to satisfy the two factions of his party and the wider Greek electorate.[82] As long as the tension between Greece and Turkey remains, the foreign policy of Greece will be formulated based on these elements.

THE EMU: A GREEK PANACEA

There is no doubt that one of the main objectives of Greek foreign policy was the participation in the European single currency. This opinion was stressed by the late Deputy Foreign Minister Yiannos Kranidiotis in an interview in *Hermes* magazine in October 1998. He stated:

> A key aim of our foreign policy is Greece's full and equal participation in European developments … (The) effort for Greece's entry into EMU on January 1, 2001 is an imperative choice, not only from an economic angle but also politically. It is linked with the security of the country itself. Greece will then be part of a core of European countries where political decisions are made.[83]

Simitis believes that the security of the country and modernisation of the Greek economy pass through Greece's participation in the EMU(European Monetary Union). Simitis perceives Europeanism and specifically Greek equal participation in the EMU as a panacea due to the fact that it will provide economic and political stability for Greece.[84] Moreover, as long as NATO cannot provide a mechanism for solving the disputes between Greece and Turkey, a strong and effective economy is seen as guaranteeing the capability of the country to stand up to any potential aggressor (for the Greeks, Turkey is the main threat).

GREECE AND TURKEY: AN ETERNAL DEADLOCK?

As mentioned earlier one of the most important priorities (from a defence standpoint) in Greek foreign policy objectives is the military balance between Greece and Turkey. Greek bipartisan policy calls for the maintenance of an adequate balance of forces (especially in the air and at sea) while avoiding the destabilisation of the economy with a costly arms race.[85] However, this has not been achieved, since Simitis failed to find a formula which he could use to start talks with Turkey. The NATO Summit in Madrid in July 1997 indicated the possibility of improved relations with Turkey. The Greek and Turkish leaders made a pledge to respect each other's rights and avoid the use of force against one another in the future.

Yannos Kranidiotis, the late Greek Foreign Affairs Undersecretary, said about the new agreement:

> What happened in Madrid was a positive first step. Turkey has accepted to abide by international law and by international agree-ments as regards its relations with Greece. At the same time, Turkey has accepted to withdraw its threats of force against Greece. We hope that more positive steps will follow … Its value will have to be proved in practice and in its application.[86]

The Madrid Joint Statement, however, did not contribute to a gradual improvement of bilateral relations because both sides are inflexible with regards to the procedure that needs to be followed.

Greek Foreign Minister Theodoros Pangalos asked Turkey to

> acknowledge that any future issues raised as well as those problems that already exist will be dealt with by legal means provided for by international law and specifically the International Court of Justice (ICJ). Such a step would open possibilities for a gradual build-up of good-neighbour relations and the establishment of confidence and co-operation in every field.[87]

Pangalos has also urged NATO to consider seriously the development of an intra-NATO dispute settlement mechanism which would help resolve differences peacefully as well as strengthen the appeal of the Atlantic alliance as an institution providing collective security and collective defence. On the other hand Turkey does not accept the jurisdiction of the ICJ and insists on 'meaningful and result oriented negotiations between Greece and Turkey'.[88]

Under these circumstances Simitis was affected by the Imia incident, and endorsed a major rearmament programme as well as reaffirming the commitment of Greece towards the 'Integrated Defence Doctrine' (with Cyprus) devised by Papandreou in 1993. In 1998 the Simitis government announced a mammoth seven hundred and fifty billion drachma rearmament programme over the following five years.[89] In 1999, KYSEA reiterated the interest expressed by the Hellenic Navy in acquiring four US-made, KIDD-class destroyers. It also approved the procurement of more fighter aircraft for the Hellenic Air Force.[90] National Defence Undersecretary D. Apostolakis justified the necessity of the rearmament programme by expressing the opinion that 'the Turkish threat exists and Greece will be faced with instability, threats and uncertainty which necessitates an effective and well-armed army'.[91]

It is widely believed that with the end of bipolarity, the post-war security arrangements in the Balkan region have been rapidly replaced by the emergence of local national rivalries and disputes. Greece and Turkey are two of the major players in the current unstable strategic environment of the Balkans. Their bilateral relations have rarely been smooth. Even today the issues that divide the two countries are complex and rooted in years of conflict and mutual distrust.

Since the end of the Cold War there has been no fundamental progress toward a comprehensive Greek–Turkish settlement. On the contrary, on 31 January 1996 the stalemate turned to a hot incident in the Aegean over the Imia (Kardak) islets. The confrontation between the two states over the Aegean islets has injected, according to the Greek elite, a disturbing new element into their tense relations. For the first time ever, Turkey is questioning Greek sovereignty over a portion of its territory, namely Imia and a large number of Aegean islets. Most probably the escalation of Turkish claims was ostensibly triggered by a Greek plan to populate some of the islets. However, for the last fifty years Greece has exercised unfettered sovereignty over the Imia islets. Turkish official maps, including naval maps, acknowledge Greek sovereignty over the islets as do British Admiralty maps, official US naval maps and Italian maps.[92]

Contrary to the cynical interpretation by the US and British media and by some US officials and British academics[93] that the Imia/ Kardak incident was over 'rocks and goats', the issue was the respect and continued validity of international agreements and of established international boundaries.[94] The US and the western European position during and immediately after the crisis was to avert war and avoid taking sides between the two NATO allies. This neutrality deeply disturbed the Greeks, who felt they deserved greater solidarity from their allies in the face of Turkey's aggressive acts.[95]

In the week after the crisis, Turkish Prime Minister Tansu Ciller escalated Turkish claims. She first stated that Ankara would re-examine the status of one thousand islets and threatened Greece with war over the issue. Subsequently, Ciller declared that the extension of Greek territorial waters to 12 miles would be a cause of war, for Turkey.[96] Successive Turkish governments have adopted the same position. From 4 to 9 February 1996, both the US and the EU began to move towards a position favouring Greece, albeit without coming down firmly on the Greek side. The Clinton administration advised the two sides to take their dispute to the International Court of Justice, a position implicitly favourable to Greece. The European Commission expressed its solidarity with Greece and pointed out that Turkey's customs union with the EU was intended, among other things, to promote Turkey's relations with Europe in the context of respect of international law and the absence of the threat or use of force.

Thus far, the positions of Greece and Turkey remain irreconcilable. Greece seeks to uphold the Aegean status quo as defined by bilateral and multilateral treaties. Turkey (according to the Greeks) seeks to revise that *status quo*, if necessary by threat of war in contradiction with UN principles and more specifically Article 2(4) of the UN Charter which 'prohibits the threat or use of force against the territorial integrity of the other states'.

An attempt to ease tensions between the two states was initiated by the Dutch Presidency of the EU in spring 1997. The two sides decided to form a committee composed of two nationals of each country. The Greek representatives were Professors Fatouros and Ioannou, both experts in international law. Turkey was also represented by a professor of international law, Bilge, as well as by a diplomat, Elegdag. During these negotiations no agreement was reached on any of the subjects that constitute the essence of the Aegean question. A deadlock on the key issues of the disputes has remained ever since.

Moreover, Greece has asked Turkey to accept the six principles embodied in the 24 March 1996 EU–Turkey Association Council statement and in the 15 July 1996 Declaration of the Council of the EU Foreign Ministers, namely:

- commitment to the principle of respect for international law and agreements and to relevant international practice;
- respect for the sovereignty and territorial integrity of EU members;
- acceptance that disputes should be settled solely on the basis of international law;
- restraint and avoidance of any action liable to increase tensions, and specifically the use or threat of force;
- dialogue for the improvement of bilateral relations and establishment of a crisis prevention mechanism;
- resort to the ICJ for disputes created by territorial claims.[97]

These principles constitute the cornerstones of the Greek foreign policy toward Turkey.[98] If Turkey accepts them, they could establish a *modus vivendi* between the two countries, which could lead to a settlement of the disputes between Greece and Turkey on the basis of international law.

Turkey, on the other hand, ignores the rules of international law and its obligations under international treaties; therefore, Greece cannot start negotiations on the substance of the Greek–Turkish differences.[99]

THE CYPRUS IMBROGLIO

Another thorn in the Greek–Turkish relations is the Cyprus issue. Even though a potential resolution will improve the political climate between the two countries, it cannot be characterised as a panacea for a permanent solution of the Greek–Turkish disputes. Since 1989, there have been numerous efforts to reach a negotiated settlement but to no avail. The Greek–Cypriots were persistently seeking and are still pursuing a prompt solution to the problem. At the same time Turkey and the Turkish–Cypriots have systematically undermined the initiatives of the UN leading them to an impasse. Fully aware of the situation, the UN Secretary General in his 30 May 1994 report referred to the lack of political will of the Turkish–Cypriot side for the achievement of any solution as a 'well-known scenario'.[100]

The EU's decision to open negotiations with Cyprus for full membership offers a unique opportunity for a solution to the political problem of the island. It is in the interest of all concerned, including Turkey, to take advantage of its opportunity and embrace a solution. It is hoped by the Greek–Cypriots that both Turkey and the Turkish–Cypriots will acknowledge the beneficial effects of accession to all domains of public life, including the economic, the political and the institutional field, and will finally give their consent to Cyprus's joining the EU. For it is a paradox that Turkey, while aspiring to become a member of the EU herself, at the same time, purporting to act in the interests of the Turkish–Cypriots, denies them the security and prosperity they would enjoy from Cyprus's EU membership.

At the same time, membership of the EU may offer a new insight and furnish new ideas as to the best way for dealing with the problem. The union's *acquis* could give the opportunity for accommodating – in a most satisfactory way – the basic parameters of the problem while keeping in line with the UN provisions. Moreover, membership of the EU for the Republic of Cyprus would exaggerate its economic supremacy over northern Cyprus. This might conceivably lead to internal pressure on Denktash (political leader of the Turkish–Cypriots), although hitherto the already considerable economic disparities have not led him to modify his political position in the direction of significant compromise. Denktash argues that accession 'will secure the full integration of the Turkish Republic of Northern Cyprus with Turkey' a position echoed by Turkish Prime Minister Ciller when she said, 'if southern Cyprus is accepted into the EU before a final solution is reached on the island then we unite with northern Cyprus'.[101]

The same stance has also been adopted by successive Turkish governments including the Yilmaz and the Ecevit government.[102] The EU has made it clear that it wants to see a solution to the Cyprus problem before the island joins the EU, although that is not a condition for allowing Cyprus in. 'It has been clear to us that they will judge who is the guilty party if a solution is not found' said Cypriot President Clerides in an interview:

> If they judge that it is the other side, then that would not be an impediment to our joining. But if they judge that because we know we are going into the EU we have raised our stakes, then that would be held against us. They are using the carrot and the stick on both sides.[103]

Taking these developments into account one should argue that the Cyprus imbroglio remains and most likely it will remain for some time. However, one should also bear in mind that a potential solution of the political problem would further enhance the image of Cyprus as a stable and reliable strategic partner because it already possesses all those 'stability-generating' prerequisites lacked by other states in the region: a democratic system of governance, a pluralistic society and a dynamic market economy.

NATO AND GREECE: STRONG PARTNERSHIP, WEAK FOUNDATIONS

The defeat of the Greek communists in 1949 and the entry of Greece into NATO three years later seemed to settle the question of whether Greek defences would be land or sea oriented for the duration of the Cold War. As far as NATO was concerned, the principal threat to Greek security came from the north. Greece's NATO mission was to defend its northern and north-western borders from communist attack. Under these arrangements, Greece provided port and communication facilities for the US Sixth Fleet and tried to co-ordinate the air and sea defences of the Aegean and the Dardanelles with Turkey. Moreover, Greece received over $7 billion worth of military aid from the US and from NATO infrastructure funds between 1949 and 1995. In the same period, Turkey received $10 billion in military aid.[104]

However, after 1955 Greek and NATO defence doctrines began increasingly to diverge. Greek–Turkish relations began to worsen instigated by anti-Greek riots in Istanbul and Izmir during 1955 and culminated in the summer of 1974 when a *coup d'etat* against the Cypriot government, supported by the Greek military junta, allowed Turkey to invade northern Cyprus.

Since that time no Greek government has put more emphasis on Greece's northern defences than on its eastern defences. No Greek government until now has seen a threat to Greek security more dangerous than the threat perceived from Turkey. Greek and NATO defence doctrines not only diverged in the last fifteen years of the Cold War, they became antithetical. Instead of directly addressing Greek–Turkish differences, NATO tended to disparage their importance while trying to limit their impact on the alliance's planning and operations.

Given their differing perceptions of where the main threat to Greek security lay, it is no surprise that the disintegration of the Soviet Union and eventually the collapse of the Warsaw Pact were less disorienting for Greece than for NATO.[105] Greek defence officials, unlike their counterparts in Brussels, felt no need to redraw defence plans, re-examine their order of battle, or search for new missions to justify their existence. From the 1970s, consecutive Greek governments from both sides of the political spectrum (Conservative and Socialist) started to cultivate cordial relations with Warsaw Pact countries. In Greek eyes, when NATO finally declared the Cold War to have ended, the main threat to Greece's security remained where it had always been, in the east.

Since 1991 the NATO alliance has undergone fundamental changes. Alliance doctrine has changed and NATO's standing military forces have been reduced radically because the alliance is no longer postured against an extended military threat or enemy to the east.[106] As NATO Secretary General Javier Solana pointed out in 1997, 'NATO has changed beyond recognition' as it has adopted a new security approach which embraces the principle of co-operation with non-member countries and other institutions.[107]

Specifically, the NATO role in the post-Cold War era has been focused on the following directions:

- NATO no longer considers the countries of the former Soviet Union to be adversaries.
- All former eastern-bloc communist states are welcome to co-operate with NATO through programmes such as PfP.
- NATO does not seek to isolate any country in the former eastern bloc.
- The alliance seeks to erase division on the European continent.[108]

Based on these directions, NATO Defence Ministers agreed on a new military command structure which would provide an efficient, cost-effective answer to the alliance's military needs in the new century. Under these new arrangements Greece was given a Sub-regional Command (SouthCentre in Larissa) which will be part of the RC in Naples, Italy. This new structure would help NATO to develop a more flexible approach for the conduct of alliance mission requirements with a leaner, multifunctional command structure in the new security environment.[109]

Greece's long-standing objective within the NATO alliance is to play a stabilising role in the Balkans and the eastern Mediterranean. For this purpose, it is restructuring and upgrading its armed forces in response to the new security environment and to various potential instabilities. The goal is to achieve a cost-effective, flexible and efficient force structure which can ensure a robust defence of the national territory (mainly from the Turkish threat), and contribute to NATO and regional stability. However, it is not clear that Greece can do both. NATO is encouraging Greece to boost its land forces for use in the Balkans. The logic of the Turkish threat is emphasis by Greece on air and naval forces.

In addition, the modernisation of the Greek armed forces will result in a more efficient Greek participation in missions undertaken by the NATO alliance. Since 1991, Greece has demonstrated its commitment to the new NATO dogma by its support for PfP and the CJTF concept as well as by its participation in the Implementation Force or Stabilising Force in Bosnia (IFOR/SFOR) and in Kosovo (KFOR). However, the five-year modernisation plan also has the dual aim of facing the imminent threat from its neighbour and NATO 'ally' Turkey.

In the 1990s, with the end of the Cold War and the passing from the scene of a charismatic Prime Minister who had come to prominence by denouncing Greek dependence on the US and NATO, Greek elites have adopted a much more pragmatic view of the NATO alliance and the role of the US in the post-Cold War era. They see that the US is the only superpower left, whose main interest is to promote liberal capitalism and global security and stability.

Nevertheless, the Simitis government, having seen that NATO does not offer any legal or political grounds for support against the perceived threat from another NATO ally like Turkey, tried to pursue a fully developed EU CFSP as a clear alternative to NATO. To this end, the current government has been working under the present CFSP to secure a resolution that commits the EU to the territorial integrity of its member states' present borders, albeit with no success.[110]

Given Greece's foreign policy priorities presented earlier, Greece has been characterised as a strategically located, medium-sized power which managed to be an integral part of the western multilateral institutions such as NATO and the EU. Given the new role of NATO in the post-Cold War era, Greece has managed to meet the challenges and the engagements of the new NATO whose main objective is to provide the values of collective defence and collective security to its member states. However, NATO's continuous unwillingness to consolidate security and stability in the southern flank has spoiled in Greek eyes the foundation of NATO as a collective defence organisation whose aim is to provide security guarantees to all of its member states regardless of the source of threat.

According to the Greek elites NATO clearly needs to take a more proactive role in resolving the Greek–Turkish dispute. The realisation that a possible armed conflict between these two allies would be disastrous for the alliance and the vital interests of NATO in the eastern Mediterranean (oil, out-of-area operations, basing) can work as a catalyst for a potential intervention. NATO officials have accepted the fact that the end of the east–west competition has shifted attention toward dormant but simmering inter and intra-state rivalries which could present security threats affecting the entire region.[111]

US Secretary of Defence William Perry urged NATO to 'build trust and improve relations in the Aegean region'.[112]

The introduction of a 'hot line'[113] and the Madrid Declaration of 8 July 1997[114] between Greece and Turkey must be seen by NATO as an opening for a further and systematic attempt to stabilise relations in the Aegean. Both countries (including Greek and Turkish elites) have acknowledged that NATO is probably the only organisation which can play a useful role in bringing the two sides together. NATO needs to acknowledge this fact and to engage in energetic diplomacy. An open conflict in the Aegean will be a lose–lose outcome for all parties involved, including NATO. It is a paradox that most academics and NATO officials have realised the importance of the eastern Mediterranean and the disastrous consequences for the alliance in the case of a regional conflict, but at the same time NATO has focused obsessively on the European Northern Tier and the issue of expansion based on opinions expressed by Huntington, Schopfin, Kennan or Brzezinski.[115] All of the aforementioned claim the incompatibility of the Balkan culture with the western European civilisation or western Christianity which is basically located in central Europe and includes countries like the Czech Republic, Hungary and Poland.

A policy of completely equal distance will not be feasible and would have to be abandoned in the event of open warfare between these two 'allies'. It is not clear that the NATO alliance could survive a war between two of its members.

NOTES

1. For further analysis see Jopp Mathias et al., *Integration and Security in Western Europe: Inside the European Pillar*, Chapter 15 (Boulder: Westview, 1991). For more information about Greece's foreign policy objectives see T. Veremis and T. Couloumbis, *Eliniki Exoteriki Politiki: Dilimata mias Neas Epoxis, Sideris* (Athens: Sideris, 1997). See also T. Veremis, 'Greece', in Douglas T. Stuart (ed.), *Politics and Security in the Southern Region of the Atlantic Alliance* (London: Macmillan Press, 1988) pp.140–2.
2. For further study see 'Security Strategy in the New Europe', in C. McInnes, F. Carr and K. Ifantis (eds) *NATO in the New European Order* (Houndmills: Macmillan Press, 1996).
3. See R. Ware, 'The End of Yugoslavia', *House of Commons Background Papers* 290, 91/42 (1992); J. Eyal, *Europe and Yugoslavia: Lessons from a Failure* (London: Whitehall Papers, RUSI, 1993) and Report of the South Balkans Working Group, *Toward Comprehensive Peace in Southeast Europe: Conflict Prevention in the South Balkans* (New York: Twentieth Century Fund Press, 1996).

4. For further study about the history of Greece see N. Forbes, *The Balkans: A History of Bulgaria, Serbia, Greece, Rumania, Turkey* (Oxford: Clarendon Press, 1915). You can also see D.G. Kousoulas, *Modern Greece: Profile of a Nation* (New York: Scribner, 1974) and Y. Kourvetakis and Dobratz, *A Profile of Modern Greece in Search of Identity* (Oxford: Clarendon Press, 1987).

5. For example, in order to restrain Greece from siding with Russia during the Crimean War, British and French warships occupied the Piraeus harbour from 1854 to 1857. Two decades later diplomatic pressure from London and Paris prevented Greece from entering the Russo-Turkish War of 1877–8. The same scenario was repeated after Bulgaria annexed eastern Roumelia in 1885. The Greeks mobilised, only to find their coasts once again blockaded by the British and the French in May 1886. For the involvement of European powers in Greek political life see Theodore Couloumbis, *Foreign Interference in Greek Politics: An Historical Perspective* (New York: Pella Publishers, 1976). See also C. and B. Jelavich, *The Balkans* (Englewood Cliffs: Prentice-Hall, 1966) and Barbara Jelavich, *The History of the Balkans* (Cambridge: Cambridge University Press, 1983).

6. See William H. McNeil, *The Metamorphosis of Greece Since World War II* (Oxford: Blackwell, 1978).

7. See R. Clogg, *A Short History of Modern Greece* (Cambridge: Cambridge University Press, 1979) p.103. He provides an insightful concise history of Greece from the downfall of Byzantium to the return of democracy.

8. For further details see D.G. Kousoulas, *Profile of a Nation* (New York: Scribner 1974) pp.97–128.

9. For further details about the Treaty of Lausanne see also Tozun Bahcheli, *Greek–Turkish Relations since 1955* (Boulder: Westview Press, 1990) pp.10–13. See also the Treaty of Lausanne, www.zeus.hri.org/docs/lausanne.

10. Kostas Tsipis (ed.), *Common Security Regimes in the Balkans* (Boulder, Colorado: East European Monographs, 1996) p.237.

11. For further information about the Greek Civil War see W.A. Heurtley, H.C. Darby, C.W. Crawley and C.M. Woodhouse, *A Short History of Greece: From Early Times to 1964* (Cambridge: Cambridge University Press, 1965) pp.143–61.

12. Soviet leader Joseph Stalin did not directly support the Greek communists, partly out of recognition of the realities of the spheres of influence emanating from his October 1944 agreement with British Prime Minister Winston Churchill, and partly out of the Greek communists' initially close association with the independent-minded Yugoslav leader Josip Tito; see Victor Papacosma, 'NATO, Greece and the Balkans in the post-Cold War era', in Van Coufoudakis et al. (eds), *Greece and the New Balkans: Challenges and Opportunities* (New York: Pella Publisher, 1999) p.48.

13. Greece's position in the post-war order was decided in the famous 'half sheet of paper', exchanged between Stalin and Churchill on the night of 9–10 October 1944, by which Greece was placed within the British sphere of influence, W.S. Churchill, *The Second World War: Triumph and Tragedy* (Boston, Mass.: Houghton Miffin, 1953).

14. See A. Beaufro, *NATO and Europe* (London: Faber, 1967) pp.19–20.

15. See M. Bentick, 'NATO's Out of Area Problem', *Adelphi Paper*, 211 (1986) p.7. For more details about the US military and economic assistance to Greece and Turkey, see Constantide P. Arvanitopoulos, 'The Politics of U.S. Aid to Greece and Turkey', *Mediterranean Quarterly*, 7, 2 (1996) pp.123–41.

16. As some political analyst argued, Greek governments 'in the 1947–55 period faced a condition of structural dependency vis-à-vis the United States that could be referred to as a patron–client relationship'. Between 1946 and 1953, 'Economic aid was channelled mainly into the struggle against communism, rather than to programs of development and industrial-isation', George M. Stathakis, 'Approaches to the Early Post-War Greek Economy: A Survey', *Journal of Modern Hellenism*, 7, 2 (1999) p.164.

17. A. Platias, 'Cost and Benefits of the US Military Bases in Greece', in Jane M.O. Sharp (ed.), *Europe After An American Withdrawal: Economic and Military Issues* (London: Oxford University Press, SIPRI, 1990) p.219.

18. See John Chipman (ed.), *NATO's Southern Allies, Internal and External Challenges*, Chapter 6 (London: Routledge, 1988).

19. For further details see T. Coloumbis, *The United States, Greece and Turkey the Troubled Triangle* (New York: Praeger, 1983) pp.13–14. See also C.P. Arvanitopoulos 'The Politics of US Aid to Greece and Turkey', *Mediterranean Quarterly*, 7, 2 (1996) pp.123–41.

20. Arvanitopoulos, 'The Politics', p.124. For more details about the role of the US in Greece see *BBC Cold War Documents Series*, Episode 1 (1999).

21. The Balkan Treaty of Friendship and Co-operation brought Yugoslavia, Greece and Turkey together against the Soviet Union. It received a covert encouragement from the US and led to the Bled Alliance of 1954, a narrowly drawn mutual defence pact, affirming that the signatories would regard an attack against one as an attack against all. The alliance began to weaken when Yugoslav–Soviet relations improved after the Khrushchev visit to Belgrade in 1955.

22. Turkish direct involvement in the Cyprus dispute was triggered off 'by the consequent inter-communal bloodshed (about 100 people on each side had been killed by June 1958 and Turkish Cypriots had been evacuated from about 33 mixed villages to safe areas', Raouf Denktash, 'The Crux of the Cyprus Problem', *Perceptions: Journal of International Affairs*, IV, 3 (1999) www.mfa.gov.tr/grupa/percept/IV-3/denktas.htm, p.2; see also Michael Stephen, 'Cyprus and the Rule of Law', *Perceptions: Journal of International Relations*, IV, 3 (1999), www.mfa.gov.tr/grpa/percept/IV-3/stephen.htm, pp.3–4. For a series of articles which justify the current Turkish–Cypriot stance and explain the reasons behind the Turkish invasion in Cyprus see also Ergun Olgun, Undersecretary to the President of the Turkish Republic of North Cyprus, 'Cyprus: A New and Realistic Approach', *Perceptions*, IV, 3 (1999) www.mfa.gov.tr/grupa/percept/IV-3. For more information about the Turkish perspective read Clement Dodd, *The Cyprus Imbroglio* (Huntingdon: Eothen, 1998). For the Greek perspective see Thanos Veremis, 'Greek Security: Issues and Politics', *Adelphi Paper*, 179 (1982) pp.10–14.

23. Veremis, 'Greek Security', p.12.

24. Following the intervention of the Turkish air force on 8 and 9 August 1964 to protect Turkish–Cypriots under attack in the Kokkina and Mansura areas, the Soviet Union announced on 15 August 1964 that it was prepared to help Cyprus in the event of foreign invasion, and was ready to begin negotiations on the matter right away.

25. See Van Coufoudakis, 'Greek–Turkish Relations 1972–1983', *International Security*, 9, 4 (1985).

26. For in-depth analysis about the Cyprus dispute see R. Haas, 'Alliance Problems in the eastern Mediterranean – Greece, Turkey and Cyprus', *Adelphi Paper*, 231 (1988). See T. Couloumbis and M. Stearns, *Entangled Allies: U.S. Policy Toward Greece, Turkey and Cyprus* (New York: Council on Free Press, 1992).

27. See Veremis, 'Greek Security', p.15.

28. While public opinion and some western governments regularly criticised the Greek junta, it never experienced serious pressure from NATO or the US. The junta carefully served US interests in the region during a period of constant turmoil in the Middle East and Soviet pressure in the Mediterranean. It is instructive to mention that US President B. Clinton on his visit to Greece on 19 November 1999, accepted that the Americans supported the Greek junta during 1967–74, see 'Mea Culpa Kai Therma Logia', *To Vima*, 21 November 1999.

29. See D. Bolles, V. Coufoudakis, J. Kozyris, B. Kuniholm, A. Philon, E.T. Rossides and N. Rudolph, 'United States Foreign Policy Regarding Greece, Turkey & Cyprus: The Rule of Law and American Interests', *AHI Conference Proceedings* (1988) p.72.

30. See G. Kourvetaris, 'Survey Essay on the Cyprus Question', *Journal of Political and Military Sociology* (1976) pp.151–64. This article reviews five books on the Cyprus crisis. Even though the Greek junta's intention was to undermine Makarios's government and subsequently to annexe (unite) Cyprus with Greece, up to today the majority of the Greeks believe that the military junta was supported and influenced by the US government.

31. See G. Kourvetaris, 'Attilas 1974: Human, Economic and Political Consequences of the Turkish Invasion of Cyprus', *Journal of the Hellenic Diaspora* (1977) pp. 24–7. This assesses the human, economic and political consequences of the 1974 Turkish invasion of Cyprus.

32. 'The key aim of the U.S. effort was to avoid an all-out war between the two NATO allies', *Washington Post*, 21 July 1974, p. A6. Emphatically, Henry Kissinger devotes only four pages to the July 1974 Cyprus crisis (Turkish invasion) in a 1,283-page memoir. He attributes the July 1974 events to the traditional animosity between Greeks and Turks, to Makarios's imprudence in taking on simultaneously the Athens colonels and Turkey, to the Athens junta's political obtuseness to carry out a coup against Makarios, thus providing Turkey with a perfect excuse for an invasion, and to Watergate which had affected decision-making and crisis-management in Washington. However, he does not explain why he did not use US leverage or his personal status to overthrow a highly US-dependent regime. See Henry Kissinger, *Years of Upheaval* (Boston: Little, Brown, 1982) pp.1188–92. US policy towards Greece and Cyprus during the junta period left its trademark in the Greek political life. On November 17, yearly anti-US mass demonstrations take place in commemoration of the Polytechnic events (the brutal killing of 13 Polytechnic University students at the hands of the junta on 14 November 1973). The Polytechnic anniversary has now assumed a symbolic role for communists, socialists and university students who want to express their feeling of bitterness against the US' embrace of the junta and against its subsequent pro-Turkish tilt. Many Greeks still believe that the US supported the Greek military rulers. They also blame Washington for failing to prevent Turkey's occupation of the northern sector of Cyprus since its 1974 invasion in response to a pro-Greek coup there; see David Storey, 'US Still Unhappy over Greek Security Efforts', *Reuters Agency*, 10 November 1999.

33. T. Couloumbis, 'Strategic Consensus in Greek Domestic and Foreign Policy Since 1974', in Van Coufoudakis et al. (eds), *Greece and the New Balkans* (1999) p.411.

34. This view has been reiterated by all post-junta Greek political leaders from all political spectrums.

35. T. Couloumbis, *The United States, Greece, and Turkey: The Troubled Triangle* (New York: Praeger, 1983) p.141.

36. See Andrew Wilson, 'The Aegean Dispute', *Adelphi Paper*, 155 (1980) p.5.

37. See Bahcheli, *Greek–Turkish Relations*, pp.130–2.

38. For an excellent analysis about the delimitation of the continental shelf see M.N. Schmmitt, 'The Greek–Turkish Dispute', *Naval War College Review*, XLIX, 3 (1996) pp.52–9. See also Jon M. Van Dyke, 'The Aegean Sea Dispute: Options and Avenues', *Marine Policy*, 20, 5 (1996) pp.397–40 and Fotios Moustakis, 'Conflict in the Aegean', *Contemporary Review*, 274, 1596 (1999) pp.8–12.

39. See official opinion of the Greek MFA, www.zeus.hri.org/MFA/foreign/bilateral/aegean.htm.

40. See *Turkish Official Gazette*, 177708, 29 May 1982; reprinted in *Mediterranean Continental Shelf*, 2 (1988) p.957. This action was contemporaneous with the conclusion of UNCLOS III and the completion of the 1982 LOS Convention.

41. The previous law of the sea conferences were convened in Geneva in 1958 (UNCLOS I) and 1960 (UNCLOS II). Despite numerous conventions, attempts to reach agreement on territorial seas were elusive.

42. See Wilson, 'The Aegean Dispute', pp.36–7.

43. Schmitt, 'The Greek–Turkish', pp.48–9.

44. ibid., pp.60–1.

45. For detailed information about Greece's and Turkey's arguments about the Aegean *status quo*, see *www.hri.org/MFA/foreign/bilateral/aegeen.htm* and *www.mfa.gov.tr/grupa/ad/ade/adeb/default/htm*.
46. For further details see C. Sazanidis, 'The Greco-Turkish Dispute Over the Aegean Airspace', *Hellenic Review of International Relations* (1980).
47. See the Preamble of the Montreaux Convention and Statement of Foreign Minister to Grand National Assembly, *Record of the Grand National Assembly*, 12 (1936) p.309.
48. Schmitt, 'The Greek–Turkish', p.64.
49. See L.S. Kaplan, R.W. Clawson and R. Lurangi, *NATO and the Mediterranean* (Wilmington, Delaware: Scholarly Resources, 1985).
50. Wilson, The Aegean Dispute, p.16. This latter position would appear to be supported by the principle of international law that rights and obligation are created only among parties to a treaty: *pacta tertiis nec nocent prosunt*.
51. See Couloumbis, *The United States*, p.133.
52. Anti-US sentiment was running high and in some cases it was manifested with attacks on US property throughout the country.
53. Turkey requested the US to suspend operations at all major US installations except the Incirlik air base. President Jimmy Carter, reversing his 1976 campaign position, ended the embargo in September 1978.
54. Greeks and Greek/Cypriots accused NATO and the US of Turkish favouritism with regard to the Turkish invasion of Cyprus.
55. For more information about Papandreou's foreign policy with regards to Turkey, see Van Coufoudakis, 'PASOK and Greek–Turkish Relations', in Richard Clogg (ed.), *Greece, 1981–89: The Populist Decade* (London: Macmillan Press, 1993) pp.167–80.
56. For more details about PASOK's foreign and defence policy see G. Tsoumis, 'The Defense Policies of PASOK', pp.91–114 and Y. Kapsis, 'The Philosophy and Goals of PASOK's Foreign Policy', pp.41–62, in N.A. Stavrou (ed.), *Greece under Socialism* (New York: Orpheous Publishing, 1988).
57. See J. Schaffer, 'Andreas Papandreou: [Political] Portrait of a Modern Socialist', pp.63–90 and R. Pranger, 'US–Greek Relations Under PASOK', pp.251–79 in Stavrou, *Greece under Socialism*.
58. 'In the aftermath of the 1974 crisis (a process that began, however in mid/late-1960s), the re-orientation of Greece's security doctrine (which followed from the necessary redeployment of forces from the north to the Greek–Turkish border in Thrace and the islands of the Aegean), led to an instinctive de-emphasis of developments within the Warsaw Pact. During the late 1970s and 1980s, there was little evidence that Greeks were concerned about any danger of direct attack by Warsaw Pact forces on Greece's narrow and difficult to defend land strip in Thrace and Macedonia', Thanos Dokos, 'Greek Defense Doctrine in the post-Cold War era', in Van Coufoudakis et al. (eds), *Greece and the New*, p.245.
59. Coufoudakis, *Greece and the New*, p.169.
60. Tom Frinking, 'Draft Interim Report of the Sub-Committee on the Southern Region', Brussels, *North Atlantic Assembly* (November, 1984) p.24.
61. In the contingency plans of the Soviet General Staff, the Balkan region was included in the south-western Theater of Strategic Military Action (TVD) providing the Soviet High Command with five different 'Operational Directions', see Phillip Petersen and Joshua Spero, 'The Soviet Military View of Southeastern Europe', in Paul Shoup and George Hoffman (eds), *Problems of Balkan Security* (Washington: Wilson Centre Press, 1990) pp.207–34.
62. Henry Kissinger, *The Troubled Partnership* (New York: McGraw Hill, 1965) p.35.
63. It is widely believed that the Americans have realised for some time now, that Turkey is the main concern of Greek security policy and the driving force behind most foreign policy initiatives. According to a former US ambassador to Greece, 'It would be only a slight

exaggeration to say that Greek foreign policy for 160 years has taken no major initiative that was not directly or indirectly, intended to create a more favourable balance of power with Turkey', Monteagle Stearns, 'Greek Foreign Policy in the 1990s: Old Sign Posts, New Roads', in Dimitris Constas and Nikos Stavrou (eds), *Greece Prepares for the 21st Century* (Baltimore: Woodrow Wilson Center Press, 1995) p.60.

64. James Brown, *Delicately Poised Allies: Greece and Turkey* (London: Brassey's, 1991) pp.6–7.

65. Pedro Moya, 'Frameworks for Co-operation in the Mediterranean', *North Atlantic Assembly*, (October, 1995) p.4, pp.11–12.

66. Rodrigo de Rato, 'NATO's Mediterranean Initiative', *North Atlantic Assembly* (October, 1995) p.11.

67. For further study about Greece's European orientation see A. Moschonas, *European Integration and Prospects of Modernisation in Greece* 3 *Research Paper*, University of Reading (1997). See also M.J. Tsinizelis and D.N. Chryssochoou, *Between 'Disharmony' and 'Symbiosis': The Greek Political and European Integration*, University of Reading, Research Paper, Unpublished (1997).

68. For further study see K. Arvanitopoulos, 'The Politics of US Aid to Greece and Turkey', *Mediterranean Quarterly* 7, 2 (1996) pp.123–41.

69. Thanos Veremis, 'Greece: The Dilemmas of Change', in F.S. Larrabee (ed.), 'The Volatile Powder Keg: Balkan Security after the Cold War', *RAND Study*, American University Press, Washington (1994) pp.124–5.

70. Jaques Delors, 'European Integration and Security', *Survival* (March/April, 1991) pp.99–110; see also Vasso Papandreou, 'The Role of Greece as a New Europe Takes Shape', *Occasional Research Paper – Special Issue* (October, 1992), Panteion University, Athens, p.14.

71. See M. Ward, 'The Enlargement of WEU', Political Committee, *Report*, 19 April 1993, p.5, *www.fumet.fi/pub/doc/world/AWEU/documents/enlargement-weu.*

72. This view has been expressed by Greek officials from the Greek Ministry of Foreign Affairs during a series of interviews which were conducted between December 1996 and March 1997.

73. See C. Iordanides, 'Greece and European Security', *Kathimerini*, 13 November 1991.

74. For further study about minorities in Greece see C.L. Rozakis, 'The International Protection of Minorities in Greece', in Kevin Featherstone and Kostas Ifantis (eds), *Greece in a Changing Europe* (Manchester and New York: Manchester University Press, 1996) pp.95–115.

75. For further study see T.A. Couloumbis and 'Greek-US Relations in the 1990's: Back into the Future', in Harry Psomiades and S.B. Thomadakis (eds), *Greece, the New Europe and the Changing International Order* (New York: Pella, 1993).

76. See 'Problems and Opportunities for Post-Election Greece', *Cosmos*, 1, 8 (1996) p.1.

77. See 'Who Runs Your Country: Greece', *The Economist*, 28 September 1996, p.60.

78. 'Greece: Rocky Start', *The Economist*, 22 June 1996, p.50.

79. See R.J. Guttman, 'Greek Foreign Policy', *Europe*, Commission of the European Communities (October, 1997) p.1.

80. Andreas Kazamias, 'The Quest for Modernization in Greek Foreign Policy and its Limitations', *Mediterranean Politics*, 2, 2 (1997) p.71.

81. Kostas Simitis, *Gia Mia Ischiri Koinonia Gia Mia Ischiri Ellada* (Athens: Plethron, 1995).

82. For further study see Kazamias, 'The Quest', pp.71–94.

83. Kranidiotis Points to EMU accession as Key for Greece's Stability, *Athens News Agency*, 15-10-98, *www.zeus.hri.org/news/greek/ana/1998/98-10-15.ana.html.*

84. As of January 2001 Greece became a member of EMU, the government's main policy goal of the past four years. For more information on the political and economic policy outlook see 'Greece: A Country Report', *The Economist Intelligent Unit*, October 2000 and January 2001.

85. See Couloumbis, 'Strategic Consensus in Greek Domestic and Foreign Policy Since 1974',

       www.hti.org/MFA/thesis/winter 98/consensus.html/ (p.2).
86. Guttman, 'Greek Foreign Policy', p.2.
87. Theodoros Pangalos, 'Principles of Greek Foreign Policy', *Mediterranean Quarterly*, 9, 2
       (1998) p.5.
88. This view has been expressed constantly by Turkish military officials and academics.
89. 'Gov't Opts for Patriot Long Range Missiles, French and Russian Short-Range Systems',
       Athens News Agency, 10-10-98, *zeus.hri.org/news/greek/ana/1998/98-10-10.ana.html.*
90. For detailed and updated information about arms procurements between Greece and
       Turkey see *Defence Biblos 2002–2003*, (Athens: Strategiki, 2002). Overall, Greece unveiled
       plans to spend $24 billion over the next eight years.
91. *Athens News Agency*, 10-10-98.
92. See *Cosmos*, 1, 6 (February–March, 1996). Institute of International Relations, Athens. For
       maps see *www.seas/gwu.edu/student/stratos/hol/crisis1.html* (see Maps, Chapter 5). The
       Greek sovereignty over the Imia was disclosed in a Turkish map issued by the Turkish
       Ministry of Defence, *www.enet.gr/on-line/politika.htm*, 21-04-98.
93. This view was expressed on Channel 4 main news by an English academic on 31-01-96.
94. See Van Coufoudakis, 'Greek Foreign Policy in the post-Cold War era: Issues and
       Challenges', *Mediterranean Quarterly*, 7, 3 (1996) p.33.
95. This was the opinion of all the daily Greek newspapers on 1-02-96.
96. See 'Crisis Diffused, Ankara Urges Greece to Negotiate', *Turkish Daily News*, 1-02-96,
       zeus.hri.org/news/agencies/trkn/96-02-01.trkn.html.
97. See 'Greek–Turkish Talks Slowly Underway', *Cosmos*, 2, 1 (1997) p.2, p.6.
98. See the interview of Greek Foreign Minister T. Pangalos, Athens, 21-01-98, *www.hri.org/
       MFA/foreign/bilateral/aegeen.htm.* See also Theodoros Pangalos, 'Basic Principles of Greek
       Foreign Policy', *Thesis* (spring, 1997), *www.hri.org/MFA/thesis/spring97/principles. html.*
99. For further study about Greece's official stance towards Turkey with regards to the
       disputes see *www.zeus.hri.org/MFA/foreign/bilateral/aegeen.htm.* Also Thanos Veremis, 'The
       Ongoing Aegean Crisis', *Thesis* (spring, 1997), *www.zeus.hri.org/MGA/thesis/spring 97.*
100. See 'Cyprus and The United Nations', *House of Commons Research Paper*, 95/31. The EU also
       blames Rauf Denktash for the stagnation, after six months, of the latest inter-communal
       talks in Cyprus. See 'More Than Enough to Worry About', *The Economist*, 20 July 2002, p.22.
101. ibid.
102. *The Economist* suggests that most ordinary Turkish–Cypriots would like to join the EU but
       Denktash is less keen. EU membership he claims, 'would relegate his slice of Cyprus to
       the status of poor relation', *The Economist*, 7 February 1998, p.56. For more information
       about the Turkish–Cypriot perspective see Raoul Denktash, 'The Crux of the Cyprus
       Problem', *Perceptions: Journal of International Affairs*, IV, 3 (1999) *www.mfa.gov.tr/grupa/
       percept/IV-3/denktas.htm;* see also Ergun Olgun, 'Cyprus: A New and Realistic Approach',
       Perceptions: Journal of International Relations, IV, 3 (1999) *www.mfa.gov.tr/grupa/percept/
       IV-3/olgun.htm* and D. Blumenwitz, 'Cyprus: Political and Legal Realities', *Perceptions:
       Journal of International Affairs*, ibid., *www.mfa.gov.tr/grupa/percept/IV-3/blumenwitz.htm.*
103. See '1996 Could be Year of Destiny for Cyprus', *European*, 11 April, 1996.
104. Monteagle Sterns, 'Greek Security Issues', *The Greek Paradox*, pp.62–3. For further details
       see C. Migdalowitz, 'Greece and Turkey: Current Foreign Aid Issues', *Congressional
       Research Issue Brief*, Congressional Research Issue, Washington, D.C., 5 September 1995.
105. Stearns, 'Greek Security Issues', p.63.
106. *Fact Sheet: How NATO Has Changed In The Post-Cold War Era*, prepared and compiled by the
       Bureau of European and Canadian Affairs, US Department of State, 21 March 1997,
       www.usia.gov/topical/pol/atlcomm/natof321.htm, p.1.
107. ibid., p.1.
108. ibid., pp.1–2.
109. For further details see General K. Naumann, 'NATO's New Military Command

Structure', *NATO Review*, 46, 1 (1998) pp.10–14.

110. See Kazamias, 'The Quest', p.78.
111. See *NATO Sixteen Nations*, 42, 1, 1997, p.57.
112. See Rodrigo de Rato, 'NATO's Mediterranean Initiative', *North Atlantic Assembly* (October, 1995) p.5.
113. See ETHOS, *Direct Emergency Phone Link Between NATO, Greece and Turkey*, 19-02-97, *www.tagish.co.uk/ethos/news/lit1/s2fe.htm*.
114. Premier Simitis and President Demirel reached agreement on six principles by which to govern the bilateral relations of the two countries. Much of the language was amicable, encouraging the parties to undertake acts of good neighbourliness, to respect each other's sovereignty and interests, and to forswear the use of threat or force as a means of settling disputes. See also 'Greece and Turkey: CBMs', *Cosmos* (March–April, 1998) p.5.
115. For further analysis see E. Prodromou, 'The Perception Paradox of post-Cold War Security in Greece', *The Greek Paradox*, (1997) pp.126–7.

3

Turkish Security Challenges and its Relationship with NATO

In order to investigate NATO's role in Turkey, it is necessary to first provide a brief historical background of Turkey and of how Turkey entered into the North Atlantic alliance. Greek–Turkish relations will then be assessed from a Turkish perspective, with regard to Cyprus and the Aegean. Finally the chapter analyses the relationship of NATO and Turkey and how this partnership has developed during the Cold and the post-Cold War era.

A half-century after Turkey joined the North Atlantic Treaty Organisation many of the geo-political facts that justified its accession still hold. Even though there were crises of confidence and trust which created strains in the alliance the bonds between Turkey and NATO are secure, especially after the active role that Turkey played during the Gulf War. Throughout the Cold War period, Turkey's geo-strategic location and the size of its armed forces, constituted an important contribution to NATO's strategy of deterrence.

NATO's decision to accept Turkey into the alliance was justified by Turkey's proximity to the Warsaw Pact countries on the one hand and the Middle East on the other. The vital resources of oil in the Middle East, and the Soviet influence in this region determined the NATO decision to include the Turkish armed forces into the defensive line. In addition, Turkey possessed the only non-Warsaw Pact coastline on the Black Sea, and controlled the entry/exit point for all shipping moving from the Black Sea to the Mediterranean.

HISTORICAL MORPHOLOGY OF TURKEY

Turkey occupies the land mass of the Anatolian Peninsula in west Asia together with the city of Istanbul and its Thracian hinterland. The Asian and European portions of Turkey are divided from each other by the Bosporous Strait, the Sea of Marmara and the Dardanelles. The modern Turkish Republic was born at the end of the First World

War as the successor to the collapsing Ottoman Empire.[1] Its founder Mustafa Kemal (Ataturk) abandoned the ancient imperial capital, Istanbul, in favour of Ankara. He then decided to opt for Europe, or as he preferred to call it: 'civilisation'.[2] He replaced the Ottoman constitutional monarchy with republican institutions under the guidance of a single ruling party. Islam was disestablished, laws and customs were imported from Europe, and the Arabic script was replaced by the Latin alphabet. Kemal Ataturk resented any suggestion that Turkey was not part of Europe. Subsequently, Europe accepted this official Turkish view and Turkey became a member of the Council of Europe in 1950. From an outpost of the east-facing Europe, it became a bastion of Europe. The Kemalist Revolution provided the Turks with the opportunity to acquire a new identity in the contemporary world. First and foremost, the Turkish people were solidly cemented as a national identity around a firm linguistic, cultural and territorial base.[3] However, Turkey's identity is still fragile, with 25 per cent of its population being from various minorities (for example Turks, Kurds, Laz, Circassians, etc.).

Kemalism saved Turkey from a dichotomy that had divided the country between the east and the west for almost two hundred years. All previous changes had been emergency operations to meet the pressures the new world was creating. Kemalist changes had no use for temporary expedients. In the words of Professor Nail Kubali:

> The previous period accepted compromise and the outer forms. They believed that the new and the old, that the East and the West, that existence based on religion and a secular life, could co-exist and influence one another constructively. The Kemalist Revolution, rested on the indivisibility of western civilisation. It was a radical and organic revolution that rejected compromise between the old and the new, the East and the West, secularism and religion.[4]

The cultural and social dimension of the revolution outstripped its political depth. It developed, in the words of Ataturk, into a struggle for the 'creation of a new nation, a new state, a new mentality, a new way of life'.[5]

The Tanzimat (Reorganisation) of Turkey which was instigated by Ataturk started at the end of the First World War and after the foundation of the Turkish Republic (1923). The moment he secured the international status of Turkey he focused all his efforts to establish a strictly secular state. Hence, in November 1922, the sultanate was abolished and all members of the Ottoman dynasty were banished. Turkey then became a republic and Mustafa Kemal became its first President.[6] In 1937 an amendment was inserted in the Turkish constitution which enclosed the principle of secularism.[7] The religious courts were abolished, Muslim law abandoned, religious schools were closed down and the entire education system was placed under the supervision of the Ministry of Education. Western legislation was introduced in all fields, drawing on the Swiss civil code, the German criminal law and the Italian penal and commercial codes. Alphabetic and language reforms facilitated the establishment and expansion of a general, secular education system. The position of women was, at least in the major cities, effectively Europeanised. The wearing of the *fez* was forbidden and European clothing in general was recommended. The Gregorian calendar replaced the lunar calendar of Islam. The weekend holiday was moved from the Islamic holy day of Friday to Sunday.[8]

In 1928, a new Latin alphabet was introduced instead of its counterpart Arabic alphabet. Ataturk's aim was to replace Arabic and Persian words with Turkish ones. To this end, in 1932 all prayers, including the call to prayer from the mosques, were ordered to be made in Turkish and not in Arabic, the language of the Koran. During Ataturk's rule, the economy of the state was given top priority. 'We have to give absolute priority to the economic matters of our newly Turkish Republic, if we desire to reach the level of contemporary civilisation. This age, no doubt, is an age of economy.'[9]

Between 1923 and 1930, Ataturk followed a liberal economic policy and the main economic decisions were focused on spreading private ownership of land, appropriating land for landless farmers and migrants, extending state credit for capital accumulation in agriculture, promoting private enterprises, protecting domestic production by customs policies and refraining from external borrowing. Between 1923 and 1930, Ataturk implemented a mixed economic policy with special emphasis on the role of the state. This policy was pursued until the 1980s, with the exception of the Democrat Party's attempts at liberalisation. Since 1981 the strategy of import substitution as the means of industrialisation has been abolished. Subsequently, the Turkish economy transformed from being a closed, agricultural and non-competitive economy to being market oriented and liberal.[10] Despite the fact that Kemal Ataturk criticised anti-democratic ideologies and underlined the superiority of democracy in several of his speeches: 'According to us, in our understanding, popular governmental administration is possible through democracy',[11] the Cumhuriyet Halk Partisi (CHP) which was established by Ataturk in 1923, remained as the only political party until 1945. The attempt of other political parties such as the the Progressive Republican Party and the Free Republican Party to play a protagonist role in the political scene was short-lived. On his better days it seems that Ataturk

believed in liberal democracy. But when he tried to liberalise the
regime in 1930, religious reaction to the revolution and popular
hostility compelled him to abandon the democratic experiment in
the interests of the modernising revolution.[12]

In 1946, the DP was created by some CHP members and after the
1950 elections it came to power bringing an end to one-party rule.
However, since then democracy has been interrupted three times, by
military dictatorships in 1960, 1971 and 1980.[13] Kemalist foreign
policy was in nature pacifist, nourishing no territorial aspirations at
any other country's expense:

> 'Peace at home and peace in the world' were Kemal's position. Ataturk
> also declared that 'Turkey does not desire an inch of foreign territory,
> but will not give up an inch of what she holds[14]. The main desire of
> Turkey was only its territorial integrity and freedom.'[15]

TURKEY'S ENTRY INTO NATO

Turkey's accession to NATO was made possible after a guarantee of
mutual benefits and obligations between both parties. Support for
the balance of power in the Near East interlocked with support for
the balance of power in Europe.[16] The US realised that Turkey was
the only state in the eastern Mediterranean capable of substantial
resistance to the Soviets and that Turkey could provide something of
a protective screen for the region. To this end, the US was determined
to oppose with all means at its disposal, including the force of the US
army, any Soviet aggression against Turkey. Therefore, containment
of Soviet expansionism and aggression became a common objective
for both Turkey and the US, and it shaped Turkey's security policy in
the early years of the Cold War.[17]

It was Stalin who pushed Turkey into the western alliance in
1945–6 by demanding revision of the Montreux Convention of 1936
governing access through the straits, in favour of the Soviet Union.[18]
The persisting Soviet political and military expansion in eastern
Europe brought Soviet troops to Turkey's western as well as eastern
frontier, within striking distance of Istanbul. Furthermore, the
hostilities in Korea had shown US officials that the communists were
not hesitant to mount military attacks. More importantly, even before
the Korean War (1950–3), military strategists had recognised
Turkey's vital strategic role for the North Atlantic area in an eventual
war with the Soviet Union. It was also of considerable value that the
inclusion of Turkey (and Greece) would contribute twenty-five new
divisions to NATO's common defence.[19] In addition, NATO was

afraid that the Soviet Union could even exploit Greek and Turkish disillusionment at having been excluded from the alliance to lure the countries into a neutral, or even worse, submissive role in relation to Moscow.[20]

Turkey's entry into NATO in 1952 was the predictable result of these developments. The construction of air bases which would mostly be used to deter Soviet designs in the Middle East, started immediately after Turkey's entry into NATO. By 1953, Stalin had realised his mistake and renounced any territorial claims against Turkey. Nevertheless, it took a long time for the ice to melt in Soviet–Turkish relations.

TURKEY AND NATO: A TESTING PARTNERSHIP

Turkey's entry into the NATO alliance was also accompanied by continuous benefits from US military and financial support (the Marshall Plan). Between 1948 and 1959 Turkey received some $1.2 billion in economic aid almost exclusively from US sources. Of this, grants amounted to almost $700 million. Military aid is estimated at $1 billion for the years 1950–60.[21]

However, the golden era of Turkey's relationship with NATO in the 1950s was succeeded by a more complicated relationship in the 1960s and 1970s. The most important determinant to this development derived from the twists and turns of the Cyprus dispute. In 1963–4, there was serious intercommunal fighting which divided the island and pushed the Turkish–Cypriots back into a series of scattered enclaves. The failure of diplomatic efforts and UNFICYP led Turkey to contemplate military intervention to protect the Turkish–Cypriot minority. According to Turkey, Article 4 of the Treaty of Guarantee, permits unilateral action to restore the *status quo,* if collective action by the guarantor powers – Britain, Greece and Turkey – fails. In June 1964 Turkey was considering military intervention and President Johnson sent a letter to the Turkish government in which he stated in part that if Turkey invaded Cyprus and the Soviet Union reacted, there was no guarantee of NATO support of Turkey.[22]

Whether or not the 'Johnson letter' prevented a Turkish invasion of Cyprus in 1964,[23] it became something of a *cause célèbre* in Turkey, and it was regarded by Turkey as a turning point in the Turkish foreign policy based on the belief that the US had attempted to undermine and jeopardise Turkish national interests.[24] The Johnson letter 'forced' Turkey to pick up the proffered olive branch from Moscow. A series of high-level contacts eventually produced a measure of accord between the two governments. The expansion of trade and a limited Soviet aid programme to Turkey followed in due course.[25] Progressively the Soviet Union ceased to be considered as the main threat to Turkey's security, as relations with Greece deteriorated, especially with regards to the Cyprus issue.

Turkey's cordial relationship with the Soviet Union raised critical questions among Greek academics as to whether Turkey would assist the US or NATO in a conflict with the Soviet Union.[26] A further diplomatic deterioration between Turkey and the US was accelerated by two other unilateral US decisions. The US announcement in January 1963, three months after the Cuban missile crisis, that US Jupiter missiles would be removed from Turkey startled the Turks.[27] It was widely believed that Turkish territory could be traded for time, in the event of a Soviet pre-emptive nuclear attack and that NATO would favour protecting the central front instead of its flanks. The crisis of confidence and trust between the US and Turkey was widened after the invasion of Cyprus by Turkey in 1974. Between early 1975 and mid-1978 the US Congress imposed an embargo on transfers of military equipment to Turkey in an attempt to force Turkey to withdraw from Cyprus. The embargo was never watertight, since the Turks were able to buy spare parts and some other hardware for their US-equipped forces from third parties. However, the Cyprus crisis determined the relations with Greece (another NATO member) and provoked a delicate and fragile situation for NATO in the eastern Mediterranean.

Turkey's involvement in Cyprus has been uncharacteristic of its foreign policy under the republic. Ataturk had renounced any act of irredentism, but in the 1950s Prime Minister Menderes argued that the case of Cyprus was different. It was believed that the Greek nationalists were trying to alter the balance established by the Treaty of Lausanne. Consequently, the British discreetly allowed a Turkish involvement as a counterweight to Greek nationalism in Cyprus.[28] To this end, Turkish–Cypriots were involved in operations against Greek terrorists. Therefore, an assumption that one day the Turkish minority community would come under Greek rule was highly detested and rejected among the Turks. Turkish active engagement into the Cypriot dispute was also encouraged by the belief that Turkish membership in NATO should protect Turkish interests abroad, certainly where other NATO countries were involved.

TURKEY IN CYPRUS

The Menderes policy in Cyprus which was stated in contradictory slogans, such as 'Cyprus is Turkish' and 'Partition or Death' won

Turkey concrete advantages.[29] The 1959–60 independence settlement for Cyprus gave Turkey a stake on the island, as well as granting Turkish–Cypriots a privileged status as founder members of the Cyprus Republic. The Turkish government was as a result entitled to safeguard the Turkish–Cypriot minority against any Greek threat. According to Turkish officials, the Turkish Peace Operation in 1974 was a reaction to a military coup which took place with the aim of annexing the island to another country, thus destroying and annihilating an independent state for which Turkey was a guarantor by international treaties.[30] This military action was justified on the grounds that Turkey feared Cypriot union (*enosis*) with Greece, since the military coup by Greek officers of the National Guard and the EOKA-B had been encouraged by the military government in Greece. Turkey failed to persuade Britain to assist it in a joint military action and therefore launched a unilateral offensive on July 20 in order to protect the Turkish minority. A second Turkish action in August consolidated vulnerable positions and left Turkey occupying about 40 per cent of Cyprus and at the same time hardened the positions of the adversaries. In September 1974 Turkish Prime Minister Ecevit resigned partly as a result of disagreements within his coalition over Turkish attitudes toward a settlement in Cyprus, and the presence of Turkey in Cyprus became further bound up with Turkish domestic politics. However, Turkish officials agreed that the Turkish forces stationed in Cyprus should be maintained in order *inter alia* to preserve the peace until a negotiated settlement of the dispute had been reached between the Turks and the Greeks of the island and a lasting peace had been secured.[31] Since 1974 and up to now Cyprus has come to be regarded less as a problem to be solved than as a situation to be managed.

Eventually, Turkish Cold War security concerns started to recede. The Soviet Union ceased to be considered as the main threat to Turkey's security, as competitive relations with Greece intensified. Turkish Prime Minister Ecevit in May 1978[32] stated that 'I believe that détente with Soviet Union is a reality…But it has been replaced by threats from other quarters…Obviously Greece for years has been arming against her ally Turkey'.[33]

COLD WAR IN THE AEGEAN: TURKISH ASSERTIONS

Contrary to the opinion that conflict between Turkey and Greece is historically inevitable, nothing seems to support this belief until the 1960s. With the Treaty of Lausanne of 1923, Greece and Turkey settled most of their outstanding differences. This was followed by a

Friendship Pact signed in 1933, in which both states promised to provide mutual support in conferences with outside powers.[34] This rapprochement resulted from the determination of Ataturk and Venizelos to terminate the ancient and pointless enmity between their two nations. This collaboration was pursued in the post-1945 era. The approach to NATO was a common one, and the military authorities in the two countries had begun consultations even before they were admitted to the alliance.[35]

However, since the Turkish invasion of Cyprus, relations between Turkey and Greece have deteriorated to the extent that Turkey considers problems with Greece as one of its major security problems. Hence, the tension between these two allied countries started to undermine alliance harmony and had a debilitating effect on the security of NATO's southern flank. This strained relationship distracted the attention of both countries from common security questions confronted by the western alliance. Joint training opportunities were wasted because Greece usually refused to participate in joint NATO exercises in the Aegean and the eastern Mediterranean. Tension between Greece and Turkey exacerbated command and control problems and created additional complications for force deployment. As a result, this perplexing situation complicated not only the defence plans of both nations, but also their relationships with other states.

Greek–Turkish differences in the Aegean have been well documented and analysed over the past twenty years by many Turkish academics and officials. However, for the purpose of this book it will be useful to highlight the main Turkish arguments regarding the Aegean dispute.[36]

Greek–Turkish differences in the Aegean stem partly from the geographical peculiarities of the region, and partly from the respective historical perceptions of the disputants. Contrary to what many Greeks believe, the conflict according to the Turks arises not because Turkey challenges Greek sovereignty over the Aegean, but because Greece utilises the Aegean islands in order to achieve complete sovereignty over the entire Aegean. Various Greek advances in the Aegean since the 1930s are viewed by the Turks as manifestations of a revisionist policy. In 1931, Greece extended its air space to ten miles, without regard for the breadth of its territorial waters which was then three miles and was extended in 1936 only to six miles. This unilateral decision constituted a breach of international law, embodied in the 1945 Chicago Convention on International Civil Aviation, whereby the breadth of national air space must correspond to the breadth of territorial waters. Turkey claims that Greece defines the FIR in the Aegean not as a technical issue of air traffic services, according to the

International Civil Aviation Organisations Assembly Resolutions, but as a matter of sovereignty over the Aegean air space. Since 1980, the demarcation line follows Turkish territorial waters, giving Greece responsibility for all civilian air traffic over almost all the Aegean. Turkish authorities argue Greece abuses its FIR rights and restricts Turkish military exercises over the high seas in the Aegean.

The 1958 Geneva Convention and the 1982 Convention on the Law of the Sea ascribe continental shelves to islands. If this resolution were to be applied to the Greek islands in the Aegean, then the Aegean would be transformed into a Greek lake. Turkey seeks a political solution to the delimitation of the continental shelves on the basis of the principles of equity and equality.[37]

Greece also threatens to extend its territorial waters from six miles to twelve miles. Under the six-mile regime Greece possesses 43.68 per cent of the Aegean Sea and Turkey 7.46 per cent. In the case of an extension the Greek share of the sea would rise to 71.53 per cent and that of Turkey only to 8.79 per cent. Moreover, the continental shelf problem would be solved automatically in favour of Greece.[38]

The unlawful remilitarisation by Greeks of the eastern Aegean islands presents Turkey with the most direct military threat. The eastern Aegean islands are situated in the close vicinity of the Turkish mainland and precisely for this reason, their demilitarised status is considered as essential for Turkey's security. The aforementioned Greek decision constitutes a clear violation of the Lausanne Treaty of 1923 and the Paris Treaty of 1947. Nevertheless, since 1974 Greece has remilitarised these islands, citing the Turkish intervention (invasion) of 1974 in Cyprus as its rationale. A fundamental principle of international law is *pacta sund servanta* and this principle has been completely violated by Greece.[39]

TURKEY AND NATO: THE COLD WAR PERIOD

Turkey during the Cold War period was considered to be of vital importance to NATO's southern flank. The US realised that Turkey's location between the Mediterranean and the Black Sea, and Europe and Asia qualified it as one of the most strategically important countries for NATO. Turkey was responsible for guarding and defending the Turkish Straits, the passage through which the Soviet Black Sea Fleet would have to pass to reach the Mediterranean. The defence of southern Europe depended to some extent on the control of the Mediterranean and the control of the Mediterranean depended on the control of the straits.[40] NATO was concerned that Thrace, the European portion of Turkey, was a primary Warsaw Pact attack corridor in its aim to secure the straits in time of war. A quick strike through Thrace to seize the Turkish Straits was of real concern for NATO strategists.[41]

However, the eastern border of Turkey actually faced more Soviet divisions than its western border. Thus in the event of a full-scale war with the Warsaw Pact, Turkey could face a land war on two fronts as well as the naval obligation to close the straits to the Soviet navy. These strategic parameters had determined the role of Turkey within the NATO alliance.

In an event of a Warsaw Pact attack Turkey with 569,000 troops, together with Greek troops faced thirty-three relatively modernised Warsaw Pact divisions in the Balkans, while confronting another fifteen or so in the Transcaucausia. The Warsaw Pact forces out-numbered those of the Greeks and Turks by a 3 to 2 ratio.[42] Warsaw Pact ground forces were further supported by a Soviet Black Sea fleet of twenty-five submarines and forty-five to seventy-five surface ships (nearly one-third of the Soviet Union's major surface combatants) and 600 fairly advanced attack and interceptor aircraft.[43] The Soviets considered the Mediterranean and especially the straits as a key to their security. The fact that 7,000 Soviet ships transited the straits in 1978 (20 per day) proves the strategic importance of the straits and indicated that Soviet access to the Mediterranean was considered as a military requirement in the event of a Warsaw Pact attack.

Taking into account these possible theatres of military operation, Turkey primarily and Greece secondarily had to tie down the first wave of the Warsaw Pact invasion. Subsequently, NATO would mobilise the ACE/AMF which was stationed in Heidelberg, Germany. Established in 1960, the AMF force was designed to come rapidly to the aid of NATO members in the flanks.[44] However, AMF was not fully operational in the southern flank due to the Greek withdrawal from the military structure of NATO after 1974.

During the 1980s NATO exercises with the participation of the AMF emphasised the determination of the alliance to reinforce Turkey. The AMF participated in major training exercises in eastern Turkey such as ADVENTURE EXPRESS 1983, in Turkish Thrace ARCHWAY EXPRESS 1985, AURORA EXPRESS 1987 and ALLY EXPRESS in 1988. Nevertheless, the efficiency of the AMF force had been hampered by the Turkish reluctance to allow the AMF force to mix with the local population.

Furthermore, Turkey's defence within the NATO alliance had been hindered by a series of infrastructure deficiencies such as inadequate reception facilities, poor road and rail networks (particularly in the more remote regions of eastern Anatolia) and shortfalls in ammunition and fuel storage capacities.[45] These deficiencies were to a certain degree eliminated by the allocation of an infrastructure funding for the southern-eastern region in 1985–91.

Turkey's value to the alliance was significantly enhanced *via* the use of major installations. Incirlik base still provides basing for US tactical fighter bombers; Sinop, electromagnetic monitoring; Kargaburum, radio navigation; Belbasi, seismic data collection; Yumurtalik and Iskenderum, contingency storage of war reserve materials, ammunition and fuel (20 per cent of the US Sixth Fleet's Mediterranean-based fuel was stored there) and Pirinclik, radar warning and space monitoring. Along with numerous secondary facilities, which include fourteen NATO Air Defence Ground Environment early warning sites and twenty US Defence Communication System terminal sites, these installations and facilities provided 25 per cent of NATO's hard intelligence, some of which were not available from other sources on such matters as Soviet strategic nuclear activities, military systems development and force readiness and movement. Facilities in Turkey could also track Soviet air attacks in the eastern Mediterranean and would provide assistance and protection for the Sixth Fleet.[46]

NATO and US officials regarded Turkish military bases as being of significant value for NATO contingencies. It was believed that the unimpeded use and modernisation of Turkish airfields would help NATO to deter Soviet expansionism in the eastern Mediterranean and to protect western access to oil in the Persian Gulf.[47] Hence, it is not hard to understand why NATO and the US considered Turkey's security as vital for the geo-political and geo-strategical interests of the west.

Turkey with the second-largest army in the alliance initially perceived the Soviet Union and the Warsaw Pact as the primary threats to its national security. From the 1970s Turkey altered its security outlook and adopted the 'Mask Doctrine', which considers Greece (mainly), Syria and Iraq as the major threats to Turkish national security. The armed forces are based on conscription and the military personnel is approximately 528,000.

While the Turkish army is large, prior to the late 1980s its equipment was considered obsolete and it was viewed by many strategic analysts and NATO officials as ineffective and less than reassuring.[48] Turkey's modernisation needs were emphasised first during the Carter administration, and later by the Reagan administration.[49] NATO was convinced that Turkey should have to rely upon its own resources in the early stages of a war, hence the necessity of self-reliance dictated a large defence establishment.[50]

Since 1985 Turkey has designed a plan to privatise sectors of its defence industry. The legislation for the Defence Industrial Support Fund was passed in July 1985. Its purpose was to develop a local

Turkish defence industrial base to provide basic defence equipment, with the hope of attracting foreign investment and technological know-how. In the mid-1980s the Turkish General Staff produced a Six-Year Strategic (Defence) Plan and a Ten-Year Defence Industry Plan. Emphasis was placed on research and development and military procurement for the following fields: tactical wheeled vehicles, armoured vehicles, main battle tank conversion, artillery modernisation, various warships, fighter and transport aircraft and mobile radars. The outcome of this attempt was that General Dynamics established an assembly plant near Ankara in order to build F-16 FIGHTING FALCONS. The Turks own 51 per cent of the corporation set up for this joint venture. Production began in 1988 with an initial run of 160 aircraft. The F-16 Squadrons enabled Turkey to enhance its defence capabilities on air support, interdiction and air strike.

Given also the importance of the straits, Turkey and NATO considered as imperative the modernisation of the Turkish navy. Therefore, Turkey started to produce naval vessels at Golcuk naval yard, notably MEKO-200 frigates and TYPE-209 diesel submarines. In early 1989, the US announced that four frigates would be transferred to the Turkish navy under a five-year lease agreement. Although these vessels are nearly 20 years old, they have been refurbished and upgraded.[51]

NEW CHALLENGES AND OPTIONS

The assumption that Turkey would be the victim of strategic neglect after the Cold War, was soon eliminated since the Gulf War reinstated Turkey's strategic significance in the eyes of the west. However, the reassertion of Turkey's importance in the wake of the Gulf crisis emphasised its role in Middle East rather than European Security. Turkey abandoned the passive neutrality that had dominated its foreign policy approach and emerged as a regional actor. Rapid changes in the external environment confronted Turkey with numerous challenges which led to a move away from its traditionally conservative approach on foreign and security policy.[52] An active but clandestine economic and military support for Azerbaijan in the dispute with Armenia over the territory of Nagorno-Karabach and Chechen rebels in a war against Russia transformed Turkey into a 'regional arbiter' in support of its own security interests.[53] Thus, in its attempt to play an active role as a regional arbiter, Turkey may involve itself in broader conflicts, with devastating repercussions for its own economy and security. Such a danger is more likely to occur in the

Middle East since Turkey has embarked on a closer military and economic collaboration with Israel which might result in finding itself entangled in a regional conflict.

The Middle East is likely to constitute the most troublesome region for Turkey's international relations over the coming years. During the 1980s the Middle East and North Africa markets were instrumental in Turkey's export increase. Even though the Middle East region still remains the principal source of Turkey's oil imports, the Turkish trade in the Middle East and North Africa has been declining steadily over the past years.[54] Apart from close economic ties and a common Islamic heritage, two interrelated geo-strategic concerns link Turkey irrevocably to the fortunes of the region – water and the Kurds – both of which have brought Turkey to the verge of conflict with its two southern neighbours, Iraq and Syria.

The initiative of a massive South East Anatolian Project, popularly known in Turkey as the GAP (Guney Dogu Anadolu Projesi) project has been viewed by Syria and Iraq with some apprehension. The Attaturk dam and some hydro-projects may seriously threaten to deplete water resources in Iraq and Syria. Even though Turkey proposed the 'peace pipeline' scheme in 1987, which could solve the problem of water, the potential Arab recipients of the project have their reservations, mainly due to the prevalent instability in the region. There were concerns that the flow of the water could easily be disrupted by the countries participating in the scheme, due to any political tensions in the region. So the politics of water is likely to become a potential source of conflict in this region.[55] Considering Turkey's strategic interests in the water issue and the Kurdish problem, Turkey's engagement in the region, particularly in conjunction with its two southern neighbours, Iraq and Syria, is unavoidable.

Perhaps the greatest single challenge Turkey must face in the 1990s is to find ways to successfully deal with the Kurdish problem. For a long period, Turkish governments have resorted to force and persecution towards the Kurdish population. Kurdish incursions and violence instigated by the Marxist PKK brought out the worst in military and civil officials who were trying to contain them. The problem has worsened steadily since 1982. It peaked in the early 1990s and one index is the flight of over a million Kurds from the countryside to the unofficial Kurdish capital Diyarbakir from 1990 to 1994, as the Turkish army was devastating the countryside.[56]

With aspirations to reach the standards of contemporary civilisation, Turkey has found a basic goal in integration with Europe. Turkey's preference in favour of Europe is a political decision with its roots in its past. According to Turks:

a Turkey which is integrated in Europe economically, is socially powerful and stable, would be a bridge that unites the modern values of
pluralistic parliamentary democracy, the rule of law and human rights
of the West and with the East, and would constitute an antidote to the
theories of cultural conflict.[57]

However, the collapse of the eastern bloc has added a completely
new dimension to the debate concerning the future of the EU and
the possibilities facing individual states in conjunction with full
membership. Several east European countries have emerged as
serious applicants for full EU membership. A potential candidate
such as Hungary stands a better chance of obtaining membership
than Turkey, given Hungary's geo-graphical proximity, higher level of
industrial development, much smaller population and above all
cultural and religious heritage. Furthermore, it is well acknowledged
that the average European can correlate himself or herself more
easily with the former communist countries of central and eastern
Europe than with Turkey.

Considering the issue of feasibility, Turkey's full membership in
the EU has never been a strong possibility at any point in recent
history. Several structural factors had a detrimental effect and can
elucidate why Turkish membership has not been achieved so far and
most likely will continue to be unattainable in the foreseeable future.
Unequivocally, the most important constraints are economic.
Turkey's levels of industrialisation and economic development are
significantly below the western European average. Similarly, Turkey's
inflation and unemployment figures compare unfavourably with even
the least advanced EU members. Given Turkey's level of development
and population size, free labour mobility constitutes a very sensitive
issue from the perspective of the union, and probably constitutes
the single most important barrier to Turkey's graduation to full
membership.[58]

One of the main issues that is frequently put forth as a problem
hindering Turkey's relations with the EU is Turkish–Greek relations.[59]
The end of the Cold War compelled Turkish security perceptions to
respond to the anarchical process of geo-political change in the
Balkans. For nearly four decades, Turkey viewed its security interests
in the Balkans almost exclusively through the prism of the Warsaw
Pact and the Greek–Turkish conflict. The Yugoslav conflict and the
Kosovo crisis have unleashed the forces for a Christian versus Muslim
polarisation thus re-igniting in the Balkans the spectre of a 'clash of
civilisations'.[60] Hence, it has led to the entanglement of the
Greek–Turkish conflict in the regional struggle for power, thus
greatly expanding its scope beyond the limited dimensions of the

earlier era. Since the collapse of the Soviet Union, Greek–Turkish relations have remained static and according to the Turkish President Suleyman Demirel 'the present picture is not a particularly hopeful one'.[61] However, the reality of the matter is that the prospect for stability in the eastern Mediterranean will be strongly influenced and decided by the extent to which Greek–Turkish relations can be 'anchored' in NATO after the Cold War, and the longer-term evolution of relations between Europe and the Islamic world.

KURDISTAN: TURKEY'S ROUGHEST NEIGHBOURHOOD

The world's 25 million Kurds are often described as the biggest ethnic group without a state, and are certainly one of the longest-standing. Since the allies dropped their pledge of a Kurdish state, made after the First World War, the Kurds have been divided mainly between four inhospitable countries: Turkey, Syria, Iran and Iraq.[62]

Kurdish nationalism constitutes the biggest single political problem Turkey faces today. The Republic of Turkey was founded as the Turkish national state and was assumed to be nationally homogeneous. However, the truth is more complicated.

The republic was and still remains religiously homogeneous. More than 99 per cent of its inhabitants profess the Muslim faith, the founding fathers of the republic equated Muslim with Turk. Attaturk as Turkey's founder, sought to unite all the Muslims who had come as refugees when the Ottoman Empire began to contract at the end of the seventeenth century or when Russia began to expand south but more consistently after the Bolshevik Revolution. His motto 'Happy is he/she who calls himself/herself a Turk' stressed choice and personal commitment over origin. But the accompanying injunction 'Citizen, speak Turkish!' had a coercive ring. Nevertheless, none of the constitutive ethnic components of the Turkish citizenry presents a political or societal problem, with the exception of the Kurds.[63] The republic of Turkey has failed to satisfy any legitimate demands of its citizens of Kurdish ethnic heritage, who constitute between 20 and 25 per cent of the overall population.[64]

The Kemalist state aimed to transform Turkey into a country that was 100 per cent Turkish and considered any war waged towards this end as almost a holy war. It was also a state which saw itself as the vehicle of a mission, the civilising mission of the Turkish nation and it used this to justify its provision of education and civilisation to other nations – by force, if necessary. Therefore, the Kurds presented both an obstacle to the objective of homogenising the national territory and to the Turkish nation's civilising mission.[65] The fear of the loss of 'national unity' was and still is a common characteristic among most politicians and army officials.[66] During 1960 and 1961 while the soldiers were the absolute masters of Turkey, the only bank that had been created by the internal dynamism of the Kurdish regions, the Dogu Bank, was liquidated by military decree. During succeeding years, while tribunals applied the laws forbidding the Kurdish language and culture,[67] the extreme right and the army came into conflict over plans for negotiation and general strategic questions. One of the leaders of the *coup d'état* of 27 May 1960, Colonel Turkes, did not hesitate to openly threaten Kurds with a 'final solution' of the kind that had been adopted by the Unionist government towards the Armenians in 1915:

> If the Kurds run after an illusion of creating a state, their destiny will be wiped off the face of the earth. The Turkish race has shown the way in which it can treat those who covet the homeland which it has obtained at the price of its own blood and untold labours. It has eliminated the Armenians from this land in 1915 and the Greeks in 1922.[68]

Ab initio the state created by Ataturk in 1920–3 was built on nationalism and secular modernisation, it relied on military power to achieve both objectives, and it has remained dedicated to this dual purpose ever since. Its two main challenges are the Kurdish insurgency led by the PKK and the anti-modern and anti-secular reaction of large numbers of Muslims, led politically by the Welfare Party (Refah Partisi).[69] The current crisis, a civil war with the PKK that has left 24,000 dead and a confrontation between Islamic 'fundamentalism' and the military are in fact recurrent themes of modern Turkey's history. 'Both the PKK and Refah' says Turkish intellectual Dogu Ergil, 'are the illegitimate children of the system'. And they were conceived in the early, tumultuous years of the republic's proto-fascist governance.[70]

The root and branch of this intra-state conflict can be attributed to Turkish nationalism. The Turkish state for the aforementioned reasons from 1923 onward simply refused to acknowledge that Kurds even existed – they were known, until the 1990s, as 'Mountain Turks'. Turks were portrayed as founders of the great Asian civilisations insofar that the Kurds and Kurdish history were on the whole disregarded. A 'Turkification' programme was instituted in the southeast, raising the visibility of Turkish culture, moving Turks into that area, and above all promoting the dogma of Ataturk. At the same time the Kurdish regions were gradually impoverished by persecutions, deportations of Kurdish elites and the disappearance of the Christian entrepreneurial class. Furthermore, economic neglect has left the area traditional and tribal, impeding the growth of any national feeling. By the early 1990s less than 10 per cent of adults in the Kurdish south-east had industrial jobs, and most of them tended to be in low-skilled industries. The demise of viable agrarian life and the growth of the urban poor and unskilled youth radicalised large segments of the Kurdish people. As a result, radical movements such as the PKK were created in 1974 on the campus of Ankara University. The bloodless and temporary coup by the military of 1980 inaugurated and engineered a new round of systematic and methodical persecution of Kurdish nationalists. Since then the PKK has turned into a genuine guerilla movement which was significantly supported by ordinary Kurdish peasants. What was a nuisance to the Turkish state grew over the 1980s into a large-scale civil war. The Turkish government has steadily increased its military presence in the provinces under the emergency rule. According to the International Institute for Strategic Studies, the normal level of Turkish troop deployments in the area was around 90,000. This number had risen to 160,000 by June 1994. By the end of 1994, taking into account also the number of police, special forces and village guards, there were 300,000 security forces deployed in eastern and south-eastern Turkey. Approximately one-quarter of the total manpower of NATO's second-largest army was deployed in the area against the PKK.[71]

It was during President Tugrut Ozal's tenure that the current Kurdish problem began, slowly escalating and then exploding. Although Ozal at first rejected any political or democratic solution to the Kurdish problem, by the end of his life he had evolved to become the only important Turkish statesman politically and intellectually capable of conceiving imaginative, democratic solutions. Ozal in the spring of 1991 legalised the usage of Kurdish in everyday conversation and folkloric music recordings by rescinding Law No.2932, which had been enacted by the military in October 1983. Usage of Kurdish in the media and education, however, remained prohibited. Even according to the PKK leader Ocalan (Apo), Ozal 'was the one who could find a way to solve the problem'.[72]

One of the most dramatic developments in Turkey's changing Kurdish problem occurred in 1993. The PKK declared a unilateral cease-fire from March 20 and presented President Ozal and Prime Minister Demirel with a proposal for a cease-fire. However, the cease-fire failed for two basic reasons. Firstly, the Turkish authorities interpreted Ocalan's move as a sign of weakness and therefore their chance to finish his movement off, rather than as a way to achieve a permanent solution to the Kurdish problem. The second reason was the sudden death of Ozal, the Turkish leader who was most receptive to some type of compromise that might have ended the struggle. This argument was corroborated by a well-known Turkish academic, Ismet G. Imset who claimed that if Ozal had lived 'everything would have been different. A major reform package would have been underway and even the hawks (hard-liners) would have fallen in line'.[73]

The date 16 February 1999 opened a new chapter in the war between the Turkish forces and the PKK. The PKK leader Ocalan was abducted by Turkish secret forces while being escorted across Nairobi by Greek diplomats. His arrest and the Greek involvement triggered off a new series of confrontations and accusations between Greek and Turkish governments which highlighted once more the lack of basic co-operation and understanding between the two NATO allies.

Despite Ocalan's capture, the political aspirations of Turkey's 15 million Kurds most likely will not end. On the contrary the Turkish attitude and behaviour towards the Kurdish minority will continue to be under international scrutiny. It is not a coincidence that the EU put Turkey at the bottom of the league of applicants in 1999 in part because of its dismal record on human rights.

Yet, the Kurds' pursuit of some kind of autonomy or even some minority rights most probably will continue to fall on deaf ears. The geo-political reality constitutes Kurdistan as a frontier between the countries the US considers its foes and its staunchest regional allies, between the weak but rich states of the Gulf and their expansionist neighbours and until recently, between the Soviet Union and NATO.

The US fears that a break-up of Iraq or a weakening of Turkey would favour Iran, still the greatest threat to stability in the Middle East in the eyes of many Pentagon planners. In the face of such grand strategic imperatives, Kurdish self-determination is far from high on the US as well as the international agenda. Even in northern Iraq, where the Kurds have run their own affairs with US support since their uprising in 1991, the US has made sure that the local authorities cease all support for the PKK and religiously reaffirm their respect for the territorial integrity of Iraq.[74]

NEW OPPORTUNITIES FOR TURKEY IN THE CAUCASUS?

Turkey's adoption of a leading role in the Black Sea region contributed to promoting its economic pre-eminence in the Caucasus. Subsequently Greece pursued an opposing strategy which in turn served to maintain and even heighten competitive feeling between these two NATO members.

Since the end of the Cold War, the west and a number of NATO member states, predominantly Turkey, have developed strong links with the Caucasus region, driven by their aspiration to exploit hydro-carbon and mineral deposits in the Caspian basin. The Caucasus, after the collapse of the Soviet Union, has emerged as a highly complex and problematic region. The oil factor, the future economic opportunities that would follow with it and the benefits for western companies, created a great deal of tension both in terms of politics and economics in the Caucasus. Moreover, the US via Turkey is striving to ensure the safe flow of oil to western markets in order to reduce US reliance on the Persian Gulf area.

On 18 November 1999, an important agreement with regards to the construction for a new oil pipeline linking Azerbaijan's capital, Baku, to Turkey's Mediterranean coast was signed during the summit of the OSCE in Istanbul. In an attempt to bypass and reduce Moscow's ability to shape energy events in the Southern Caucasus, Turkey, Azerbaijan and Georgia, promoted by the US, signed a series of accords to build an oil pipeline, which is expected to cost $2.4 billion, and would cross through Georgia to the Turkish port of Ceyhan. Crucial to this agreement was the involvement of Kazakhstan, which agreed to pump 20 million tonnes of its oil per year through the pipeline.[75]

Russia, on the other hand, has tried to force Baku to ship its oil through Russian ports (Novorossisk) into the Black Sea. Tankers would then carry the oil through the Trans-Balkan pipeline linking the Black Sea Bulgarian port of Burgas with the Aegean port of Alexandroupolis, thus bypassing the straits. Russia's scheme is focused on an attempt to outflank Turkey by building a pipeline from the Black Sea to the eastern Mediterranean. This scheme would eventually bypass Turkey as a player in Transcaucasian energy, striking at Ankara's vital interests there and in the Balkans.[76] The implementation of this scheme would also consolidate a Greco-Russian and perhaps Bulgarian bloc against Turkey and its efforts to play a regional role in south-east Europe through the BSEZC.[77] What is more important is the scheme once more emphasises the antagonism between Greece and Turkey and tends to expand the Caucasus energy issue into the security agenda in the eastern Mediterranean and to feed into a broader Greek–Turkish geo-political competition in the Balkans, the Aegean and the eastern Mediterranean.

GREECE AND TURKEY: THE COLD WAR CONTINUES

Despite the end of the Cold War, a Greek–Turkish rapprochement remains out of reach. A catalytic factor in the preservation of the Cold

War in the eastern Mediterranean is the lack of genuine dialogue between the two countries. Lack of dialogue which brings about lack of trust has significantly hindered progress on a bilateral level and has so far prevented the development of a co-ordinated approach to help shape the post-Cold War Balkans.

However, of greater significance is the coming together of such diverse initiatives as the Turkish–Israel Axis and promotion of the Turkish model in central Asia, pipelines, all of which have combined to promote Turkey into an influential military and economic regional power. As a result, it has heightened Greek suspicions of Turkey and its role in the eastern Mediterranean. These factors have inevitably served to maintain the antagonism which exists between these two states.

Currently both countries enjoy very good relations with their Balkan neighbours. However, Turkish and Greek governments have set their respective foreign policies to a large extent with the other in mind. Turkish and Greek politicians, almost on a daily basis, have accused the rival state of being behind all developments that are found to be harmful to their national interests. In the new post-Cold War Balkan atmosphere of change and uncertainty, the media and leading politicians tend to unleash provocative and propagandistic articles and views which allow prejudices and emotions to run their course, further reinforcing mutual suspicions.

Under these circumstances, no progress and hence stability in the eastern Mediterranean, has been made or can be expected. However, the creation and activation of a Balkan rapid deployment force with the participation of Albania, Bulgaria, Greece, Italy, FYROM, Romania and Turkey constitutes one of the biggest challenges for the Balkan countries. According to the protocol which was signed on 12 January 1999, the force's headquarters will alternate every four years among the participating NATO and PfP countries in the order of Bulgaria, Romania, Turkey, Greece. The command will be assigned to each of the countries for a two-year term. Turkey will be first, followed by Greece.[78] Slovenia and the US are participating in the multinational force as observers. However, the effectiveness of this multinational peacekeeping force remains to be seen, since diametrical and divergent views have been presented and supported by Greece and Turkey on the bilateral and regional level. A joint statement issued at the end of official talks in Ankara between Turkish Foreign Minister Hikmet Cetin and Greek Foreign Minister Michalis Papakonstandinou on 19 April 1993, acknowledges this vast chasm with the following words: 'It has been announced that Turkey and Greece agree on the establishment of peace and stability in the Balkans as soon as possible, but differ on the means and the methods.'[79]

NATO AND TURKEY: NEW ERA NEW CHALLENGES

The geo-strategic role of Turkey until 1989 was clearly defined, *albeit* limited. Her position as the south-eastern rampart of NATO had a twofold strategic meaning. First, Turkey was required to control the Turkish Straits, a vital route for Soviet vessels sailing from the ports in the Black Sea to the Mediterranean. Second, it was expected to withstand any air–land operation in the direction of the eastern Mediterranean, both in Thrace and in Anatolia. Furthermore, the national strategy of the alliance's leader – the US – was aimed at controlling the pivotal area between Europe, south-western Asia, and the Indian Ocean mainly through maritime power.[80] During the Gulf War in 1991 it became evident that this traditional, well-defined but limited, Turkish role had changed. Turkey was hence for the first time openly involved in Middle Eastern affairs in the framework of the allied action. Likewise, the dissolution of the Warsaw Pact in 1991 freed Turkey from the arduous need to face the Bulgarian presence on its north-western borders while the collapse of the Soviet Union ended the threat from its north-eastern borders. Therefore, after 1989, a new arc of crisis and challenges appeared. This arc extends from Sarajevo to Samarkand, from the Balkans to former Soviet central Asia.

The cessation of the east–west confrontation, and the evolution of new challenges were the main reasons behind the transformation of the Turkish military doctrine. In a major press briefing on 24 August 1992, Prime Minister Demirel highlighted the importance of a military reform package which aimed at reducing manpower levels, shifting to a professional army and procuring and integrating high-tech weapons. Turkey's defence policy aims were defined as protecting and safe-guarding the country's borders, territorial integrity and legitimate rights and interests.[81] He also announced that according to the man-power limits set within the framework of the Treaty on CFE,[82] Turkey was required to reduce its forces to 530,000 within forty months after the agreement came into force. The result of the CFE Treaty was a *de facto* re-balancing between the NATO forces deployed to the north and those deployed to the south, a consequence of a reduction in the North American, French and north European presence in Germany and of reinforcement of Turkish and Greek arsenals.[83]

NATO during the 1990s tried to adapt to the new challenges in the post-Cold War era. Its core mission remains collective defence, but its organisation, military capability and structures have been adapted to enable it to address new tasks, in particular those involving co-operation with non-member countries and crisis management. The alliance has developed procedures and mechanisms for close co-operation with its partner countries, for example, through PfP, the

Euro-Atlantic Partnership Council, the NATO–Russia Founding Act and the NATO–Ukraine Charter.[84] At the NATO Rome Summit meeting of 7–8 November 1991, it was agreed that the CSCE process would in future include institutional arrangements and provide a contractual framework for co-operation complementary to that of NATO and the process of European integration in preserving peace.[85]

Within the new European architecture, Turkey's growing importance is clearly related to its central location within regions of high instability and conflict. The 1994 NATO Summit in Istanbul reiterated Turkey's importance for the alliance due to its centrality in an enormous geographical region. Moreover, since 1991 Turkey has participated in NATO operations in the Bosnian crisis and in Kosovo. Many western policy analysts and Turkish strategic planners perceive Turkey as a regional power capable of forging peace in a wider conflict zone.[86] The southern flank of NATO presents the alliance with a range of challenges potentially more critical than those that NATO faces in other regions within Europe.[87] In the aftermath of the Cold War, the southern flank has gained in importance, as was illustrated by the Gulf War of 1990–1 and the war in Kosovo. Turkey has the potential to play an energetic and more prominent role in the Balkans, the Caucasus and central Asia. Turkey's place within NATO and other western security systems (OSCE, Member of Council of Europe, Associate Member of the EU and the WEU) can be utilised and redefined, according to the needs arising in the region as a result of the end of the Cold War.

In line with its enhanced post-Cold War regional status, and the new NATO structure, Turkey has paid particular attention to the modernisation of its air force and navy, the two branches of its armed forces that provide it with the capability for power projection abroad. In this connection, Turkey received in 1995 two KC-135 R-type tanker aircraft. Turkey is the only US ally that has obtained the KC-135 Rs and this indicates the extent of the deepening strategic relationship between Ankara and Washington. A single KC-135 R can refuel up to 25 aircraft during a single flight. Thus, with the help of its tanker fleet, the Turkish air force will have the capability to double the 600-kilometre range of Turkey's F-16s and allow them to fly all over the eastern Mediterranean and the Middle East.

Moreover, past and recent purchases of attack and air-troop-carrying helicopters and transport planes have given the Turkish army the strongest and most modernised air transport capability in the Balkans, the eastern Mediterranean and possibly the Middle East. The procurement of 50 *Cougars*, together with the 45 US S-70 *Blackhawks*, the 19 Russian MI-17 and over 250 various other types of transport helicopters has made the ability to transport special forces and troops, up to a brigade in strength, a reality.[88]

In addition, there has been a parallel modernisation of the Turkish navy. The US Department of Defence announced the sale to Turkey of three FFG-7 PERRY class frigates and eight leased FF 1052 KNOX class frigates. The estimated cost is $205 million. With the co-production already of six out of eight MEKO frigates in Turkish and German shipyards, Turkey has taken a decisive step towards naval supremacy in the Aegean.[89] The Turkish navy will also be receiving additional support from six new mine-hunter ships scheduled for purchase at a cost of $700 million. This military procurement will improve the military capabilities of Turkey, while enhancing weapon system standardisation and interoperability.

On the other hand, it inaugurated a new area of arms competition between the two NATO allies and damages efforts to bring regional stability. Since 1990, both countries have continued to maintain levels of defence spending that are well above the NATO average, have been vigorously modernising their forces aided by the NATO 'Cascade' Programme and have acquired categories of weapons designated offensive under the CFE Treaty, such as tanks, armoured infantry vehicles, attack helicopters and anti-tank aircraft. Given these facts effective co-operation is unlikely although the NATO framework does provide military co-operation between the two countries such as the STANAVFORMED and the multinational division for the southern flank.[90]

The effects of current Turkish security policy actions together with the open support of the west have combined to sustain and heighten a climate of antagonism between Greece and Turkey.

What is also striking is that Greek–Turkish bilateral issues have clearly the potential to bring these two countries to war. This makes them exceptional in the context of NATO because it is genuinely believed that other NATO member states form a security community, but it is clear that the security community does not embrace the relationship between Greece and Turkey. It is necessary to explain this. The next chapter examines Deutsch's security community theory and analyses why it has failed to operate in the case of Greece and Turkey.

NOTES

1. For further study about the Ottoman Empire see A.J Toynbee, *A Study of History*, IV (London: Oxford University Press, 1940) pp.68–189. See also R.S. Humphreys, *Islamic History: A Framework for Enquiry* (NJ: Princeton, 1991) and Bernard Lewis, *The Middle East*, Part III (London: Phoenix Giant, 1996).
2. See A. Mango, *Turkey: A Delicately Poised Ally* (London: The Washington Papers, SAGE Policy Paper, 1975) p.3.

3. See N. Eren, *Turkey Today – And Tomorrow: An Experiment in Westernization* (New York: Praeger, 1963) p.19.

4. ibid., p.19.

5. On legal reforms see 'The Reception of Foreign Law in Turkey', *International Social Science Bulletin*, 9, 1 (1957) pp.7–81. On language reform see Heyd, *Language Reform in Modern Turkey* (Jerusalem: Israel Oriental Studies, 1954). For descriptions and evaluations of the cultural repercussion caused by Turkey's modernisation and secularisation see *The Turkish Press*, 1925–31, Athens, 1931 and Lilo Linke, *Allah Dethroned*, (London: Constable and Co, 1938). For general information about Turkey's political and economic transformation see, K.H. Karat, *Turkey's Politics: The Transition to a Multi-Party System* (Princeton: Princeton University Press, 1959). For the effect that Ataturk plays in the Turkish modern society see C. Haviland, 'Ataturk: The Man and the Myth', in *Discovery Turkey*, BBC World Service (1995).

6. For more information about Ataturk see J. Kinross, *Ataturk: The Rebirth of a Nation* (London: Weidenfeld & Nicolson, 1993); H.C. Armstrong, *Grey Wolf* (Harmondsworth: Penguin Books, 1939).

7. See Idris Bal, 'The Turkish Model and the Turkish Republics', *Perceptions*, 3, 3, Center for Strategic Research, Ankara, Turkey, 1998, p.1.

8. Philip Robins, *Turkey and the Middle East* (London: Pinter Publishers, 1991) p.7.

9. K. Hami, 'The Past, Present and Future of Turkish Industry', *Turkish Review*, 3, 15 (1995) p.62.

10. For further study see J. Wanterbury, 'Export-Led Growth and the Center-Right Coalition in Turkey', *Comparative Politics*, (January, 1992) pp. 127–42; F. Senses, 'An Overview of Recent Turkish Experience with Economic Stabilisation and Liberalisation', in F. Nas and M. Odekon (eds), *Liberalisation and the Turkish Economy* (Westport, Conn: Greenwood Press, 1988) pp.9–28; with regards to the political economy of Turkish development see Bent Hansen, *Egypt and Turkey*, Chapter 13, (Oxford: Oxford University Press, 1991) pp.421–33.

11. Bal, 'The Turkish Model', p.3.

12. See C. Dodd, 'Developments in Turkish Democracy', in Vojtech Mastny and R. Craig Nation (eds), *Turkey Between East and West: New Challenges for a Rising Regional Power* (Colorado: Westview Press, 1996) pp.131–40.

13. For further study see Andrew Mango, *Turkey the Challenge of a New Role* (Westpost: Praeger, 1997), pp.5–30; Metin Heper and Ahreed Evid (eds), *State, Democracy and the Military: Turkey in the 1980s* (Berlin: Walter de Gruter, 1988).

14. See Kinross, *Ataturk: The Rebirth of a Nation* p.458.

15. ibid.

16. Kaplan, Clawson and Lurangi, *NATO and the Mediterranean* (Wilmington, Delaware: Scholarly Resources, 1985) p.216.

17. G. Aybet, 'Turkey's in its Geo-Strategic Environment', *RUSI and Brassey's Defence Yearbook* (1992) p.92.

18. See H.N. Howard, *Turkey, The Straits and US Policy* (Baltimore and London: Johns Hopkins University Press, 1974) pp. 216–55.

19. See Frode Liland, 'Keeping NATO Out of Trouble: NATO's Non-Policy on Out-Of-Area Issue During the Cold War', *Forsvarsstudier* (4/1999) pp.36–9.

20. The US decided to include Greece and Turkey in NATO because it 'is primarily military and is based on a conviction that this is the only satisfactory means of assuring that their military resources, especially those of Turkey, will be fully available to the West in event of war. The association of Greece and Turkey is to (a) secure the Southern Flank of Europe, and (b) to lend substance to a Middle East Command', National Archives and Records Administration (US), Record Group (RG) 59, 740.5 preparations for NATO meeting, 14 September 1951.

21. See A. Mango, 'Turkey: A Delicately Poised Ally', *The Washington Papers* (London: Sage

Publications, 1975) p.34. For more information see also S. Deger, 'The Economic Costs and Benefits of US–Turkish Military Relations', in J.M.O. Sharp (ed.), *Europe After an American Withdrawal: Economic and Military Issues* (Oxford: Oxford University Press, SIPRI, 1990) pp. 243–73.

22. See Sezer, 'Turkey's Security' (1981) p.23.
23. See G.A. Harris, *Troubled Alliance: Turkish–American Problems in Historical Perspective* (Washington and Stanford: AEI-Hoover, 1972) pp.112–14.
24. See Ali Karaosmanoglu, 'Turkey's Security Policy: Continuity and Change', in D.T. Stuart (ed.), *Politics and Security in the Southern Region of the Atlantic Alliance* (Basingstoke: Macmillan Press, 1988) pp.162–3.
25. K.H, Karpat, 'Turkish–Soviet Relations', in Karpat (ed.), *Turkey's Foreign Policy in Transition, 1950–1974* (Leiden: Brill, 1975) pp.90–107.
26. For further elaboration on this view see E.T. Rossides, 'American Foreign Policy and the Rule of Law – The Aegean and Cyprus', in *United States Foreign Policy Regarding Greece, Turkey & Cyprus: The Rule of Law and American Interests*, AHI Conference Proceeding (Washington: American Hellenic Institute, 1988) pp.99–102.
27. See George Harris, 'The View from Ankara', *The Wilson Quarterly*, 6, 5 (Special Issue), (1982) p.132.
28. The appointment of Turkish–Cypriot policemen by the British in pure Greek–Cypriot villages was perceived as such a move.
29. See Mango, 'Turkey' (1975), p. 35.
30. For further study about Cyprus see, *The Rule of Law and Conditions on Foreign Aid to Turkey, Legislative Conference* (Washington: American Hellenic Institute, 1990).
31. See R. Guerdilek, 'View From Ankara', *NATO Sixteen Nations*, 38, 5/6 (1993) p.14.
32. Ecevit resigned in 1974 and was replaced by Demirel. He formed another government in January 1978 which lasted until 1979 and was once again replaced by Demirel.
33. *Prime Minister Ecevit's* speeches, published by the General Directorate of Press and Information of the Turkish Republic (1978) p.29.
34. See L. Bilman, 'The Regional Co-operation Initiatives in Southeast Europe and the Turkish Foreign Policy', *Perceptions*, III, 3 (1998), Center for Strategic Research, Ankara, pp.1–14.
35. Hale, 'Turkish Politics', p.49.
36. For the Turkish official viewpoint see *www.mfa.gov.tr/grupa/ad/ade/adea/default.htm*. For further study see D.B. Sezer, *Turkish Security in the Shifting Balkans: Reorientation To a Regional Focus*, in K. Tsipis (ed.), *Common Security Regimes* (New York: Columbia University Press, 1996) pp.113–22. See also A. Karaosmanoglu, 'Turkey and the Southern Flank: Domestic and External Contexts', in J. Chipman (ed.), *NATO's Southern Allies, Internal and External Challenges* (London: Routledge, 1988) pp.339–49.
37. Sezer, 'Turkey's' (1996) p.118.
38. Karaosmanoglu, 'Turkey and the' (1988) p.340–1.
39. For more information regarding the military and logistical capabilities of these islands see Sezer, 'Turkey's' (1996) p.120.
40. The ultimate defence of the eastern Mediterranean depended on the Greek islands and Crete which could actually prevent any Soviet advance from the Straits once the Soviet army succeeded in placing them under control. See T. Couloumbis and M. Stearns, *Entangled Allies* (New York: Council on Free Press, 1992). For more details about the importance of the Mediterranean, see L. Lemnitzer, 'The Strategic Problems of NATO's Northern and Southern Flanks', *Orbis*, XIII, 1 (1969) pp.101–6.
41. For further study see J. Brown, *Delicately Poised Allies: Greece and Turkey*, (London: Brassey's, 1991) pp.1–3.
42. See Bruce R. Kuniholm, 'Turkey and NATO', in *NATO and the Mediterranean* (1985) p.228.
43. ibid., p.228.

44. The AMF force was primarily designed to deter the enemy and it was viewed as a force capable of providing reinforcements.
45. Brown, 'Delicately', p.93.
46. See Kuniholm, 'Turkey and NATO', p.229 and L. Lemnitzer, 'The Strategic Problems of NATO' Northern and Southern Flanks', *Orbis*, XIII, 1 (1969) pp.101, 105.
47. See Congress, Senate, Committee on Foreign relations, 'United States Foreign Policy Objectives and Overseas Military Installations', 96th Congress, 1st Session (1979), pp.62–5. See *Washington Post*, 16 October 1982 and 1 November 1982.
48. For more information about Turkey's army see, *The Military Balance 1995–1996*, (London: Brassey's, 1995) pp.33–48; *Defence Biblos 2002–2003* (Athens: Strategiki, 2003); and Sezer, 'Turkish Security in a Shifting Balkans', in *Common Security Regimes in the Balkans* (1996) pp.122–33; for detailed description see Brown (1991) 'Delicately', pp.97–101.
49. See Kuniholm, 'Turkey and NATO', pp.232–3.
50. ibid., p.231.
51. See J. Brown, 'Delicately', p.100.
52. I.O. Lesser, 'Mediterranean Security: New Perspectives and Implications for the U.S. Policy', *RAND Report*, (1993) pp.86–103.
53. For more details see Suha Bolukbasi, 'Ankara's Baku-Centered Transcaucasia Policy: Has it Failed?' *The Middle East Journal*, 51, 1 (1997) pp.80–94; C. Blandy, 'Chechen Caravan Trails', *Conflict Studies Research Centre* (April, 1996). See V. Bennett, 'Crying Wolf: The Return of War to Chechnya' (London: Macmillan Press, 1998) pp. 446–58. See also R. Olson, 'The Kurdish Question & Chechnya; Turkey versus Russia since the Gulf War', *Middle East Policy*, 4, 3 (1996) pp.106–18. For information about economic and military assistance towards Chechens see Anishchenko, Vasilevskaya, Kugusheva and Mramornov, *Kommissiya Govorukhina* (Moscow, 1995) pp.41–2.
54. For data information see *The Turkish Economy in June 1992: Statistics and Interpretations*, (Ankara: State Institute of Statistics, 1992).
55. For more information about the project see F. Kolars and W.A. Mitchell, *The Euphrates River and the Southeast Anatolia Development Project* (Carbondale: Southern Illinois University Press, 1991).
56. See Noam Chomsky, 'The Current Bombings: Behind the Rhetoric', *www.ibbs.org/current_bombings.htm*, p.3 (April 1999). Interview with N. Chomsky, in WBUR Boston's NPR News Station, 12 April 1999. See also *The Economist*, 1 August 1998, pp.45–6, *The Economist*, 20 February 1999, p.57, M. Gunter, *The Kurds and the Future of Turkey* (London: Macmillan Press, 1997) p.1. See the figures listed in *Turkish Daily News*, 10 June 1995 and *Human Rights Watch Arms Project*, 'Weapons Transfers and Violation of the Laws of War in Turkey', *Human Rights Watch* (1995) pp.1, 23; citing the Turkish Human Rights Foundation (TIHV), Ismet G. Ismet, a most knowledgeable source, listed a total of 3,000,000 displaced Kurds and 3,000 torched villages at the end of 1995.
57. See Cakar, 'Turkey's Security', p.1.
58. In 1999 Turkey gained recognition as a second-tier candidate for full membership. See Malcolm Cooper, 'The Legacy of Ataturk', *International Affairs*, 78, 1 (2002), pp.115–28. For more details about Turkey's relationship with the EU see C. Balkir and A.M. Williams, (eds), *Turkey and Europe* (London and New York: Pinter Publishers, 1993); Fotios Moustakis, 'Turkey's Entry into the EU: Asset or Liability', *Contemporary Review*, 273, 1592 (September, 1998), pp.128–35; Vittorio Sanguineti 'Turkey and the European Union: Dreaming West but Moving East', *Mediterranean Quarterly*, 8, 1 (1997) pp.11–26; J. Redmond, *The Next Mediterranean Enlargement of the European Community: Turkey, Cyprus & Malta?* (Aldershot, England: Dartmouth Publishing Company, 1993).
59. US President Bill Clinton on his visit in Athens on 20 November 1999, warned Turkey that it could not join the European family unless it settled its disputes with EU member Greece, *Reuters Agency*, 21 November 1999.

60. For Professor Samuel Huntington's view that the 'clash of civilisations' is the defining conflict in world politics in the post-Cold War era see S. Huntington, 'The Clash of Civilisations', *Foreign Affairs*, 72. 3 (1993) pp.22–49. For polarisation in the Balkans see 'Not Really their Business at All', *Current Affairs* (1992) pp.9–11.

61. See S. Demirel, 'The Need For Dialogue: Turkey, Greece & the Possibility of Reconciliation', *Harvard International Review*, 21, 1 (winter, 1998/1999) p.24.

62. See 'The Kurds: An Ancient Tragedy', *The Economist*, 20 February 1999, p.58. About Syria's political regime see D.S. Sorenson, 'National Security and Political Succession in Syria', *Mediterranean Quarterly*, 9, 1 (1998) pp.69–91. For more information about Syria see Kienle Eberhard, *Contemporary Syria: Liberalisation between Cold War and Cold Peace*, (London: London Academic Press, 1994). For more details about Kurds in the aforementioned countries see S.C. Pelletiere, *The Kurds: An Unstable Element in the Gulf* (Boulder & London: Westview Press, 1984). See also David McDowall, *A Modern History of the Kurds* (London: Tauris, 1997).

63. During the First World War, most Armenians were deported from the eastern part of present-day Turkey. The Greek movement out of Turkey, which began around 1912, reached its high point in the 1920s during and after the War of Independence. As part of the peace settlement following the defeat of the Greeks, a formal exchange of populations was agreed upon. As a result, Turkey received about 500,000 Turkish immigrants in exchange for nearly two million Greeks. It is instructive to mention that the threat of foreign Christian rule, initially in the east and then, following the Greek invasion, galvanised the Muslim population into a war of resistance against the perceived invaders. As a result, the spread of nationalist ideas led to the Armenian massacres in 1915 and the expulsion in 1922 of most of the Christian minorities. It is worth mentioning that Turkey has never admitted an act of genocide against the Armenians, with the rare exception of Taner Akcam, *Turkish National Identity and the Armenian Question* (in Turkish), (Istanbul: Iletisim, 1992). For more information about minorities in Turkey see Hugh Poulton, 'The Struggle for Hegemony in Turkey: Turkish Nationalism as a Contemporary Force', *Journal of Southern Europe and the Balkans*, 1, 1 (1999) pp.15–19; see also 'Turkey: A Country Study', *Library of Congress*, Federal Research Division, Washington, (1992). With regards to the Greek population in Turkey, whose numbers have dwindled due to pogroms and expulsions, they have declined from about 110,000 at the time of the signing of the Lausanne Treaty in 1923 to about 2,500 in 1992; see 'Denying Human Rights and Ethnic Identity: The Greeks of Turkey', *Human Rights Watch* (1992) pp.1–25.

64. Michael M. Gunter, *The Kurds and the Future of Turkey* (London: Macmillan Press, 1997) p.2.

65. See Philip G. Kreyenbroek and Stefan Sperl (eds), *The Kurds: A Contemporary Review* (London: Routledge, 1992) p.103.

66. See S. Demirel, 'Demirel Warns Greece, and There is Absolutely no Resemblance Between What is Going on in Kosovo and the Southeast Turkey', *Anadolu Agency*, 29 April 1999; see also 'Down but Far from Out', *The Economist*, 1 August 1998, pp.44–5.

67. Gunter, 'The Kurds', pp.11–21.

68. Kreyenbroek and Sperl (eds), 'The Kurds', p.104.

69. The Welfare Party was banned by Turkey's highest court on 16 January 1998 and was replaced by the Virtue Party which became the third party in Turkey after the elections of April 1999 and got 111 seats in the Parliament. Welfare's leader Necmettin Erbakan and five of his colleagues were ejected from politics for five years. It is constructive to mention that the generals, once more, were responsible for overthrowing Erbakan's coalition government in summer of 1997.

70. See John Tirman, *Understanding Turkish Nationalism and its Contribution to the War against the Kurds* (January, 1998) p.1, *www.wf.org/turknational.htm*.

71. K. Kirisci and Gareth M. Winrow, *The Kurdish Question and Turkey: An Example of a Trans-State Ethnic Conflict* (London: Frank Cass, 1997) p.130.

72. *Milliyet Interviews PKK leader Ocalan*, Part II, Foreign Broadcast Information Service–West Europe, 27 March 1992, p.43. For more recent views from Ocalan see interview with Professor M. Gunter in Damascus on 13–14 March 1998 in *Middle East Quarterly*, 5, 2 (1998) pp.79–85.
73. See Ismet G. Ismet, 'Wiping out the PKK Again…Again', *Turkish Probe*, 6 July 1993, pp.4–7.
74. For further study about the Kurdish problem see R. Olson, 'The Kurdish Question Four Years On: The Policies of Turkey, Syria, Iran and Iraq', *Middle East Policy*, 3, 3 (1994) pp.36–44; R. Olson, 'The Kurdish Question and Geopolitic and Geostrategic Changes in the Middle East after the Gulf War', *Journal of South Asian and Middle Eastern Studies*, XVII, 4 (1994) 49–67; Henri Barkey, 'Turkey's Kurdish Dilemma', *Survival*, 35, 4 (1993), pp.51–70; Philip Robins, 'The Overlord State: Turkish Policy and the Kurdish Issue', *International Affairs*, 69, 4 (1993), pp.657–71; Nevzat Soguk, 'A Study of the Historico-Cultural Reasons for Turkey's Inconclusive Democracy', *New Political Science*, 26, (1993) pp.89–116.
For information about the National Liberation Front of Kurdistan (ERNK) and PKK see *www.library.cornell.edu/collde/mideast/kurd.htm*. See the Turkish view on the Kurdish problem, N.B. Atiyas, 'The Kurdish Conflict in Turkey: Issues, Parties and Prospectus', *Security Dialogue*, 28, 4 (1997) pp.439–52. For an analysis about missed opportunities and critical turning points on the Kurdish problem see H.J. Barkey and G.E. Fuller, 'Turkey's Kurdish Question: Critical Turning Points and Missed Opportunities', *The Middle East Journal*, 151, 1 (1997) pp.59–79.
75. Kazakhstan's contribution to the project helped to allay fears that the scheme will not be viable in economic terms, see 'Oil Pipeline Deal Bypasses Russia', *The Independent*, 18 November 1999 and *Turkish Daily News*, 18 November 1999. See *The Guardian*, 16 November 1999, p.16. It is instructive to mention that Turkey has signed an agreement with Moscow to develop the Blue Stream pipeline, under which Russia would build the stretch of the 1,200-km connection up to the Turkish Black Sea town of Samsum including a 400-km section under the Black Sea. Turkey's demand for gas is expected to rise to 54bcm in 2010 from 13.5bcm in 1999. As the Turkish Prime Minister explained 'We need gas, from whatever it may come from', see *Reuters Agency*, 4 November 1999. For more information regarding the issue of oil transportation and the competition between Turkey and Russia see Andre Gunter Frank, *The Centrality of Central Asia*, (Amsterdam: VU University Press, 1992). John Loyd and Steve LeVine, 'Russia Demands Veto Over Caspian Oil Deals', *Financial Times*, 31 May 1994, p.2. J. Loyd, 'Moscow Claims Caspian Energy Deals Veto', *FT*, 9 November 1994, p.3. See also Roland Goetz, 'Political Spheres of Interest in the Southern Caucasus and in Central Asia', *Aussenpolitik*, 48, 3 (1997). 'The Geopolitics of Oil in Central Asia', *Cosmos*, 1, 2 (1995) p.2. 'Conference on The Transfer of Caspian Oil to the Western Markets: The Role of Turkey', *Anadolu Agency*, 13-04-99. P. Henze, 'Russia & the Caucasus', *Studies in Conflict and Terrorism*, Vol.19, No.4, (1996). See Stephen Blank, 'Russia and Europe in the Caucasus', *European Security*, 4, 4 (1995) p.627. Barry Newman, 'Oil, Water and Politics Make a Volatile Mix in Crowded Bosporus', *Wall Street Journal*, 24 August 1994, p.1. See also 'Turkey Seeks US-Style Legislation to Stop Russian Tankers in Straits', *Turkish Daily News*, 23-05-96, *www.gri.org/news/agencies/trkn/96-05-23.trkn.html*.
76. For an analytical and theoretical study of central Asia and the Caucasus see Mehdi Mozaffari (ed.), *Security Politics in the Commonwealth of Independent Studies: The Southern Belt*, (Houndmills: Macmillan Press, 1997).
77. Kerin Hope, '*Oil Pipeline Boost for Balkans*', *FT*, 30 September 1994, p.5. See also Fiona Hill, '*Pipeline Politics, Russo-Turkish Competition & Geopolitics in the eastern Mediterranean*', *Cyprus Review*, 8 (1996) p.98.
78. See Athens New Agency, 24-11-98 and 3-01-99, *www.zeus.hri.org/news/greek/apeen/1998/98-11-24.apeen.html* and *www.zeus.hri.org/news/greek/apeen/1999/99-01-13.apeen.html*.
79. Sezer, *Turkey's*, p.109.

80. See L. Bozzo and R. Ragionieri, '*Regional Security in the Balkans and the Role of Turkey*', *The Southern European Yearbook 1992* (Athens: Eliamep, 1993) p.21.
81. For Turkey's war strategy and threats in the post-Cold War era see Sukru Elekdag, 'War Strategy', *Perceptions* (March–May, 1996) pp.1–11, *www.mfa.gov.tr/grupf/percept/I1/per1-3.htm*.
82. For more information about weapons distribution and arms control in the eastern Mediterranean see C. Tuck 'Greece, Turkey and Arms Control', *Defence Analysis,* 12, 1 (1996) pp.23–32 and *Fuelling Balkan Fires: The West's Arming of Greece and Turkey,* Project on the Arms Trade, The British American Security Information Council (1993).
83. Pedro Moya, 'NATO's Role in the Mediterranean', *North Atlantic Assembly Report,* 16 April 1997, p.6.
84. See The Alliance's New Strategic Concept, NATO Communiqué, *www.nato.int/doc/comm/c911107a.htm*.
85. See Meltem Muftuler Bac, *Turkey's Relations With a Changing Europe* (Manchester: Manchester University Press, 1997) p.34.
86. This view has been expressed by many Turkish academics in a series of conflict resolution conferences about the Balkan region which I attended during the period 1997–9. See also Carol Migdalovitz, 'Turkey: Ally in a Troubled Region', *CRS Report for Congress,* Congressional Research Center, The Library of Congress, 14 September 1993, p.2. For a different view see Marios L. Evriviades, 'Turkey's Role in United States Strategy', *Mediterranean Quarterly,* 9, 2 (1998) pp.30–51.
87. See Javier Solana, 'NATO and the Mediterranean', *www.erols.com/mqmq/solana.htm*.
88. See 'Turkey War Arsenal Grows', *Cosmos,* 1, 3 (1995) p.2. For further study about Greece's and Turkey's arsenal see '*Greece and Turkey: Current Foreign Aid Issues*', *CRS Issue Brief,* 3 December 1996, *www.fas.org/man/crs/86-065*. It is instructive to mention that Turkey has purchased pure offensive weapons such as rapid deployment bridges, hundreds of small landing boats which reveal the military intention of the country towards Greece. Moreover, through the deployment of the Turkish land and air forces, any military analyst can understand the military dogma of the country.
89. See *Reuters,* 18 November 1998, *www.diaspora-net.org/Turkey/US_Frigates_to_Turkey.html*.
90. See Naumann, *NATO's New Military* (1998) pp.10–14.

4

The Application of the Pluralistic Security Community in the Eastern Mediterranean

NATO is not sexy, nor is it extreme, nor is it the perfect solution to anybody's problem. But it is the best – and probably the only – international environment in which the concepts of peace, equality, justice and prosperity can grow.

Jane Leitner, *American Business Review*, 10 August 1997

This chapter aims at developing and testing the concept of PSC explicated by Karl Deutsch and his associates in the 1950s, and applying it to the eastern Mediterranean. Ultimately, the purpose of this chapter is to identify and characterise the nature of the PSC in the eastern Mediterranean which accounts for a dearth of solidarity, stability, unity and co-operation among the two NATO members, Greece and Turkey.

In essence, a pluralistic security community is a union in which war is no longer contemplated as a possible way of resolving conflicts among its members. However, this is not the case in the southern flank of the NATO alliance despite the fact that post-Cold War NATO constitutes a security community and considers the PSC values and principles as a *fait accompli* for all of its member states.[1] As Stephen Weber points out, NATO has never been just a mere anti-Soviet coalition, but a peculiar mixture of alliance and pluralistic security community.[2] He asserts that the cardinal goal of the alliance – to defend its territory against external invasion from the Soviet Union – was always balanced against the security community goal – to prevent the use of force among the NATO members, and particularly to solve the Franco-German security dilemma.[3]

The aim of this investigation is to argue that due to geo-political and geo-strategic demands during the Cold War and the post-Cold War period (see previous chapters), one of the three conditions required for a PSC, identity of major values, i.e. democracy in the eastern Mediterranean, has not yet been met by one member state, that is Turkey. From this perspective, there has been, to this point in

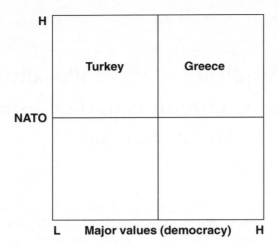

Figure 1 PSC *Hybrid Region* in the eastern Mediterranean

time, '*incomplete integration* in terms of dependable expectations of peaceful change. That is, the democracies involved exist within a not yet fully formed, or imperfectly formed, pluralistic security community'.[4] Turkey's flawed adoption of the PSC elements has led to the creation of a unique and characteristic sub-region within the organisation which I will refer to as a *Hybrid Region*[5] (Figure 1).

In order to explain the PSC *Hybrid Region*, it is imperative to attempt a comprehensive analysis of the developments of these two states with an assessment of their particular status in terms of fulfilling the conditions required for a PSC.

The outcome of this investigation will reveal the formation and the establishment of an aberrant sub-region which can be referred to as a *Hybrid Region*. The characteristics of this *Hybrid Region* can *only* be applied to the eastern Mediterranean region and are valid for the post-Cold War period *only*.

DEUTSCH'S ANALYSIS

Deutsch and his associates 'undertook this inquiry as a contribution to the study of possible ways in which men some day might abolish war'.[6] Notwithstanding the fact that the study failed to present a clear answer to the problem of war and peace, the concept of security community explicated in this work is considered as a watershed in the theory of International Relations. *Ab initio*, Deutsch and his colleagues acknowledged the possibility that 'some political communities do eliminate war and the expectation of war within their boundaries'.[7]

In particular, the concept of the PSC is the main rational explanation for the existence of long-term peace in some regions of the globe. More specifically

> a security-community is one in which there is real assurance that the members of that community will not fight each other physically, but will settle their disputes in some other way. If the entire world were integrated as a security-community, wars would be automatically eliminated.[8]

In order to have a clear and explicit illustration of the findings of Deutsch's study, it is worth introducing in its entirety the sequence of his definitions:

> A SECURITY COMMUNITY is a group of people which has become 'integrated'.
>
> By INTEGRATION we mean the attainment, within a territory, of a 'sense of community' and of institutions and practices strong enough and widespread enough to assure, for a 'long' time, dependable expectations of 'peaceful change' among its population.
>
> By SENSE OF COMMUNITY we mean a belief on the part of individuals in a group that they have come to agreement on at least this one point: that common social problems must and can be resolved by processes of 'peaceful change'.
>
> By PEACEFUL CHANGE we mean the resolution of social problems, normally by institutionalised procedures, without resort to large-scale physical force.[9]

In defining the concept of security community, Deutsch and his colleagues emphasised that a security community is created when social problems are resolved without resort to large-scale physical force. In their investigation they identified two types of security community. An amalgamated security community sees a 'formal merger of two or more previously independent units into a single larger unit, with some type of common government after amalgamation'. A pluralistic security community, on the other hand, 'retains the legal independence of separate governments'.[10] Both systems require varying levels of integration between societies within the community.

Furthermore, the authors after an investigation of historical case studies came to some interesting conclusions. They argued that the pluralistic archetype requires a lower level of integration to become operational than the amalgamated archetype. Moreover, they observed that pluralistic security communities were more resilient, responsive and maintainable than amalgamated security communities.[11] Having taken into consideration these findings, this chapter uses the pluralistic model as a framework for analysing the emergence of an eastern Mediterranean security community.

Since security and community are the main notions of Deutsch's study, it would be appropriate to explicate the definitional properties of a security community. It is true that security communities emerge from a plethora of activities and exchanges at the individual, transnational and international levels. According to Deutsch, security communities arise out of a process of regional interaction characterised by the development of transaction flows, shared understandings and transnational values. Transaction flows involve the regular, institutionalised interaction not only of national governments but of members of civil society as well. This interaction, in turn leads to 'dependable expectations of peaceful change', where states believe that disputes among members of the community will not be settled by force. Furthermore, security communities are not defined merely by the absence of war, but they are also characterised by what Deutsch called 'we-feeling', or shared identity.[12]

With regards to the question of what defines a political community, Michael Taylor adopted a three-pronged definition.[13] First, communities are identified by the existence of shared values and beliefs which means that members of a community share identities and meanings. Community is usually defined as 'a collectivity, the members of which are linked by a strong feeling of participation'[14]. Charles Taylor asserts:

> Intersubjective meaning gives a people a common language to talk about social reality and a common understanding of certain norms, but only with common meanings does this common reference world contain significant common actions, celebrations and feelings. These are objects in the world everybody shares. This is what makes community.[15]

Second, those in a community have diverse and direct relations. And third, communities exhibit a reciprocity that expresses some degree of long-term interest and perhaps altruism. Altruism can be understood as a sense of obligation and responsibility.[16]

After 1945, security and defence were treated as being virtually synonymous.[17] Security was closely associated to the following: that a state is free from a threat of war; that it is able to pursue its national interests and preserve its 'core values'[18] and that it feels safe against potential aggressors. These traditional ideas about security were based upon three assumptions: the belief that security is centred upon states, that security policy seeks to preserve the *status quo*, and that military threats and the need for effective military defence are the primary concerns. Hence, security has been correlated with the military power of individual states.[19]

Despite the fact that these ideas were cemented and widely accepted, since the 1980s there has been a consistent demand for reconsideration and broadening of the notion of security. Barry Buzan identified five main kinds of threats: i) military; ii) political; iii) economic; iv) ecological; v) societal.[20] What emerged was an increasing recognition of the desirability of a more holistic and dynamic concept: in other words, a concept of security which focuses not just on the state, but includes individuals and the world community; and finally a concept which is not only identified with military problems, but which encompasses a broad agenda of threats (economic and environmental for example) which hinder human progress and normal living conditions.[21]

As a consequence, two views of security studies are now available, the new one of the wideners and the old military and state-centred view of the traditionalists.[22] The 'wide' versus 'narrow' debate grew out of dissatisfaction with the intense narrowing of the field of security studies imposed by the military and nuclear obsessions of the Cold War. This dissatisfaction was stimulated first by the rise of the economic and environmental agendas in international relations during the 1970s and 1980s and later by the rise of concerns with identity issues and transnational crime during the 1990s.[23]

Those arguing explicitly for widening include Ullman, Nye and Lynn-Jones, Brown, Crawford, Haftendon, and Waever et al., most taking off from the urgency of new, often non-military sources of threat.[24] On the other hand, traditionalists fought back by reasserting conventional arguments about the enduring primacy of military security.[25] Some traditionalists such as Chipman have argued that there was simply a return to the natural terrain of the subject after the artificial nuclear narrowing only inasmuch as it could be linked to concerns about the threat or actual use of forces between political actors:

> Non-military aspects of security may occupy more of the strategist's time, but the need for peoples, nations, states or alliances to procure, deploy, engage or withdraw military forces must remain a primary purpose of the strategic analyst's inquiries.[26]

Similar, if not stronger statements have been presented by Stephen Walt who defines security as 'the study of the threat, use and control of military force'.[27]

As states move toward community, they no longer need to rely on the balance of power mechanisms to protect their security. Instead, says Adler, states focus on 'assurance, not deterrence'. Collective security, joint military planning and integration, unfortified borders and free movement of people across borders, and common definitions of both external and internal threats are all hallmarks of security communities. Once established, security of the community is based on what Adler calls an 'inside-out model', where states see their interests as best served by being inside the community. No longer is security defined exclusively as the protection of sovereign national borders from military threat. Rather, security is also achieved through benefits accrued from participating in 'zones of peace', prosperity and stability and a vision of a common future.[28]

THE PLURALISTIC SECURITY COMMUNITY CONCEPT: AN OVERVIEW

The application of the PSC in the sub-region of the eastern Mediterranean can be seen as conceivable due to historical and current difficulties involved in forging a unified, amalgamated, governmental structure. Amalgamated security communities are often unstable and prone to disintegration due to their inflexible nature whilst pluralistic structures are more flexible and workable.[29]

Furthermore, Deutsch et al. also argued that the emergence of a PSC increased the unattractiveness and improbability of war among the political units concerned.[30] This view was adopted since in a pluralistic structure states maintain their sovereignty while at the same time the respective societies embrace common values, norms and practices. One appraisal of successful integration has been suggested by Richard Ned Lebow, who argues that 'perhaps the best evidence for the existence of a pluralistic security community is the general absence of military plans by one community member for operations against another'.[31]

E. Adler also stated that one essential component in the creation of a pluralistic security community is democracy:

> A Group of democratic sovereign states that, agreeing on the unbearable destructiveness of modern war and on political, economic, social and moral values consistent with democracy, the rule of law, and economic freedom ... allowed their civil societies as well as their institutions to become integrated to the point that the idea of using force loses any practical meaning and even becomes unthinkable.[32]

Both of these notions will be examined later.

During their investigation, Deutsch et al. concluded that whilst twelve conditions appeared to be essential for the success of an amalgamated security community, the pluralistic one requires only three. Any additional conditions may enhance the chances of successful integration and consolidation; however, they were not considered indispensable. These essential conditions were: i) the compatibility of major values relevant to political decision-making; ii) the capacity of the participating political units or governments to respond to each other's needs, messages and actions quickly, adequately and without resort to violence; iii) mutual predictability of behaviour.[33]

COMPATIBILITY OF MAJOR VALUES

When Deutsch et al. referred to major values, they defined them as those 'which seem to be of major importance in the domestic politics of the units concerned'.[34] The adoption of these common values by the states can sway and eventually eliminate any substantial divisions between states. Examples of major values cited by Deutsch are 'basic political ideology ... covered for the most part by the terms "constitutionalism" and "democracy"'.[35]

Kant, Montesquieu and Schumpeter argued that liberal[36] domestic constitutional and institutional mechanisms would make liberal states inherently more peaceful. Montesquieu realised that constitutional form had implications for foreign policy and regarded the root of liberal pacificism as lying in notions of the peaceful and moderate nature of republics and also in commerce. Kant claimed that because a government would be responsible to that same citizenry that would itself bear the costs of war in terms of blood and money, the government would need to exercise caution and restraint in its foreign policy. Schumpeter also argued that the combination of democracy and capitalism would lead states to become more peaceful as those interests which depended upon a peaceful world order for the pursuit of trade and commerce prevailed over those interests served by territorial expansion and conquest.[37]

The concept of democracy has evolved in the twentieth century especially in the last fifty years, and it is usually identified with a voting franchise for a substantial fraction of citizens, a government brought to power in contested elections, and an executive either popularly elected or responsible to an elected legislature, often with requirements for civil liberties such as free speech.[38] Huntington also identifies similar criteria such as

[a] twentieth century political system is democratic to the extent that its most powerful collective decision-makers are selected through fair, honest and periodic elections in which candidates freely compete for votes and in which virtually all the adult population is eligible to vote.[39]

Furthermore, he regards a free election for transfer of power from a non-democratic government as the critical point in the process of democratisation.

The twentieth century and especially the post-Cold War era presented another possible factor which distinguishes democracy from other governmental forms, which is 'transparency'. Democratic transparency – the openness of the political processes and the vast amount of economic, political and social information which is public and generally available – is a prerequisite for democracy as conceptualised in terms of the challenge for political leadership, regardless of the specific definition used.[40] Such a conceptualisation sees democracy as providing an environment within which oppositions can effectively challenge incumbent governmental office holders for power in a legal, legitimate manner through prescribed procedures. It is only through transparency that a society or outside observers can monitor, scrutinise and know the abuses of political and civil liberties. Hence, only transparency can provide the safe environment for effective governmental opposition that is the core of democracy as conceptualised in terms of the challenge for political leadership.

It is also quite clear that democracy did not mean quite the same to the ancient Greeks as it does to the people of the late twentieth century. Conceptually, the Greek city state democracies differed significantly from twentieth-century liberal representative democracies.[41] Moreover, nineteenth-century democracies could hardly be identified as democracies since most of them had property qualifications for the vote and typically excluded women, whilst the US disenfranchised blacks.

By the middle to late twentieth century the question of guaranteed and respected civil rights, including rights to political organisation and political expression, also became a key element in any common-sense definition of democracy.[42] In most cases the exercise of such civil rights tends to be highly correlated with the existence of democratic institutions. Furthermore, most scholars have identified as democratic the countries which embody the criteria specified by Small and Singer: i) free elections with opposition parties; ii) a minimum suffrage (10 per cent); iii) a parliament either in control of the executive or at least enjoying parity with it.[43] In addition, Schweller applauds Doyle's definition of 'representative government' with a suffrage level of at least 30 per cent (and female suffrage granted within a generation of its initial demand); and further requires the government to be iv) internally sovereign over military and foreign affairs; and v) stable (in existence for at least three years). He also includes: vi) individual civil rights; and vii) private property and a free-enterprise economy.[44]

Since the end of the nineteenth century, the notion that democracies do not fight against each other or the issue of what is widely called 'democratic peace' has received considerable attention and scrutiny from academics, policy analysts and world leaders. In almost all of the available studies, across different time frames, different levels of analysis, and quite different levels of violent conflict, it is unquestionably clear that democratic dyads are far more peaceful than non-democratic and mixed dyads.[45] The democratic peace thesis contends that while democratic states are as war prone as other regimes, they are less likely to fight wars against each other.[46] In their social psychological analysis of the phenomena, Herman and Kegley list twenty-nine factors that have been postulated as contributing to the democratic peace.[47] Dixon's analysis of regime type and conflict resolution demonstrates that democracies engaged in a dispute are more likely to turn to non-violent forms of resolution such as arbitration.[48] Moreover, Russett and Antolis derive four competing hypotheses from the literature. Democracies are peaceful towards one another because

> 1) they share common ties through a network of international institutions; 2) up to World War II, the few democracies rarely shared common borders, which often generated the opportunities for war; 3) in the post-World War II era democracies faced a common enemy in the Soviet Union and its allies; and 4) the cost-benefit ratio for one advanced industrial state against another was not attractive, and most post-World War II democracies were stable economically advanced states.[49]

In analysing domestic constraints on war, Bueno de Mesquite and Lalman identify a number of 'democratic puzzles', the first of which is that democracies do not fight one another. They outline three hypotheses (called hunches) as to why this may be:

> 1) that democracies are like-minded, sharing similar liberal economic and political policies; 2) that democracies share a political culture based on individual rights and liberties and thus abhor violence to resolve conflict; and 3) that the democratic process makes it relatively easier for domestic oppositions to mobilise against the use of force, constraining leaders and making them more unwilling to use it against others similarly constrained.[50]

These hypotheses inaugurated a series of extensive investigations into the relationship between liberal and non-liberal states and the likelihood of war between democratic/democratic countries and democratic/non democratic states.[51] In a thorough and comprehensive examination Bruce Russett and his associates managed to justify the democratic peace which was explained by cultural/normative and structural/institutional reasons. The former assumes that democracies are less disposed to fight each other due to the impact of their shared norms which proscribe the use of violence between them while the latter posits that constraints on the policy-making choices of democratic leaders act as a brake on their foreign policy decision-making with regard to escalating conflict with other democracies.[52]

A summary of his results can be found in a set of propositions and it is as follows:

1. In relations with other states, decision-makers (whether they be few or many) will try to follow the same norms of conflict resolution as have been developed within and characterise their domestic political processes.
2. They will expect decision-makers in other states likewise to follow the same norms of conflict resolution as have developed within and characterise those other states' domestic political processes.

A. *Violent conflicts between democracies will be rare because:*

3. In democracies, the relevant decision-makers expect to be able to resolve conflicts by compromise and non-violence, respecting the rights and continued existence of opponents.
4. Therefore democracies will follow norms of peaceful conflict resolution with other democracies, and will expect other democracies to do so with them.
5. The more stable the democracy, the more will democratic norms govern its behaviour with other democracies, and the more will other democracies expect democratic norms to govern its international behaviour.
6. If violent conflicts between democracies do occur, at least one of the democracies is likely to be politically unstable.

B. *Violent conflicts between non-democracies and between democracies and non-democracies, will be more frequent because:*

7. In non-democracies, decision-makers use, and may expect their opponents to use, violence and the threat of violence to resolve conflict as part of their domestic political processes.
8. Therefore non-democracies may use violence and the threat of violence in conflicts with other states, and other states may expect them to use violence and the threat of violence in such conflicts.
9. Democratic norms can be more easily exploited to force concessions than can non-democratic ones; to avoid exploitation democracies may adopt non-democratic norms in dealing with non-democracies.

THE STRUCTURAL/INSTITUTIONAL MODEL

A. Violent conflicts between democracies will be infrequent because:

1. In democracies, the constraints of checks and balances, division of power, and need for public debate to enlist widespread support will slow decisions to use large-scale violence and reduce the likelihood that such decisions will be made.
2. Leaders of other states will perceive leaders of democracies as so constrained.
3. Thus leaders of democracies will expect, in conflicts with other democracies, time for processes of international conflict resolution to operate, and they will not fear surprise attack.

B. Violent conflicts between non-democracies and between democracies and non-democracies, will be frequent because:

4. Leaders of non-democracies are not constrained as leaders of democracies are, so they can more easily, rapidly and secretly initiate large-scale violence.
5. Leaders of states (democracies and non-democracies) in conflict with non-democracies may initiate violence rather than risk surprise attack.
6. Perceiving that leaders of democracies will be constrained, leaders of non-democracies may press democracies to make greater concessions over issues in conflict.
7. Democracies may initiate large-scale violence with non-democracies rather than make greater concessions demanded.[53]

Figure 2 The cultural/normative model   *Source:* Russett (1991), p.35

The outcome of this research suggests that to use or threaten to use force is not usually normatively acceptable behaviour in disputes between democracies, even in the form of symbolic, ritualised bargaining behaviour. As a result, relations between democracies can be part of the category of stable peace[54] or a security community in which states not only do not fight each other, they do not expect to fight each other. Under these circumstances, it is expected that disputes will be decided without recourse to threat and military deterrence.[55]

The observation that democracies do not fight each other was made almost three decades ago by Babst. Babst had examined data on 116 major wars from 1789 to 1941 from Wright and found that 'no wars have been fought between independent nations with elective governments'. Applying a probabilistic argument to the two world wars of this century, he concluded that it was extremely unlikely all elective governments (10 out of the 33 independent nations participating in the First World War; 14 out of 52 in the Second World War) should be on the same side purely by chance.[56] After nearly a decade of debate following Doyle's and Rummel's[57] articles, there is a near consensus on two points: that there is little difference in the amount of war participation between democracies and non-democracies, but that war (or even military conflicts short of war) are non-existent (or very rare) among democracies. Indeed, several scholars have echoed Levy's statement that this 'absence of war between democratic states comes as close as anything we have to an empirical law in international relations'[58]. This empirical regularity has never been seriously called into question.

THE QUESTION OF MUTUAL RESPONSIVENESS

The second essential condition for the emergence of a pluralistic security community, according to Deutsch, is

> the capacity of the participating political units or governments to respond to each other's needs, and actions quickly, adequately and without resort to violence. In the case of a pluralistic security community, such capabilities for political responsiveness required in each participating state a great many established political habits, and of functioning political institutions, favoring mutual communication and consultation. To be effective, such habits and institutions had to ensure that messages from other member governments or units would not merely be received, but would be understood, and that they would be given real weight in the process of decision making.[59]

Deutsch believed that the accomplishment of integration by different groups and societies postulates adequate responsiveness to each other's needs, anxieties and perceptions. For this purpose, the actors would require 'continuous mutual attention and responsiveness'.[60]

Adequate facilities for efficient communication between actors are vital to avoid confusion, dispute or outright conflict. This responsiveness must be a continuous process in order to guarantee the establishment and maintenance of a security community. Moreover, attainment of mutual responsiveness is feasible only through the formulation and fulfilment of certain criteria.

An essential feature of mutual responsiveness is the presence of regional integration. Haas argued that the study of regional integration is concerned with explaining how and why states cease to be wholly sovereign, how and why they voluntarily mingle, merge, and mix their neighbours so as to lose the factual attributes of sovereignty while acquiring new techniques for resolving conflict between themselves.[61]

Consequently, resolving discord requires the existence of open communication channels which would be vital in the attempt to achieve mutual understanding. Keohane and Nye believe that

> *multiple channels* connect societies, including: informal ties between governmental elites as well as formal foreign office arrangements: informal ties among non-governmental elites (face to face and through telecommunications); and transnational organisations (such as multi-national banks or corporations). These channels can be summarised as interstate, transgovernmental, and transnational relations. *Interstate* relations are the normal channels assumed by realists. *Transgovernmental* applies when we relax the realist assumption that states act coherently as units; *transnational* applies when we relax the assumption that states are the only units.[62]

The coexistence of the aforementioned communication channels is imperative since the needs and demands of member units of a security community cannot be met by the utilisation of one of these channels.

The notion of understanding is also closely associated with the process of learning. These two notions of learning and understanding constitute the essence of the social communication model developed by Deutsch:

> The Deutschian model represents a process of integration based on a wide array of inter-societal transactions that are of mutual benefit to the people involved. The process is based on *learning* – learning that such transactions provide benefits, that such benefits outweigh the costs involved, and that there are positive payoffs to continue such interactions and even expand them. As such interactions occur, and expand, the peoples involved become more and more interdependent and develop greater responsiveness to one another. At some point this produces the 'we-feeling', trust and mutual consideration that Deutsch called community.[63]

The insistence of Deutsch on the process of mutual responsiveness can even be ascribed to the hypothesis that eventually founded his cybernetic approach. Deutsch's viewpoint of cybernetics suggests that the systematic study of communication and control in organisations of all kinds ... That all organisations are alike in certain fundamental characteristics and that every organisation is held together by communication ... Communication, that is the ability to transmit messages and to react to them, that makes organisation.[64]

Therefore,

at the heart of Deutsch's *pluralistic, cybernetic* or *transactionalist* approach was the assumption that *communication* is the cement of social groups in general and political communities in particular.[65] Communication alone enables a group to think together, to see together, and to act together.[66]

Moreover, communication processes and transaction flows between peoples become not only facilities for attention, but factories of shared identification. Through transaction flows such as trade, tourism, cultural and educational exchanges, and the use of physical communication facilities, a social fabric is built not only among elites, but also among the masses instilling in them a sense of community. This process of communication implies the ability of the actors to emit and receive stimuli. This constitutes a significant pre-condition since the establishment of ways of communication can *ipso facto* ensure the emission and the reception of all messages.

The process of mutual responsiveness is likewise closely correlated to the notion of interdependence.[67] It is believed that if the needs of the community are completely interconnected then a practice of mutual responsiveness exists in that specific area. Oran Young perceives interdependence:

in terms of the extent to which events occurring in any given part or within any given component unit of a world system affect (either physically or perceptually) events taking place in each of the other parts of component units of the system. By definition, therefore, the greater the extensiveness and weight of the impact of events occurring in any given part of a system for each of the other parts, the higher the level of interdependence in the system.[68]

As a result, in a situation of interdependence, the acts of the units would consider as a panacea the avoidance of any kind of damage to the lives of the other units.

Despite the difficulty of defining and understanding the concept of mutual responsiveness, the fact is that attainment of the aforementioned conditions would bring about a substantial transformation of normal inter-state relations. Relations would cease to be viewed as a zero sum game, instead they would be considered as a mutually enriching and rewarding experience.

THE QUESTION OF MUTUAL PREDICTABILITY OF BEHAVIOUR

According to Deutsch the third prerequisite for the successful creation of the pluralistic security community is viewed as less important than the previous two conditions and is emanated from the foregoing:

> a third essential condition for a pluralistic security community may be mutual predictability of behaviour; this appears closely related to the foregoing. But the member states of a pluralistic security community have to make joint decisions only about a more limited range of subject matters. Consequently the range and extent of the mutual predictability of behaviour required from members of a pluralistic security community is considerably less than would be essential for the successful operation of an amalgamated one.[69]

Deutsch clearly thinks that in conditions of mutual responsiveness, messages and demands of the member units would be received and understood whilst in conditions of mutual predictability of behaviour, the behaviour of the member units would be easily foreseen. Deutsch also believes that mutual predictability of behaviour is more easily obtained in a pluralistic security community as the scope and range of the common action is not as broad as in the case of an amalgamated one. This manifestation cannot be achieved effortlessly since reaching mutual predictability is a continuous process which demands constant attention.

Mutual predictability of behaviour will also facilitate mutual understanding and co-operation. On the other hand, mutual inhibition will destabilise the security community by causing antagonism and a lack of transparency. Hence, the building of confidence[70] between members of the security community would create an important momentum for integration and would diminish any possibility of shock or surprise which might destabilise security community relations and create uncertainty and fear. This requires the creation of trust.

Deutsch claims that a minimum level of predictability emerges from familiarity. For example, state X may not fully comprehend why state Y behaves in a specific manner, but it generally knows how it will respond to various situations and thus to what extent state Y can be relied upon. As a result, simple familiarity can lead to the growth of mutual trust. Yet this can be strengthened by a more proactive approach.

Deutsch suggests an introspective approach i.e. trying to predict another's behaviour by placing oneself in their situation. This requires a certain amount of sensitivity to another's interests as well as a certain amount of similarities that allow one to fully understand the other and appreciate the situation they are in. However, the success of such an approach is heightened when a civic structure exists between countries and such a common identity is established. The existence of common values between states enhances their understanding of each other's moves and allows a more accurate level of prediction of behaviour. This is further assisted by high levels of communication and knowledge of other democratic systems which increases the transparency of decision-making between states, and allows fewer surprises.[71]

The development of genuine mutual predictability of behaviour will also bring about the existence of a reliable and persistent state of international co-operation. 'At the international level, community formation has transformed the very character of the states system – states have become integrated to the point that peaceful change becomes taken for granted'.[72]

However, the emergence of mutual predictability of behaviour which completes the three essential conditions of a pluralistic security community, is characterised by a rule which proclaims the resolution of disputes without resort to large-scale inter-state violence. This fact outlines the sense of strong confidence within the community but at the same time, paradoxically, reveals its weak and fragile character.

A breach of trust[73] in a security community is bound to cause enormous repercussions. Once the trust and co-operation has been shattered, it is extremely difficult to bring it together again. Deception has a price which is measured by the difficulty of re-establishing trust among the partners once the damage is done. The loss of confidence will disrupt and destroy the pattern maintenance of the security community *per se*, and it will diminish the possibility for the system to survive, as confidence is the core basis of the structure.[74]

On the other hand, one cannot ignore the self-interest character of a security community. Deutsch himself highlighted the importance of self-interest by stating:

> integration does have a price, one which must be met by government and is, in part, set by those who are governed. In fact it is the capabilities and performances of government that provide the key to integration and cohesion in societies. By their very nature, governments have the

means to establish and maintain certain standards of well-being for their populations which are basic conditions for integration.[75]

By stating that integration has a price, Deutsch emphasises the significance of rational behaviour of a government which aims at maximising self-interest gains through the integrative process. Albeit, every country seeks to gain and profit once it enters a security community; this can only be accomplished via mutual co-operation. It is in this respect that mutual predictability of behaviour is of great value and importance. The absence of it would result in lack of co-operation; utilisation on the other hand, would result in a constructive process with co-operation at the pinnacle of the security community objectives.

MEETING THE FIRST CRITERIA: THE CASE OF TURKEY

This section attempts to assess the degree of democratisation in Turkey. One vital condition of the PSC is the acceptance and adoption of major values such as liberal democracy. Having identified the prerequisites that countries require to fulfil in order to be considered *ipso facto* as democracies, it is necessary to examine whether Turkey can be categorised as one.[76] A combination of inductive and deductive methods can be employed to investigate the degree of democratisation. *Ab initio,* an inductive approach will be utilised to assess the current situation in Turkey.

Recent evaluations of Turkish society and politics have emphasised Turkey's 'exceptional' position in the entire Middle Eastern region for its relative success in establishing a representative democratic system and a market-oriented economy.[77] For some political and social researchers, one of the most important factors in this relative success in democratisation was Turkey's strong state tradition. Paradoxically Turkey's strong state tradition can also be held responsible for democracy's only relative success. Hence, it is appropriate to argue that Turkish democracy still lags well behind the standards of western 'polyarchy' because of this impregnable, centralist state tradition, deeply entrenched by the idea and practice of the state during almost 600 years of Ottoman history.[78] A very important tenet of the Ottoman period was that the Ottoman conception of politics cast out the existence of civil society. It assumed that only the Sultan and his bureaucrats (servants) were able to know what the common good was. Accordingly, there was no place in the Ottoman mind for any idea of citizen participation in political affairs and politics was left exclusively in the hands of the centre.[79]

The inception of the republic and the reforms that were initiated and implemented by Mustafa Kemal Attaturk embraced nationalist and solidarist components of statist–centralist thought of the past. Principles of Kemalism still prevail in most legal documents, including the 1982 Constitution. They include republicanism,[80] nationalism,[81] populism,[82] etatism,[83] laicism/secularism,[84] and reformism[85] and were mainly aimed to legitimise centralist, authoritarian rule (1923–45) under a single party (RPP).[86] Kemalist ideology and authoritarian single-party rule[87] were generally justified as a tutelary ideology and a regime that attempted on the one hand to democratise the Turkish society and on the other hand, to reinforce the role and the power of the state (etatism).[88] Therefore, Kemalist republicanism granted to the state a powerful regulatory role not only in the economy but also in other spheres, including cultural politics.[89] Cultural politics can be explained as a preponderant idea which aims at creating a new Turk obedient and in the service of the new state and allegedly equal to representing the unity of the Turkish nation. Hence, Kemalism rejected any radical democratic transformation of the state and on the other hand, maintained the state–centralist frame of the Ottoman past. Kemal had envisioned for Turkey an organised, well-articulated, linear process of modernisation through which the whole nation was going to move simultaneously and with uniform experience. At the end of this process, there would emerge a militantly secular, ethnically homogeneous republic well on its way to catching up with the civilised nations of the west. However, according to Resat Kasaba

> the Turkish experience appeared in 1997 to be culminating in economic backwardness and social flux, with Muslim and secularist, Turk and Kurd, rural and urban – in short the old and the new – existing side by side and contending with, but more typically strengthening, each other.[90]

Furthermore, Frey emphasised that the main weakness of Kemalism was the total lack of participation of the masses in the political life of the country.[91] This manifestation was explicated, by some, by the absence of large landlords.[92] Because of this absence, the nationalist intelligentsia (military) did not have to confront any serious opposition. Without a strong landlord class that might have demanded economic liberalism and civil and political rights for its narrow constituency (for example, Latin American oligarchies, or the interests around the Wafd party in Egypt during the 1920s), no group in society found it possible to challenge the absolutism of the state. Caglar Keyder asserted that absent a revolutionary break in the class basis of the state, the fundamental division between the state class and the masses was perpetuated.[93]

Another significant factor which reinforced the status and authority of the state elite was the material resources it had acquired throughout the First World War and the war with Greece. Since most of the non-Muslims who had served as the politically disenfranchised merchant bourgeoisie of the Empire were eliminated and driven away, their property as well as the positions they vacated became part of the dowry of the new state. This resulted in the creation of a native bourgeoisie which became beholden to the state. Moreover, in the 1940s due to world economic conditions which shifted in favour of a state-directed economy, the course of capitalist accumulation came under the full control of the state. Hence, the state was granted expanded prerogatives in the economic socio-political sphere which curbed any challenge of the businessmen towards the state.[94]

Ataturk saw that the only group which revealed strong pro-western feelings was the military, and entrusted the members of this group with the realisation of his goals. As a result, the military in Turkey became one of the central institutions of the republican elite and a traditional and uncompromising stronghold of secular and territorial nationalism. Furthermore, he made certain that most political and state institutions were infiltrated with personnel who had a military background.[95] However, while he instituted the involvement of the military in the political affairs, he raised legal barriers to the direct involvement of active officers in the country's everyday electoral and democratic political life.[96]

In a social context characterised by the domination of a strong state, the absence of established civil rights implies the reversibility of political arrangements such as procedural democracy.[97]. A country can be called democratic not only by following procedures which determine the choice of a government, but also with regard to the existence of civil rights and their embodiment in a legal framework.[98] In this case, Turkey's transition to democracy appears incomplete. Only the entrenchment of civil rights and the construction of an inviolable private sphere would constitute a sufficient basis for the consolidation of political rights and of a public sphere founded on these. When we refer to civil rights we mean the rights of freedom of speech, press, assembly, the right to vote, freedom from involuntary servitude and the right to equality in public places. Discrimination occurs when the civil rights of an individual are denied or interfered with because of their membership in a particular class or group.

Since it was nationalism which constituted the founding ideology of the new republic, the state class acts as a safeguard mechanism for the protection of the Kemalist ideology in modern Turkey. After 1945 it became apparent that bourgeois democracy based on civil rights was not considered important since rapid economic development was what had to be accomplished. The emphasis on the economy somehow justified the subordination of political and civil rights. As a result

> citizenship was devalued; being a people extolled. Populism came to identify citizenship with social rights: access to education, health, employment, migration and economic opportunity. Neither the state nor the political parties brought the establishment of a legal framework for civil rights onto the agenda.[99]

National development as an ideology was favoured by state elites and as a result became the sum of nation building and populism. Both Lehmann and Wallerstein among others explore this theme and offer a world historical perspective on national development.[100]

Likewise, three military interventions (1960, 1971, 1980) served to frighten all potential challengers for civil and political rights – but especially the bourgeoisie. Since national economic development was controlled and regulated by the state, the coups also convinced them that involvement in the higher realm of politics was not worth it. It was unthinkable for the bourgeoisie to risk their potential for wealth accumulation by getting directly involved in political life. On the contrary, their energy was focused on an attempt to remain on the right side of the state elite.[101]

The three military interventions eventually led to three transitions to democracy. However, Turkish consolidation to democracy has been so far unfulfilled. As noted earlier, consolidation to democracy can only be achieved in correlation with the existence and respect of civil rights. Nevertheless, none of the transitional regimes has considered civil rights as an issue to be included in their manifesto. In all three interventions the military came to power declaring that their goal was to re-establish the right conditions for democracy. In fact, after carrying out their disciplinary function, changing the rules of the game, and legislating for a gradual transition they retired to their barracks. The brevity of these interventions served two purposes. First, on each occasion the military left the political scene before becoming fully discredited and held responsible for the economic failure. Second, it hindered the civilian political elite from setting and establishing the proper rules for democracy.

In other words, Turkish transition to democracy was implemented by reform from above rather than negotiation. This meant that the path to parliamentary democracy was closely manipulated and orchestrated by the military.[102] The political elites exhibited a remarkable inability to act since they accepted the justification and *carte blanche* posed by the military for the interruption in civilian rule. Any rhetoric about civil rights came into direct collision with the state class which claimed that 'in the present chaotic world situation, with "enemies" on all the borders, it would be risky to undertake any reform'.[103]

It was the rise of the DP to power in 1950 and the new economic and social policies that it implemented which inaugurated a new era in the involvement of the military in the political affairs of the state.[104] As a result, a coup was staged in the spring of 1960 and members of the DP were severely punished.[105] Subsequently, the military did not embrace any return to a monoparty political system and hence they introduced a new set of rules. The creation of a new, liberal constitution, the formation of a second political institution, the Senate and the establishment of the NSC as an advisory body to the Council of Ministers on issues of national security, were measures which were intended to reduce the political power of the GNA and party leaders while at the same time legalising the intervention of the military in the country's political and economic affairs.[106]

The insistence of the military to encourage the development of small parties and the formation of weak coalition governments turned the attention of political elites to partisan gains rather than to the treatment of the severe socio-economic problems which the country was experiencing during the 1970s. Since the political elites were unable to curtail the political power of the military,[107] it was no surprise when the latter staged a third coup in 1980. Unlike the previous coups, the military this time decided to reform the economic and political structure of the country without the participation of the political leaders.[108]

The officers responsible for the 1980 coup had clearly intended their efforts to be long lasting. The military junta had an ambitious plan for restructuring the political institutions. Hence, the introduction of a new constitution[109] and its acceptance by the people, indicated that the process of reconstructing the country's major political institutions was irreversible. The military leaders imposed a new constitution in 1982 and a new electoral system. The bicameral parliament was replaced by a unicameral one. They reduced the membership of the GNA to 400 with an increased term of five years and reinforced the executive at the expense of the legislature and the judiciary.[110]

The 1982 constitution severely restricted individual freedoms. Freedom of the press was removed *de facto* from the constitution.

Following the new constitution religion courses became compulsory in primary and secondary schools.[111] New restrictions were also introduced on the activities of trade unions and associations. The new constitution required unions to abstain from all political activity, and prohibited them from supporting or receiving any support from political parties. These restrictions curbed the union's power in industrial relations and in public life. All these changes were intended to depoliticise society, reduce the influence of organised opposition, and increase the state's ability to monitor and control their activities.[112]

After the adoption of the constitution in November 1982, the NSC allowed a gradual and controlled recovery of political activities by announcing on 24 April 1983 the law governing the formation of political parties. The former party leaders were banned from the formation of new political parties, political activity for ten years and also political activity either orally or in writing. The junta reserved the right to examine lists of the founders of the new political formations and to decide on eventual replacements for those who were considered unacceptable by the military.[113] Furthermore, the military ensured its continuing presence at the highest level of political decision-making. According to Constitutional Article 118, the NSC would submit to the Council of Ministers its views on taking decisions and ensuring necessary co-ordination on issues regarding the preservation of the existence and independence of the state, the integrity and indivisibility of the country and the peace and security of society. As a result, the NSC although not responsible to the GNA, had become almost the 'highest non-elected, decision making body of the State'.[114]

Determined also to prevent the proliferation of small parties and the resulting instability, the military tried deliberately to create a two-party system. To ensure the emergence of a two-party system, electoral provisions were crafted to favour larger parties. A party was required to win at least 10 per cent of the vote at the national level in order to get a representative elected. While 15 new parties were set up after the adoption of the new Political Parties Law,[115] one of the parties (the Great Turkey Party supported by the current President Demirel) was dissolved by a military decree and 11 others were denied the right to register for the polls as a result of the junta's vetoes. As a result only three political parties registered for the polls: the MDP, headed by the retired army General Turgut Sunalp, the ANAP, headed by Turgut Ozal, and the HP headed by Necdet Calp. The two parties directly inspired or organised by the military, HP and MDP, lost while ANAP obtained 45 per cent of the votes and Turgut Ozal became the new Prime Minister.[116]

Ozal dominated the political scene of Turkey from 1983 up to 1993. His sudden death occurred at a period when the President of the Republic had started, once more, to seriously challenge the political power of the military institution.[117] However, despite his attempts to challenge the ultimate authority of the military, his death in April 1993 established once more a 'foretold outcome'.[118] As Hale emphasised, despite the move for significant changes in the country's civil–military relations, one cannot suggest 'that by 1992, the civil power had yet established the full degree of control over the military which is the norm in most democratic systems'.[119] Furthermore, two years later retired Air Force General Sadi Erguvenc would argue that 'civil authorities [are] not in command of the military'.[120]

After the brief encounter of the Welfare Party of Erbakan in power, the last elections of 18 April 1999, where Ecevit and his DLP formed an unlikely coalition government with the NAP of Devlet Basheli[121] and the Centre Right Motherland Party of Yilmaz, reveal some specific characteristics.[122] The NAP and to some extent the DLP, rode a rising tide of nationalism in Turkey, fuelled not only by the struggle with the PKK and the arrest of its leader, Abdullah Ocalan, but far more profoundly by the sense of rejection by Europe. At the same time, Turks feel that they can emerge as a regional power backed by growing military prowess, as well as close links with the US and Israel. The country is now more dismissive than ever of western, particularly European, efforts to convince it to compromise on Cyprus and Greek–Turkish relations.[123] Most importantly, the Turkish elections highlighted once more the determination of the Generals to keep the Islamists out of power,[124] and the formation of weak governments. Without electoral reform that produces stronger majorities it is likely that Turkey would witness not only growing fragmentation and extremism, but also increased involvement of the military in decision-making.[125] Up to now, Turkey has failed to achieve a stable multi-party system, and chronically suffers from a series of coalition governments whose component interests are so diverse that no coherent economic policy can be implemented in a sustainable way.[126]

In explaining the persistent domination of the military on the political scene and over the politicians of modern Turkey, some specific elements should be taken into consideration. First of all, the military class was and still is able to reproduce itself and its values and regard itself as the only legitimate guardians of the Kemalist character.[127] Furthermore, any interference from the civilians is minimal if not non-existent.[128] Second, the presence and the maintenance of the second-largest army within the NATO alliance has been justified by the existence of internal and external enemies.[129] Therefore, any attempt to reduce the size or the social status of the army could well result in another military coup.

Also significant has been the establishment of an independent economic power of the military. In their attempt to safeguard the financial independence of the officers, the army decided to create a number of militarily controlled financial groups that gave the officer corps a large stake in Turkey's corporate economy. OYAK has been developed into one of the largest financial conglomerates of Turkey.[130] In addition, the Turkish Secret Service, known as MIT, and three identical foundations, the Naval, Air Force and Land Force Foundations 'also have shares in a variety of civilian public sector enterprises'.[130]

Most significantly, the military elite has been actively involved in the development of a domestic defence industry.[132] According to Ahmad Feroz, the Turkish Armed Force's economic activities have been so intertwined with capitalism that 'no longer can they afford to be neutral or above politics'.[133]

It has been argued that their economic activities have been assisted and augmented by the closer and direct ties between the military establishment and leading industrialists both in Turkey, for example, Koc, Eczacibasi and Sabanci, as well as abroad, for example, US, German, French, Israeli military and high-tech companies.[134]

Moreover, taking advantage of the geo-strategic importance of their country for the NATO alliance during the Cold War[135] period, the Turkish military elite managed to overcome any external pressures on Turkey's poor human rights, the extensive use of state violence in its south-eastern provinces and the persecution of Members of Parliament, and journalists who struggled for the application of democratic principles.[136] In the current situation, the forces of inertia have found an excellent pretext for their defence of the *status quo* in the ethno-nationalist struggle of the Kurdish minority in the south-east. Once the state elite were able to define the situation as one of insurrection and separatism, rather than as a struggle for civil rights and administrative devolution,[137] the argument for national security became unassailable. As a result, repressive actions were facilitated by Turkey's antiquated legal system and restrictive constitution, which reflect the country's authoritarian past.[138] The present constitution was introduced in 1982 by military authorities after the coup of 1980. It replaced the liberal constitution of 1961, which ironically was adopted after the coup of 1960.

Currently there are a host of laws that punish free expression in Turkey. The 1982 Constitution grants the right of free expression, while at the same time qualifying the exercise of that right to an absurd degree. Its preamble states for example:

> no protection shall be given to thoughts or opinion that run counter
> to Turkish national interests, the fundamental principle of the existence
> of the indivisibility of the Turkish state and territory, the historical and
> moral values of Turkishness or the nationalism, principles, reforms
> and modernism of Ataturk, and that as required by the principle of
> secularism there shall be absolutely no interference of sacred religious
> feeling in the affairs of state and politics.[139]

Articles 26, 27 and 28 of the constitution which grant respectively,
freedom of expression, science and art, and the press, contain more
paragraphs limiting these rights than granting them. The legal
framework still lags far behind developments in society. Successive
governments since 1990 have sought to liberalise laws that are used to
punish free expression without addressing the underlying rationales
for creating such legislation in the first place. In 1991, the government repealed a law passed in 1983 that prohibited the use of Kurdish
(Law No.2932) together with Articles 141, 142 and 163 of the penal
code that penalised respectively, writers found guilty of communist,
Kurdish–nationalist and Islamist activities. In place of these laws,
however, the governments passed the Anti-Terror Law. Articles 7 and
8 of that law are often used to punish free expression dealing with the
Kurdish question. Moreover, laws exist that prevent broadcasting in
Kurdish, teaching Kurdish in private or state schools, and using
Kurdish in political campaigns.[140]

Currently, the US State Department's human rights reports have
documented Turkey's flagrant human rights abuses year after year in
a pattern that is clearly consistent. Arms exports to Turkey contravene
President Clinton's PDD 34, issued in February 1995, which directs
the State Department to factor into arms export decisions the impact
of an export on regional stability and on human rights and democracy
in the recipient state.[141] At present, according to an April 1999 Human
Rights Watch report, many journalists, prominent human rights
leaders and Kurdish and Islamic political leaders are in prison for
violating laws against inciting 'racial' or 'religious hatred' or for
issuing 'separatist propaganda'.[142] For example, Turkey's top human
rights defender, Akin Birdal, was jailed under the sedition laws on 3
June, 1999 for a speech he made calling for a peaceful solution to the
Kurdish problem, as well as granting the country's 12 million or so
Kurds the right to broadcast and educate their children in their own
language.[143] The arrest and trial of PKK leader Ocalan[144] provided
an excuse to once again lash out against those calling for a peaceful
end to the war. After the Ocalan arrest, the Turkish military
heightened its attacks on the PKK, both in Turkey and across the
border into northern Iraq[145] and the Iran border.[146] Turkey's renewed

faith in the ability to win the war probably encourages the military to continue using indiscriminate and disproportionate force, though Turkish authorities have prevented US officials and international human rights groups from monitoring their activities in the region.[147]

The war with the PKK also carries repercussions for stability in the region and within Turkey. The CIA's 1997 'State Failure Task Force' report identified Turkey as a nation in danger of collapse. The military's heavy-handed, destabilising role in domestic politics can only be justified as long as the war continues. The conflict has also created entrenched governmental corruption, touching all central political actors in Ankara.[148]

It has been argued that the Kurdish problem must be treated as a problem of human rights and must be conceived as part of the overall project of consolidating and strengthening Turkish democracy.[149] Human rights abuses in Turkey are a result not of malpractice by individuals, but of continuous intrusion of the military and security forces into areas of life where it is inconceivable they would be allowed to intervene in a truly democratic country.[150] Since these characteristics are part of the Turkish political reality, it is highly unlikely that transition to full democracy[151] will be implemented and established[152] in the near future.

The great obstacle that Turkish politics continually confronts is the challenge of legitimacy. Since the beginning of competitive politics in the mid-1940s, severe tensions between the government and the opposition have repeatedly jeopardised the legitimacy of civilian rule and multipartism. Government opposition conflict played a major role in sparking the three overt military interventions (of 1960, 1971 and 1980) that have punctuated Turkish politics since the Second World War.[153]

According to Turkish political analysts the last coup of 1980 demonstrated that 'one can not insulate a specific institution from the rest of society'.[154] During times of internal crisis the armed forces are faced with an uncomfortable choice between preserving the sanctity of the Turkish reforms or accepting the primacy of civilian rule.[155] It is generally believed that the loyalty of the armed forces to the memory of Ataturk as the founder of the modern state and to his reforms has made them the guardian of those reforms. Therefore, the generals intervene to thwart Islamic revivalism and Kurdish separatism which are sapping Attaturk's secular, centralised state. Moreover, after the 1980 military coup, the re-written constitution asserts a debt to Turkey's 'founder, immortal leader and unparalleled hero' and is used to justify denying minority rights to Kurds and jailing more than 1,000 prisoners of conscience.[156]

Undoubtedly, the Ataturkist legacy is an ambiguous one. On the one hand, it forbids the serving army officers from playing any part in the legislature; on the other, it encourages them to think of themselves as the ultimate guardians of the Ataturk revolution.[157] The Turkish modern military forces are still much the largest organisation body in Turkey, just as they were in Ottoman times. Many critics of the military assert that the Kurdish problem has been approached and executed on an imperial concept and basis, that the 1974 Cyprus invasion and occupation was seen as an expansionist and neo-imperialist engagement and that most of the Turkish military commitment was aimed to defend western interests throughout the Cold War period.[158]

The Turkish constitution remains an important factor in national political life, and the role of the armed forces in the constitution is central. If the document is read in one way, it can be seen as providing a framework for the army to dominate the country. In a key passage, its purpose is defined not merely in terms of defending Turkey against external aggression, as any military does; its function is also to make

> the timely and correct identification of threats to the unity of the country and the nation ... and to protect the territory against internal threats which may necessitate the use of the Turkish armed force within the framework of the Constitution and law against any overt or covert attempt to destroy the democratic parliamentary system ... and the indivisible integrity of the Turkish nation, regardless of the source of the threat.[159]

The reality of the matter is that the armed forces have *ad infinitum* power to intervene and to play a vital political role in the domestic affairs of the country whenever they feel it is necessary, or are ordered to by the NSC. In this respect the Turkish constitution is a document that has no parallel in any European country. Its defenders claim that all armies have this power, but most constitutions do not spell it out as clearly. If Turkey was as democratic a state as is claimed, the clauses would not be needed and should be deleted from the constitution. However, reforming or changing anything that appears to have been laid down as law by Ataturk is extremely difficult.[160] Any change is *ipso facto* linked with the constitutional role of the military forces. The Turkish army is interwoven with the Turkish culture and psyche.[161]

Another debatable issue is the actual role of the army as a defending mechanism. Turkey has hardly been involved in military operations since 1945, and unlike most other NATO countries who have reduced the defence budget and downsized their armies since 1989, Turkey has continued to spend heavily on the military. The British, German and US governments continue to provide Turkey with the latest military technology and equipment allowing Turkey to turn into a regional superpower.[162] Furthermore, Turkey (and Greece) have been the recipient of NATO central theatre equipment with the purpose to rebuild their arsenals under the Cascade Programme.[163]

Another factor which determines the rationale of the military towards involvement in the domestic affairs of the country derives from the current party system. The party system constituted the central political problem of the 1970s preceding the intervention of the military in 1980 and it continues to be the central issue following redemocratisation. According to Ikay Sunar, in the 1970s there was a breakdown of democratic politics and persisting economic and political crises and eventually military rule due to the lack of co-operation and compromise from centre-right and centre-left parties.[164]

The predominant style of political government in Turkey since 1983 (when democracy was restored) can be characterised as 'plebiscitarian' democracy.[165] Under that rule an executive controlled a wide margin of discretionary authority albeit there were low levels of party institutionalisation, low levels of institutionalised consultation, low accountability to the legislature and interest groups and unstable bases of social support.[166]

The situation at the beginning of the twenty-first century is probably not a replica of the 1970s. However, military interventions in the domestic affairs can still emanate from escalating economic crisis, weak governments or persevering lack of co-operation between centrist parties.

THE CONSOLIDATION OF DEMOCRACY IN GREECE: FACT OR FICTION?

This section will attempt to shed some light on the question of whether consolidation of democracy in Greece has been achieved. It is important to examine the existence or not, of the liberal democracy in Greece, since the outcome of this investigation will reveal the full pattern of the eastern Mediterranean model.

As noted previously, in the case of Turkey one can identify the predominant and powerful role of the army in the political, economic and social structure of the country. *Au contraire*, Greece has witnessed the presence of powerful local landowners, rich merchants, politicians[167] and above all the intrusive and meddlesome foreign powers which forced the military into a marginal role. *Ab initio*, the establishment of a Greek state was facilitated by the direct involvement of the foreign powers.[168] Furthermore, the history of modern Greece, up to the 1930s, was marked by the inability of the army to establish a disciplined and homogeneous force while their economic dependence on the political elite allowed the latter to dominate and monopolise the economic, political and social arena of the country. Despite the attempts of both Ioannis Kapodistrias (President of Greece from 1828 to 1831) and King Otto (first Monarch of the modern Greek state, from 1833 to 1862) to form a well-organised national army, both leaders and their successors established strong patron–client relations with the military which resulted in the preservation of the supremacy of the former.[169]

Although the right-wing forces emerged victorious in the civil war (1945–9) in the post war period,[170] a number of junior officers refused to accept the ultimate authority of the political elite and 'they saw themselves as independent protagonists of Greek politics rather than as a supporting staff to the civilian leaders'.[171]

Encouraged by the continuous involvement of the monarchy in the formation of governments, especially during 1965–7, and the inability of political leaders to subjugate the political power of non-elected institutions, such as the military, it was no surprise that the military staged a coup on 21 April 1967, and abolished all parliamentary democratic procedures for the next seven years.[172] The military encounter with power ended with a disaster for the Greek–Cypriots since the former instigated the Turkish military intervention on Cyprus in summer 1974 (see previous chapters).

The year 1974 unquestionably marks a watershed in the political development of the country. The establishment in that year of full political democracy for the first time, changed the structures of political life in profound and lasting ways. The most salient changes can be identified as: i) the emancipation of the conduct of foreign policy from foreign tutelage; ii) the democratisation of domestic politics, with significant consequences for society and culture; iii) the Europeanisation of politics and culture, a development intimately connected with accession to the European Community.[173]

To understand the process of democratic consolidation in Greece, one should also place particular attention on the role played by the political parties.[174] Historically, Greece suffered from limited industrialisation, weak class structures, disorientation from the influx of refugees and rapid urbanisation which all resulted in the delayed emergence of a strong pluralistic infrastructure.[175] These characteristics created a weak and suppressed civil society which appeared, especially after the authoritarian experience, incapable of articulating any strategy for transition 'from below'. Hence, the weight of the democratisation process had to fall on the shoulders of a dominant political leader while the transition–consolidation process was to be initiated by a 'from above' source. The emergence of a new democratic order occurred gradually, under the delicate and charismatic guidance of the first post-authoritarian Prime Minister, K. Karamanlis.

Karamanlis attempted to consolidate democracy by adopting specific measures. First and foremost, the abolition of the monarchy facilitated the democratisation of the new political system.[176] The failure of an attempted coup in February 1975 impelled Karamanlis to confront swiftly more sensitive issues such as the junta's supporters.[177] Notwithstanding the fact that Karamanlis enjoyed an unprecedented acceptance among the political and military elites, there were political voices such as Papandreou's newly founded PASOK and the KKE who challenged and questioned Karamanlis's definitions of parliamentary democracy.[178] Nevertheless, he introduced a series of constitutional provisions which aimed at securing parliamentary democracy. Karamanlis emphasised the importance of political parties and parliament for the consolidation of democracy. He himself stated

> that it is political parties rather than governments to which peoples attach themselves and that a regime's fortune is more affected by the number and behaviour of political parties than by its formal framework.[179]

At the same time he recognised that an elected parliament would be the cornerstone in the consolidation of democracy. In a defiant and significant initiative, Karamanlis instigated an Act (23 September 1974) to legalise all political parties and to overturn Law 509 of 1948. The legalisation of political parties most significantly involved the KKE, which had been banned since 1947. Previous legislation discriminated against left-wing supporters since it required a certificate of 'healthy views' for state employment, a driver's licence, a passport and (for a time), university entrance.[180] The 1974 Act abolished such discrimination, and the 1975 Constitution safeguarded individual liberties. The first succession of power which occurred under the new democratic regime was recognised, without disturbance, with the election of PASOK in October 1981. Unquestionably, the new constitution abolished the para-constitutional networks and the practices of political exclusion from civil liberties, which are now guaranteed. In addition, it recognised a number of social rights in the economic sphere that brought the new Greek polity closer to the constitutional trends of its European counterparts and the principle of the welfare state.[181] Furthermore, Karamanlis inaugurated the reorientation of foreign policy away from US tutelage and closer to the European Community. The crisis unleashed by the Turkish invasion of Cyprus and Greece's inability to prevent it or reverse it resulted in a number of structural changes in its international relations.[182] Thus, the European/EC realignment of the country's foreign policy was elevated to a major national interest. In Karamanlis's words the benefits for Greece's EC membership was of prime national interest since it was not only able to guarantee 'balance of power, to contribute to peace and order'[183] but also because it would render 'the democratic institutions more secure'[184].

Meanwhile, having established democracy strictly in terms of parliamentary procedures, he declared the role of parties as fundamental to democracy and 'the role of citizens was confined to that of consensus provider with respect to a predetermined pattern of power distribution and mode of economic development'.[185]

Having understood the importance of civil–military relations for the consolidation of parliamentary democracy, it was no surprise that Karamanlis attempted to reassemble the role of the military on the Greek political arena. The 1975 coup marked the last attempt by the military to undermine political supremacy over the civilians.[186] Fearful that a continuous vendetta would further enfeeble a demoralised military in the face of the Turkish threat or provoke a backlash from the hard-liners of the junta regime, the Karamanlis government and later the Papandreou government, introduced sensible but efficient measures aimed at controlling government–military relations in favour of democratic rule. The process of 'de-juntification' was unavoidable and necessary, though Karamanlis insisted that legal procedures should be respected. He postulated strongly that the armed forces and police must not be demoralised, nor the civil service and judiciary reduced to impotence. He emphasised that 'the army must be strong enough to withstand Turkish threats, but its strength must not threaten the civil power'.[187]

Ab initio, Karamanlis moved away from the capital an important number of military units that constituted a source of possible threat to the elected government with the justification that the army was needed close to the borders with Turkey. He also brought back to the military almost one hundred high-ranking officers that the junta had forced to resign, limiting the chances of junta sympathisers to take control once more, over the military. However, he permitted the military institution to maintain its own radio station and control one of the country's two TV stations.[188] In addition, he replaced only the upper echelons of the military leadership, increased military spending and pointed out that 'the careers of army officers shall be judged by their future behaviour, not the past'.[189]

In his attempts to ease military anxieties towards the administration, he also increased the retirement allowances, medical care and housing benefits of military personnel, and when the leading figures of the junta were sentenced to death, Karamanlis immediately commuted their sentences to life imprisonment. Most significantly, he passed the 660 Act of 1977 which reinstated the role of government as solely responsible for national defence and abolished the dictatorship's concentration of power in the single post of 'Chief of the Armed Forces'.[190]

The domination of PASOK in the Greek political scene since 1981 did not alter the careful and moderate stance towards the military. Despite Papandreou's over-inflated and ambiguous rhetoric before coming to office, which called for a thorough de-juntification of the armed forces, at the end he praised the military's 'total devotion to their duties: the preservation of national independence and protection of the country's democratic institutions'.[191]

Papandreou's cordial relations with President Karamanlis restrained the military from objecting and challenging the new *status quo* in the political scene of the country. During the 1980–5 period

> 'Papandreou asked President Karamanlis – the constitutional commander in-chief – to take a more visible role in military-related matters' and the latter who enjoyed the support of the military 'responded favourably to the government's call'.[192]

Having encountered the *realpolitik* of Greece's strategic location, regional problems and socio-economic conditions, Papandreou's foreign policy and stance towards the military could be summarised in the aphorism, 'signal left and turn right'. This observation is based on the fact that despite Papandreou's assertive and defiant third world-type rhetoric, when it came to important choices involving the country's national interests, he adopted according to Couloumbis 'lock, stock and barrel the policies of his predecessors'.[193]

Hence, contrary to pre-election rhetoric, he renewed the US bases' agreement in 1983. The presence of the US bases, from the PASOK perspective, was to be made conditional on the preservation of the Greek–Turkish military balance in the Aegean – understood in terms of a 7 to 10 ratio in US military aid and sales to Greece and Turkey respectively. He chose to keep Greece in the European Community, did not withdraw from NATO, and continued to pursue a policy of deterrence based on military balance *vis-à-vis* Turkey, which could on the one hand lead eventually to a settlement of the Greek–Turkish dispute and on the other hand would ease the anxieties of the military.[194]

Most importantly, Papandreou followed a moderate and pragmatic approach towards the military's corporate interests. According to Karabelias, Papandreou consistently devoted nearly 20 percent of total government spending to defence expenditures, offered generous retirement allowances, medical care and housing to the officer corps and made certain that the promotion of younger and the retirement of senior officers was taking place annually.[195]

Papandreou also succeeded in installing radical changes in the structure and character of military institutions. He upgraded the military academies and brought them to an academic level equal to that of state universities, causing the entrance of new cadets to be based on their own skills rather than on the powers of their patrons. He reformed the curricula of the service academies and removed stringent anti-communist propaganda and at the same time tried to promote the values of pluralism. Furthermore, he managed to strip the control of mass communication networks from the army while he appointed Naval or Air Force Generals to the position of the Chairman of the General Staff, an exclusive domain of Army Generals since the end of the Second World War.

Further amendments to the constitution which the PASOK government implemented, entailed the substantial reduction of the authority of the President and increase of the power of the Prime Minister and parliament. These were accepted by the military as a *fait accompli*.[196] In sum, one can argue that the case of Greece might be considered by many students of democratic transition and consolidation processes as a textbook example of how an outgoing authoritarian regime dominated by a traditionally politicised military came to the eventual realisation that its proper role did not entail intervention in the civil and political life of the country.

However, in explaining the rapid consolidation of democracy in Greece, some specific facts should be taken into consideration. First of all, attitudinal support for democracy appears to have followed from behavioural support of the democratic regime in Greece and thus completed the military's submission to civilian control. N. Karakatsanis argues that

> behavioural submission to democracy is simply not enough for sufficient consolidation to take place ... it is only after the military had been attitudinally democratised that a fuller consolidation of democracy can occur ... and the Greek case shows that such changes in military attitudes can occur.[197]

Second, the skilful handling of military affairs by Karamanlis in the 1970s and Papandreou in the early 1980s convinced the military that civilian administration was capable of protecting the military's corporate interests and respecting the military's role in society. Furthermore, the realisation that the main threat to the territorial integrity of the country came not from the inside (communists) but from outside the borders and more specifically from a NATO ally (Turkey), resulted in a radical shift of attention from the military point of view. The parallelism of the foreign policy goals of the civilian government with those of the post-junta officers contributed paradoxically towards the country's democratic orientation and eventual consolidation.[198]

Greece's entry into the European Community in 1981, instigated by Karamanlis, was driven by his belief that Greece could exercise greater leverage on international affairs as part of the EC than a secondary power could exercise on its own. In Greek eyes, the new (as from 1974 onwards) situation in the eastern Mediterranean required additional adjustments of support in its international relations which led to a close European 'partnership' to counterweight the ever-increasing military threat from Turkey. It was also perceived as the most appropriate context to facilitate national economic develop-ment. Karamanlis's strategy was based on a theory of 'induced modernisation' where Greece would have to adjust in order to survive in this 'exclusive' and 'competitive club'. 'Adjust' or 'perish' then was his philosophy of westernisation.[199]

Furthermore, from the very beginning, accession to the EC was also seen by the Greek government as a means of political stabilisation and development. As Karamanlis put it, a united Europe with its 'democratic structure and functions', cannot but 'consolidate the democratic regimes of each country'.[200] Regime consolidation was thought to be the ultimate outcome of a process of gradual changes, reinforced by accession itself, in the economy and in the political culture of Greek society and polity.

Finally, as noted earlier, political parties are central actors in transitions to democracy and their role was proved to be vital in the democratisation process in Greece. Although political parties were relatively new formations with the establishment of the Third Greek Republic, both the 'format' and the 'mechanics' of the party system were conducive to the transition–consolidation process. Despite the novel character of the party system in all spheres – ideological, organ-isational – Greek political parties displayed strong elements of the pre-authoritarian party-political practices.[201] The existence of a strong state, and clientelistic relationships between politicians/political parties and the electorate continued to dominate Greek politics.[202] As Sassoon argues:

> political life became characterised by strongly personalised links between patron–politician and client–voter, and by the exchange of

rousfeti (political favours). Politics was a necessary evil, a self-defence mechanism used to uphold a traditional way of life, not an instrument of emancipation.[203]

The other side of the coin is the weakness of civil society in the Greek social formation. This affects all aspects of society. The state has, for instance, traditionally been involved in every part of economic activity. This has had important consequences for the nature of the private sector which had concentrated its activities on expanding the degree of protection or level of subsidy rather than relying on its own dynamism to improve its competitiveness or restructure its production.[204] In addition, public sector employment is also central to clientelestic policies. Greek public administration is embedded in clientelistic politics and relationships which can ease access to state subsidies, licences and other forms of protection.[205] Moreover, Greece is handicapped by the development of an enormous self-employed sector, arguably the largest in the EU, absorbing, at present, over 40 per cent of the Greek labour force. This sector of the labour market was dominated by extremely small and often non-competitive productive structures, dependent on state regulation and protection for survival, thriving on illicit or illegal practices and tax evasion and links with the state apparatus.[206]

Of particular concern, is the lack of an independent labour movement. Schmitter argues, that while class interests are represented by monopolistic institutions such as the GSEE, this is the result of deliberate state policy. Parties, especially PASOK, have made concerted efforts to penetrate and capture leadership positions in the GSEE.[207]

All these factors generate practices that are obstacles to the further modernisation and renewal of the Greek polity and society. Nevertheless, the democratisation of Greek politics succeeded due to the existence of specific factors: first, the elevation of democratically accountable institutions, such as parliament and the governments issuing from it, to positions of political pre-eminence typical of fully democratic political systems; second, the significant expansion of 'political space' and the occupation of power by PASOK, a non-communist party of the left; third, the modernisation of the Greek Right, which abandoned its identification with fanatical anti-communism and its half-hearted commitment to fully democratic politics and decided to form a new, moderate centre-right party, appropriately named New Democracy (Nea Democratia); fourth, the emergence for the first time in Greek history, of mass political parties capable of effectively organising and mobilising their adherents in support of or against particular policies or goals; and finally the acceptance by the army of an outward oriented security goal. Taken together, these changes signalled the normalisation of Greek politics and its convergence with modern, democratic political systems elsewhere. Furthermore, the election in January 1996 of Constantine Simitis as the new Prime Minister and his adoption in the last four years of specific economic policies has led to a rapid economic development of the country.[208]

Last but not least, democratic consolidation in Greece has been spurred on by Greece's adoption of the neo-liberalist approach.[209] The outcome of my interviews together with evidence from the current Greek government, and some Greek think-tanks (mainly ELIAMEP) discloses a tendency to support this liberalism view.[210] According to the neo-liberalists, in the post-Cold War era, the driving force of International Relations is economic power (geo-economics) and not geography and military power (geo-politics). For the neo-liberalists, the expansion of an open economy and free market, in correlation with the enactment of pluralistic democracy, could enhance co-operation and diminish the prospect of inter-state confrontations. To sum up, neo-liberalists emphasise

- economic co-dependence, which is seen as an ultimate goal of attainment
- expansion of pluralistic democracy
- enhancement of International Institutions.

Au contraire, Turkey is a stalwart supporter of the realist school in International Relations which entails the 'state' and 'power' as two of the most important characteristics of this school.[211] As noted earlier, these two elements are deeply embedded in the Turkish social and political psyche and as a result eliminate the adoption of a different approach in the International Relations of the country.[212] The application of the realist approach in Turkey has been consistent and uninterrupted throughout its modern history. However, enactment of pluralistic democracy – one of the main prerequisites for the adoption of a neo-liberalist view – in Turkey has been limited and feeble.[213]

Therefore, the analysis of this chapter proved the unequal democratic evolution in Greece and Turkey and as a result managed to unravel the flawed creation of a pluralistic security community in the eastern Mediterranean (*Hybrid Region*). The following chapter will attempt to introduce a series of measures which can lead to the stabilisation of the southern flank of the NATO alliance.

NOTES

1. This assumption is also based on Ole Waever's analysis which contends that Europe has become a security community. For further analysis see Ole Waever, 'Insecurity, Security and Asecurity in the West European non-war Community', in E. Adler and M. Barnett (eds), *Security Communities* (Cambridge: Cambridge University Press, 1998) pp.69–118. NATO has always demonstrated its adherence to the idea of security community. See the *North Atlantic Treaty, NATO Handbook* (Brussels: Nato, 1990). The view that NATO is a security community has been expressed by Javier Solana in 'NATO – A Reliable Alliance for Dynamism and Leadership', *NATO's Sixteen Nations*, 1 (Brussels: Nato, 1997) pp.7–10. Evidence of a PSC can be found also in the 23 April 1999 Washington Declaration for the 50th anniversary of NATO. See also *www.usembassy.org.uk/nato85.html*. See 'NATO is a club of democracies whose stated aims include the promotion of lofty ideals like the rule of law and civilian control over the armed forces', *The Economist*, 7 August 1999, p.46.
2. Stephen Weber, 'Does NATO Have a Future', in B. Crawford (ed.), *The Future of European Security* (Berkeley, CA: Center for German and European Studies, 1992) p.366.
3. ibid., p.366.
4. Harvey Starr, 'Democracy and Integration: Why Democracies Don't Fight Each Other', *Journal Of Peace Research*, 34, 2 (1997) p.156, emphasis in original.
5. The *Hybrid Region* is not a complete pluralistic security community nor a traditional antagonistic situation. It entails elements of both.
6. Karl W. Deutsch et al., *Political Community and the North Atlantic Area: International Organisation in the Light of Historical Experience* (Princeton, NJ: Princeton University Press, 1957) p.3.
7. ibid., p.5.
8. ibid., p.5.
9. ibid., p.5.
10. ibid., p.6.
11. ibid., p.65.
12. See *Security Communities in Comparative Perspective*, Merill House Conference, 1–2 December 1995, p.1, *www.cceia.org/security.h.t.m.*
13. Charles Taylor, *Community, Anarchy, and Library* (Cambridge: Cambridge University Press, 1982) pp.25–33.
14. G.A. Hillery, 'Definitions of Community: Areas of Agreement', *Rural Sociology*, 20 (1995).
15. Charles Taylor, 'Interpretation and the Sciences of Man', in Paul Rabinow and William Sullivan (eds), *Interpretative Social Science: A Reader* (Berkeley: University of California Press, 1979) p.51.
16. Emanuel Adler et al., 'Governing Anarchy: A Research Agenda for the Study of Security Communities', *Ethics & International Affairs*, 10 (1996) pp.63–98. This notion suggests a *Gemeinshaft* rather than a *Gesellschaft* conception; the former refers to an organic community involving bonds generated by tradition and culture while the latter sees society as a more contractual arrangement that emerges from self-interested behaviour. For different definitions about community see Andrew Linklater, 'The Problem of Community in International Relations Theory', *Alternatives*, 2 (1990). See also Antony P. Cohen, *The Symbolic Construction of Community* (New York: Tavistock, 1985).
17. For further study see K. Booth, 'A New Security Concept for Europe', in P. Eavis (ed.), *European Security: The New Agenda* (Bristol: Saferworld Report, 1990).
18. The notion of core values is very difficult to confine. They can be material (territorial integrity) and immaterial (democracy, freedom). K.J. Holsti states that 'core values can be described as those kind of goals for which most people are willing to make ultimate sacrifice', *International Politics. A Framework of Analysis* (Englewood Cliffs, NJ: Prentice-Hall, 1983) p.129.
19. See C. McInnes, *Security and Strategy in the New Europe* (London: Routledge, 1992) p.4.

20. See B. Buzan, *People, States and Fear: The National Security Problem in International Relations* (Brighton: Wheatsheaf, 1983, Chapter 3). See also K. Booth, 'Security and Anarchy: Utopian Realism in Theory and Practice', *International Affairs*, 67, 3 (1991) pp.527–45; B. Buzan, *People, States and Fear: Agenda for International Security Studies in the post-Cold War Era* (Brighton: Wheatsheaf, 1990).

21. McInnes, 'Security', p.4.

22. For an excellent analysis see B. Buzan, O. Waever and J. De Wilde, *Security: A New Framework for Analysis* (London: Lynne Rienner Publishers, 1998).

23. ibid., p.2.

24. For further analysis see R. Ullman, 'Redefining Security', *International Security*, 8, 1 (1983) pp.129–53; J.S. Nye and S.M. Lynn-Jones, 'International Security Studies', *International Security*, 12, 4 (1988) pp.5–27; N. Brown, 'Climate, Ecology and International Security', *Survival*, 31, 6 (1989) pp.519–32; N. Crawford, 'Once and Future Security Studies', *Security Studies*, 1, 2 (1991) pp.283–316; H. Haftendon, 'The Security Puzzle: Theory-Building and Discipline-Building in International Security', *International Studies Quarterly*, 35, 1. (1991) pp.3–17; Waever et al., *Identity, Migration and the New Security Order in Europe* (London: Pinter, 1993).

25. See C. Gray, *Villains, Victims and Sheriffs: Strategic Studies and Security for an Inter-War Period*, (Hull: University of Hull Press, 1994).

26. J. Chipman, 'The Future of Strategic Studies: Beyond Grand Strategy', *Survival*, 34, 1 (1992) pp.109–31.

27. S.M. Walt, 'The Renaissance of Security Studies', *International Studies Quarterly*, 35, 2 (1991) pp.211–39.

28. See Merill House Conference, p.1.

29. Deutsch et al., 'Political Community', p.65.

30. ibid., p.115.

31. R.N. Lebow, 'The Long Peace, the End of the Cold War, and the Future of Realism', *International Organisation*, 48, 2, (1994) p.269.

32. E. Adler, *Europe's New Security Order: A Pluralistic Security Community, The Future of European Security*, in Crawford (ed.), p.294.

33. Deutsch et al., 'Political Community', pp.66–7.

34. ibid., p.123.

35. ibid., p.124.

36. The use of the terms 'liberal state', 'democracy', 'liberal democracy' signify virtually the same subject.

37. John MacMillan, 'Democracies Don't Fight: A Case of the Wrong Agenda', *Review of International Studies*, 22, 3 (1996) pp.278–9. For more details about the cosmopolitan views of the aforementioned authors see C.L. de Secondat de Montesquieu, *The Spirit of the Laws* (Cambridge: Cambridge University Press, 1989); I. Kant, 'Perpetual Peace', in H. Reiss (ed.), *Kant's Political Philosophy* (Cambridge: Cambridge University Press, 1991); J.A. Schumpeter, *The Sociology of Imperialism, in Imperialism and Social Classes* (New York, 1955); Doyle analyses Kant's and Schumpeter's stances in 'Kant, Liberal Legacies and Foreign Affairs', Part I, *Philosophy and Public Affairs*, 12, 3 (1983) pp.205–35 and 'Liberalism and World Politics', *American Political Science Review*, 80, 4 (1986) pp.69, 1151.

38. A good measurement discussion can be found in R. Merritt and D.A. Zinnes, 'Democracies and War', in A. Inkeles (ed.), *On Measuring Democracy: Its Consequences and Concomitants* (NJ: New Brunswick, 1991) pp.207–34.

39. Samuel Huntington, *The Third Wave: Democratisation in the Late Twentieth Century* (University of Oklahoma Press, 1991) pp.7, 9.

40. For further and detailed analysis see R.A. Dahl, *Democracy and Its Critics* (New Haven: Yale University Press, 1989).

41. For more details see Bruce Russett et al., *Grasping the Democratic Peace: Principles for a post-Cold War World* (Princeton: Princeton University Press, 1991) pp.43–71.

42. For further analysis see Dahl, *Democracy and Its Critics*.

43. Nils Petter Gleditsch, 'Democracy and Peace', *Journal Of Peace Research*, 29, 4 (1992) p.370.

44. For more details see R.L. Schweller, 'Domestic Structure and Preventive War. Are Democracies More Pacific', *World Politics*, 44, 2 (1992) pp.235–69. In my opinion, free elections, civilian control over the military, respect for civil rights are fundamental factors for the identification of a pure democratic country.

45. Douglas A.Van Belle, 'Press Freedom and the Democratic Peace', *Journal Of Peace Research*, 34, 4 (1997) p.405. Even in the Greek–Turkish case when Turkey invaded Cyprus Greece was not a democracy.

46. Ze'ev Maoz and Nasrin Abdolali, 'Regime and International Conflict 1816–1976', *Journal of Conflict Resolution*, 33 (1989) pp.3–35; Small Melvin and J.D. Stinger, 'The War-Proneness of Democratic Regimes, 1816–1965', *Jerusalem Journal Of International Relations*, summer, 1 (1976), pp.50–69.

47. Margaret Herman and Charles Kegley, 'Rethinking Democracy and International Peace: Perspectives from Political Psychology', *International Studies Quarterly*, 39, 4 (1995) p.513.

48. W. Dixon, 'Democracy and the Peaceful Settlement Of International Conflict', *American Political Science Review*, 88, 4 (1994) pp.14–32.

49. Harvey Starr, 'Democracy and War: Choice, Learning and Security Communities', *Journal Of Peace Research*, 29, 2 (1992) pp.207–8.

50. ibid, p.207; for more details see Bueno de Mesquite and Lalman, *War and Reason* (New Haven: Yale University Press, 1992).

51. See MacMillan, 'Democracies', pp.275–99.

52. The same view has been expressed by M. Doyle, 'Liberalism and World Politics', *American Political Science Review*, 80, 14 (1989) pp.1151–70; S. Kober, 'Idealpolitik', in Richard K. Betts (ed.), *Conflict After the Cold War, Arguments on Causes of War and Peace* (New York: Macmillan, 1994) pp.250–62; T.C. Clifton and S. Campbell, 'Domestic Structure, Decisional Constraints and War', *Journal of Conflict Resolution*, 35 (1991) pp.187–211; John Owen, 'How Liberalism Produces Democratic Peace', *International Security*, 19 (fall, 1994) pp.87–125.

53. Russett, 'Grasping the Democratic', pp.35, 40.

54. See Kenneth Boulding, *Stable Peace* (Austin: University of Texas Press, 1979).

55. For a debate about the credibility of the democratic peace see Russett, Layne, Spiro and Doyle, 'Correspondence: The Democratic Peace', *International Security*, 19, 4 (1995) pp.164–84.

56. Nils P. Gleditsch, 'Democracy and Peace', *Journal of Peace Research*, 29, 4 (1992) p.369.

57. R.J. Rummel, 'Libertarianism and International Violence', *Journal of Conflict Resolution*, 27, 1 (1983) pp.27–71.

58. Gleditsch, 'Democracy', p.370.

59. Deutsch, 'Political Community', pp.66–7.

60. K. Deutsch, *Political Community at the International Level*, (United States: Archon, 1954) p.43.

61. E.B. Haas, 'The Study of Regional Integration: Reflections on the Joy and Anguish of Pretheorizing', *International Organisation*, 24, 4 (1970) p.610.

62. R.O. Keohane and J.S. Nye, *Power and Interdependence* (New York: Harper Collins Publishers, 1989) pp.24–5, emphasis in original.

63. Harvey Starr, 'Democracy and War: Choice, Learning and Security Communities', *Journal Of Peace Research*, 29, 2 (1992) pp.210–11, emphasis in original.

64. K. Deutsch, *The Nerves of Government: Models of Political Communication and Control* (New York: Free Press, 1966) pp.76–7.

65. E. Adler and M. Barnett (eds), *Security Communities* (Cambridge: Cambridge University Press, 1998) p.7, emphasis is added.

66. Norbert Wiener as cited in K. W. Deutsch, *The Nerves of Government* (New York: Free Press, 1996) p.77.
67. See Keohane and Nye, 'Power', pp.24–5.
68. Oran R. Young, 'Interdependencies in World Politics', in Ray Maghroori and Bennet Ramberg (eds), *Globalism Versus Realism: International Relations' Third Debate* (Boulder: Westview Press, 1982) pp.57–8. For further analysis about the notion of interdependence see Kenneth Waltz, 'The Myth of National Interdependence', pp.81–96.
69. Deutsch et al., 'Political Community and the North Atlantic Area', p.67.
70. For further study about confidence building measures see Jonathan Alford (ed.), 'The Future of Arms Control, Part 3: Confidence Building Measures', *Adelphi Paper*, 149 (1978); see also James Macintosh, *Confidence and Security Building Measures: A Sceptical Look*, Working Paper 85 (Canberra: Peace Research Centre, 1990); M.A. Desjardins, 'Rethinking Confidence-Building Measures', *Adelphi Papers*, 307, (1996).
71. Deutsch, 'Political Community at the International Level', pp.56–8.
72. E. Adler and M.N. Barnett, *Security Communities*, Paper presented at the 1994 Annual Meeting of the American Political Science Association, p.13.
73. It is constructive to point out that this depends on the nature and scale of the breach of trust.
74. Deutsch outlines the outcome of failure in a political system in his 'Nerves of Government', pp.221–2.
75. K. Deutsch, 'Integration and the Social System: Implications of Functional Analysis', in P.E. Jacob and James V. Toscano (eds), *The Integration of Political Communities* (New York: J.B. Lippincot, 1964) p.143.
76. It is instructive to mention that I will examine the Greek–Turkish dyad in relation to the PSC criteria, and mainly the value of liberal democracy.
77. On the challenges confronting the process of democratic consolidation in Turkey see Ergun Ozbudum, 'Turkey: How Far from Consolidation', *Journal of Democracy*, 7. 3 (1996) pp.123–38; see also Bernard Lewis, 'Why Turkey is the Only Muslim Democracy', *Middle Eastern Quarterly*, 1, 1 (1994) pp.41–9; see also Metin Heper and E. Fuat Keyman, 'Double-Faced State: Political Patronage and the Consolidation of Democracy in Turkey', *Middle Eastern Studies*, 34, 4 (1998) pp.259–76.
78. Levent Koker, 'Local Politics and Democracy in Turkey: An Appraisal', *The Annals of the American Academy of Political And Social Science*, 540 (July, 1995) p.53.
79. See S. Mardin, 'Power, Civil Society and Culture in the Ottoman Empire', *Comparative Studies in Society and History*, 12 (1969) p.259.
80. Kemalism accords legitimacy only to the Republican regime for Turkey. Kemalism believes that it is only the Republican regime which can represent the unconditional sovereignty of the people.
81. Kemalist nationalism believes in principle that the Turkish state is an indivisible whole comprising its territory and people.
82. The Kemalist revolution was a social revolution in terms of its content and goals. This was a revolution led by an elite with an orientation toward the people at large.
83. In the application of the principle of etatism, the state emerged not only as the principal source of economic activity but as the owner of the major industries of the country.
84. Kemalist secularism did not merely mean separation of state and religion, but also the separation of religion from educational, cultural and legal affairs. It meant the independence of institutions and thought from the dominance of religious thinking and religious institutions.
85. One of the most important principles that Ataturk formulated was the principle of reformism. It meant that traditional concepts were eliminated and modern concepts were adopted.
86. In the 1920s Kemal Ataturk established six of the fundamental principles of Turkish reforms, which are still part of the Constitution today.

87. The Republican People's Party was established by Ataturk in 1923, and remained as the only political party until 1945, when multi-party elections became reality.
88. For further elaboration on these points see S. Kili, 'Kemalism in Contemporary Turkey', *International Political Science Review*, 1 (1980) pp.387–92.
89. The Turks perceive the state as their *devlet baba* (Daddy state) and they know that in an hour of need the paternalistic state will not let them down, *The Economist*, 28 August 1999, pp.39–40.
90. Resat Kasaba, 'Kemalist Certainties and Modern Ambiguities', in Bozdogan and Kasaba (eds), *Rethinking Modernity and National Identity in Turkey* (Seattle: University of Washington, 1997), p.17.
91. F. Frey, 'Patterns of Elite Politics in Turkey', in G. Lenczowski (ed.), *Political Elites in the Middle East* (Washington, DC: American Research Enterprises, 1975) p.70.
92. For further analysis see Ellen Kay Trimberger, *Revolution from Above: Military Bureaucrats and Development in Egypt, Peru, Turkey, and Japan* (NJ: Transaction Books, 1977).
93. Caglar Keyder, 'Turkey in the 1990s', in *Rethinking Modernity and National Identity in Turkey*, p.40.
94. For further study see Aysa Bugra, *State and Business in Modern Turkey: A Comparative Study* (New York: New York Press, State University, 1994).
95. Frey argues 'that persons conditioned by military experience, accessible to military contracts and trusted by military personnel were at the mainspring of power'. Frederick Frey, 'The Army in Turkish Politics', *Land Reborn* (1966) pp.7–8, cited in G. Karabelias, 'Civil–Military Relations: A Comparative Analysis of the Role of the Military in the Political Transformation of Post -War Turkey and Greece: 1980–1995', *NATO Final Report* (June, 1998) p.21.
96. Article 148 of the Military Penal Code prohibited 'any member of the armed forces to join a political party, hold or participate in political meetings, give a political speech in public, or prepare, sign or send to the press any declaration of a political character', quoted from F. Frey, *The Turkish Political Elite* (Cambridge: MIT, 1965) p.61.
97. Caglar Keyder, 'Democracy and the Demise of National Developmentalism: Turkey in Perspective', *IEA Conference*, 113 (1995) p.193.
98. See Schweller, 'Domestic Structure' and Gleditsch 'Democracy and Peace'.
99. Keyder, 'Democracy and the Demise', p.196.
100. See D. Lehmann, *Democracy and Development in Latin America* (Cambridge: Polity Press, 1990); I. Wallerstein, 'The Concept of National Development, 1917–1989: Elegy and Requiem', *American Behavioural Scientist*, 35, 3–4 (1992) pp.517–29.
101. ibid., p.196.
102. The military was responsible for the draft of the new Constitution in 1961 and 1982; furthermore, they forced the civilian parliament to alter the Constitution in 1971. For further analysis see E. Ozbudun, *Making Constitutions During the Process of Democratisation* (in Turkish), (Ankara: Bilgi Yayinevi, 1993), on the relationship between types of transition and constitutions.
103. See Keyder, 'Democracy', p.202.
104. An officer interviewed by Karpat after the 1960 coup argued that during the DP regime 'the prestige of the army was declining. Money seemed to have become everything. An officer no longer had status in the society. It hurt ... to see officers ... wear civilian clothes and feel proud in them'. Kemal Karpat, 'The Military and Politics in Turkey 1960–64: A Socio-Cultural Analysis of a Revolution', *American Historical Review*, 75 (1970) p.1665. See also George Harris, 'The Causes of the 1960 Revolution in Turkey', *Middle East Journal*, 24 (1970).
105. Over 20,000 members of the DP lost their political rights while Prime Minister Menderes, Minister for Foreign Affairs Zorlu and Interior Minister Polatkan were hanged. The punishment of DP founders and associates was intended as a message from the military to

future political leaders that the latter must not violate the limits of political behaviour that the Turkish Armed Forces have set.

106. For a more elaborate and in detail analysis about the role of the military in Turkey and Greece during 1945–1980 see G. Karabellias, *O Rolos Ton Enoplon Dynameon Stin Politiki Zoi Tis Tourkias Kai Tis Elladas: Sigkritiki Analisis ton Metapolemikon Stratiotikon Epembaseon 1945–1980* (Athens: 1998).

107. Semih Vaner, 'The Army', in Irvin Schick and Erdugul Tonak (eds), *Turkey In Transition* (New York: London: Oxford Press, 1987).

108. Ahmet Kemal, 'Military Rule and the Future of Democracy in Turkey', *Merip Reports* (March/April, 1984) pp.12–15.

109. According to official results of the referendum that was held on 7 November 1982, 91.4% of the voters in a 91.3% turnout said 'yes' to its implementation. Of course there are valid objections about the final outcome of elections conducted under any martial law government. An important point is that the people did not have a choice. PM Bulent Ulusu mentioned on 14 July 1982, 'if the people vote "no" in the referendum, then the military would not return to the barracks but remain in power'. General Kenan Evren seemed to share the same view. Hasan Cemal, *Tank Sesiyle Uyanmak* (Ankara: Bilgi, 1986) p.550.

110. With regard to his executive function, the President's powers were: appointing the Prime Minister and accepting his resignation, presiding over the meetings of the Council of Ministers whenever he deems it necessary, calling a meeting of the NSC and presiding over it, proclaiming martial law or state of emergency in collaboration with the Council of Ministers, appointing the chairman and members of the State Supervisory Council as well as the members of the Board of Higher Education, appointing the Chief of the General Staff and appointing university rectors. Ergun Ozbudun, 'The Status of the President of the Republic Under the Turkish Constitution of 1982', in Metin Heper and Ahmed Evid (eds), *State, Democracy and the Military: Turkey in the 1980s* (Berlin: Walter de Gruter, 1988) p.39.

111. The Generals decided to put a bit of Islam into politics as an antidote to the Marxism they were chiefly worrying about.

112. Ali H. Bayar, 'The Developmenal State and Economic Policy in Turkey', *Third World Quarterly*, 17, 4 (1996) p.781.

113. For further details see G. Karabelias, 'Civil–Military Relations: A Comparative Analysis of the Role of the Military in the Political Transformation of Post-War Turkey and Greece: 1980–1995', *NATO Final Report* (June, 1998) pp.27–30.

114. *Cumhuriet*, 19 January 1989.

115. This is according to Articles 4, 5, 8 of the Political Parties Law No.2820. Parties must have at least thirty founder members who were not vetoed by the military. Moreover, they ought to be attached to the principles and reforms of Attaturk and should not adopt any of the aims deemed inadmissible under Article 14 of the constitution. In other words 'the by-laws and programs of the parties may not be in conflict with the principle of national unity and territorial integrity of the state, human rights, national sovereignty and the democratic and the secular character of the republic'. Articles 78–90 of the Political Parties Law pointed out that 'communist parties and parties oriented toward ethnic separatism, religious distinctions and racial differences were not going to be allowed to appear'. Ilter Turan, 'Political Parties and the Party System in Post-1983 Turkey', in Heper and Evid (eds), pp.69, 74.

116. For more information about the elections of 1983 see Ahmad Feroz, 'The Turkish Elections of 1983', *Merip Reports*, (March/April, 1984).

117. He overruled the appointment of General Ozturtun to the position of the Chief of the General Staff; he brought into public discussion the taboo issue of the defence funds; he became involved in the Kurdish issue and suggested that the Turkish government should

show some kind of 'goodwill gestures'. He even started discussion with Kurdish leaders, *Turkish Daily News*, 31 March 1993. He called for military intervention in Armenia, *Turkish Daily News*, 5 March 1993, *Milliyet*, 5 April 1993, all this knowing that the NSC did not approve his proposals. Ozal's death a few days before submitting a major proposal for Kurdish reforms to the NSC raised a lot of questions.

118. Whereas Ozal had closed the doors to the military ... in the Kurdish dispute ... [using] this policy to restore civilian democracy in Turkey ... Demirel who became President, opened the door for the military in fear of losing his own authority if he limited the authority of the military ... Ciller who became the first female PM, allowed the military to walk through the door opened by Demirel and has given 'full authority' to the military; see *Turkish Daily News*, 24 March 1994 and *The Observer*, 26 March 1995.

119. William Hale, *Turkish Politics and the Military* (London: Routledge, 1994) p.294.

120. *Turkish Daily News*, 14 March 1995. It is worth mentioning that after the formation of the new post-Ozal government, in July of 1993, rumours of an imminent military takeover started to circulate in Ankara. The issue of military intervention was back in the agenda in February 1994, January 1995 and the summer of 1997; see also 'The Chill Descending on Turkey', *The Economist*, 24 January 1998, pp.51–2.

121. During the violence-ridden 1970s, when the NAP was linked with armed militias that targeted leftists, the social democrat Ecevit regularly denounced the party as 'fascist'.

122. The DLP got 136 seats, the Islamist Virtue Party, successor of the Welfare Party, 110, the True Party 86, the Motherland Party 88, and the National Action Party (NAP), 130, 'Nation and Tribe the Winners', *The Economist*, 24 April 1999, p.57.

123. Alan Markovsky, 'Turkey's Nationalist Moment', *Policywatch*, 384, 20 April 1999, p.2.

124. This fact seems to have scared many voters away from backing them again. On 11 June 1997, the General Staff headquarters issued a statement threatening that 'weapons would be used if necessary in the struggle against fundamentalism'. One week later Erbakan resigned. In February 1998, after a trial in the Constitutional Court, the Welfare Party was closed. Several of its leaders, including Erbakan, were barred from politics for five years.

125. The head of Turkey's powerful military warned that the state must fight Islamic radicals for '1,000 years if necessary' and called on Parliament to pass tougher laws curtailing religious extremism. General of Chief of Staff Huseyin Kivrikoglou criticised the government and past administrators, saying they had approved only four of the 18 laws proposed by the military on 28 February 1999. 'We expect parliament to look speedily into the other draft left from February 28 when it convenes on October 1', see *Associated Press*, 4 September 1999. Huseyin Kivrikoglou officially retired on 28 August 2002 when he handed over his duties to his successor at the post, General Hilmi Ozkok, in a ceremony in Ankara.

126. See Z. Onis and J. Riedel, *Economic Crises and Long-term Growth in Turkey* (Washington: The World Bank, 1993).

127. Karabelias, 'Civil–Military' p.37.

128. If there is a case of civilian interference in the military schools or in the officer corps, the high ranking officers quite often expel undesired cadets and officers from the military. The expelled are not able to take their case to court since the 1982 Constitution stipulates that decisions of the Supreme Military Council cannot be contested judicially.

129. See previous chapters, including Ihsan Gurkan, *NATO, Turkey and the Southern Flank* (New York: NSIC 1980) pp.17–18.

130. OYAK derived its income from the obligatory contribution of all active and reserve officers as well as civilian employees of the Ministry of National Defence, deducting 10% from their military salary, and from its financial investments in various sectors (in the Automotive Industry with OYAK-Renault, Motorlu Acalar Imal ve Satis and Goodyear, in the Cement Industry through Cukorova Cimento, Unye Cimento, Mardin Cimento, Bolu Cimento and YASAS, in the Electronic Industry through ASELSAN, in the Service

Industry through OYAK Sogorta, in the Construction Industry through OYAK Insaat A. S., OYAK-Kutlutas konut and OYAK-Kutlutas Paz; in the Food Industry through Tam Gida, Tukas, Entas Tavuk Pinar Et and Eti Pazarlama; in the Petroleum Industry through Turkiye Petrolleri A.O., Petro-Kimya A.O. and Seylak; and in the Stock Exchange Industry through AXA). See Serdar Sen, *Sihahli Kuvvetler ve Modernizm* (Istanbul, Sarmal, 1996) pp.148–62.

131. Karabelias, 'Civil–Military', p.40; see also the Turkish newspaper *Yeni Yuzul,* 17 October 1995.

132. Some of the companies involved in the domestic defence are: the Military Electronic Industries Inc. (ASELSAN), the Military Battery Industry (ASPILSAN), the Electric Industry (ISBIR), the Silvas Textile Industry (SIDAS), the Machinery and Chemical Industries Establishment (MKE), the Turkish Aircraft (TUSAS), the Turkish Engine Industries (TEI), the Turkish Airspace Industries (TAI), the Turkish Electronics Industry and Trade Corporation (TESTAS), the Taskizak and the Golcuk shipyards, and others; see Omer Karapasan 'Turkey's Armaments Industries', *Middle East Report,* 144 (Jan–Feb, 1987) pp.29–30; for more updated information about the Turkish Defence Industry see *NATO's Sixteen Nations, Special Supplement* (1998).

133. Ahmad Feroz, *The Turkish Experiment in Democracy, 1950–1975* (Boulder: Westview, 1997), p.281.

134. Karabelias, 'Civil–Military', p.41.

135. See Moustakis, 'Turkey's', pp.133, 134; see also *NATO's Sixteen Nations, Special Edition* (1992) pp.14–24.

136. See Department of State Report, U.S. Military Equipment and Human Rights Violations (1997) pp.1–11. The Department of State submitted this report to the Chairman of the Senate Foreign Relations Committee on I July 1997, pursuant to Senate Committee Report 104–295, accompanying H.R. 3540, *www.fas.org/asmp/library/state/turkey_dos_ usweapons.htm.*

137. One prominent Kurd, Yilmaz Camlibel, argues that after fifteen years of war thousands of Kurdish villages in the south-east have been emptied by the Turkish army but 'Kurdish rights have not advanced even a single centimetre', *The Economist,* 14 August 1999, p.41.

138. The Chief Justice of the Supreme Court of Appeal, Sami Selcuk, asserts that the current constitution had almost no legitimacy. He attacked the traditional notion of a strong centralised system in which the state has more rights than the individual. He also proclaimed that 'the Turkish Constitution was an obstacle to democracy and it had to be changed' while he also attacked the influence which Turkey's military wields over the political process; see Chris Morris in Ankara, *BBC, 6* September 1999.

139. See *Human Rights Watch Report* (1999), *www.hrw.org/reports/1999/turkey/turkey993-09.htm.*

140. For a complete, detailed and updated investigation about the lack of free expression, human rights and suppression of the Kurdish minority in Turkey see *Human Rights Report* (1999); although Turkey is a member of the UN, the Council of Europe and the CSCE and it should abide with the Universal Declaration on Human Rights, Art.2, Art.7, Art.21/2, Art.22, Paris Charter, International Agreement on the Eradication of all Forms of Racial Discrimination, Art.2, Art.27, there is clear evidence that the fundamental rights and freedoms of Kurds are denied. i) It is forbidden for Kurds to give their children Kurdish names; see Personal Status Nr.1587, Art.16, Enforcement Order on Personal Status Regulations, 8 March 1997, Nr.7/13269, Art.77. ii) Kurdish people may not express their thoughts in their native language; see Constitution of the Turkish Republic, Art.3 Section 4, Art.28, Art.26, Art.42. iii) No one in Turkey may claim that Kurds exist as a separate people or minority; see Anti-Terror Law Nr.3713, Art.8, Art.2/2; it is true that Ozal repealed Articles 141, 142 and 163 of the old criminal code, an act which the Turkish and European public praised as a major reform, and a remarkable display of democrati- sation. Sections 2 and 3 of the discarded Article 142 stated 'the thoughts of Kurdish

nationalists are a form of separatism' and proposed heavy sentences. After it was abolished it was 'transplanted' into the Anti-Terror Law which made certain forms of expression [Kurdish] criminal offences. Kurds cannot produce publications in the form of newspapers, magazines, see Constitution, Art.28 Sections 5 and 7, Art.30, Press Law Nr.5680, Art.31/1, or produce films, video cassettes, theatre works, see Law Nr.3257, Law Nr.2559 concerning police powers, Art.8d or establish radio/TV stations, see Law 2954 concerning radio and TV, Art.4a, 5f and so on; for a complete explication see *www.burn.ucsd.edu/archives*. All but 22 of the 177 Articles of the Turkish Constitution ensure that the Kurds are not allowed to possess their fundamental rights and freedoms. Hence, neither the Constitution nor the Criminal Code makes use of the word 'Kurd', rather Kurdish nationality and Kurdish identity are covered by the notion of that which 'violated the territorial and national integrity of the state'.

141. Tamar Gabelnick, 'In Focus: Turkey: Arms and Human Rights', *Foreign Policy in Focus*, 4, 16 (May, 1999) p.3.

142. The European Court of Human Rights ruled on 7 August 1999 that Turkey has denied citizens the right to free speech and a fair trial. Turkey was found guilty of human rights violations. All cases involve Turkish nationals of Kurdish origin, *Associated Press*, 7/8/1999; the Council of Europe accused Turkey on 9 June 1999 of 'repeated and serious' human rights violations by government security forces against Kurds, *Agence France-Presse*, 10 June 1999. According to a law which was approved recently Turkey's Parliament wants to free common criminals (26,538) but keep its political prisoners behind bars (10,000 mainly Kurdish dissidents and Islamic militants). Semi Selcuk, the chief of Turkey's appeal court was blunter 'It's impossible to understand the contents of this bill.... Either you have democracy or you don't. In Turkey there is no democracy', see 'An Ill-Judged Amnesty', *The Economist*, 4 September 1999, p.48.

143. 'Going Wolfish', *The Economist*, 12 June 1999, p.55. Even Izzet Sedes, a columnist on the daily 'Aksam' newspaper, stated that 'the soldiers' interruption of politics in Turkey is still continuing' and 'Turkey has been unable to fulfill democracy and human rights fully', *Aksam*, 6 October 1999.

144. The United Nations High Commissioner for Human Rights, Mary Robinson, expressed concern that certain aspects of the legal proceedings deviated from international standards on the right to a fair trial before an independent and impartial tribunal. Robinson said Ocalan's lawyers were repeatedly subjected to threats and harassment, and stated it was particularly disquieting that the Court had sentenced him to death. The London based Human Rights International said that Ocalan was sentenced to death 'at the conclusion of a trial that violated both national law and international standards for fair trials'; see Niccolo Sarno, 'Rights-Europe: Ocalan's Sentence Drives Turkey away from EU', *World News, Internet Press Service*, 30 June 1999, *www.oneworld.org.*

145. See 'Ocalan and the Taboo', *The Guardian* 23 June 1999.

146. See *Daily Telegraph*, 19 July 1999, and *BBC News*, 23 July 1999.

147. A blunt message which is making it plain that it would like to see better treatment of the Kurds was delivered by Harold Koh, the American Assistant Secretary of State, during a 'listening tour' which included the south-east, *The Economist*, 14 August 1999, p.41.

148. Gabelnick, 'In Focus', p.4.

149. Onis, 'Turkey in the Post', p.66.

150. Characteristically in an interview with the newspaper *Peloponisos*, 9 January 1998, the former Greek Chief of the General Staff Admiral Liberis, mentioned that former Turkish Chief of the General Staff Karadayi, jokingly suggested to Liberis to 'stage a coup', and 'they do not need the politicians in order to solve Greek–Turkish problems'.

151. Even a columnist of a right wing Turkish newspaper *Turkiye* highlights the lack of democracy in modern Turkey, 'in order to obtain the standards that the EU wants, we should adopt democracy sincerely', *Turkiye*, 7 October 1999. In August 2002 the Turkish parliament

overwhelmingly approved a raft of sweeping reforms, in an attempt to meet the EU's preconditions for taking Turkey's bid for membership seriously. For more details on the reforms see 'Great – If They Really Happen', *The Economist*, 10 August 2002, p.35. Even though the new laws look good on paper, the EU would like to see if they will materialise in practice.

152. Taking into consideration the aforementioned analysis about Turkey's lack of democracy I should also cite that Conway Henderson points out the more democratic the government, the less likely the government will choose repression as a means of rule. It is expected that the worse the conditions of democracy, socio-economic needs, inequality, the rate of economic growth, and economic level, the worse will be the conditions of repression. For further study see C.W. Henderson, 'Conditions Affecting the Use of Political Repression', *Journal of Conflict Resolution*, 35, 1 (March, 1991) pp.120–42. Shannon Lindsey Blanton stresses 'that the more democratic a country, the less likelihood a repression of human rights'; see S.L. Blanton, 'Instruments of Security or Tools of Repression: Arms Imports and Human Rights Conditions in Developing Countries', *Journal of Peace Research*, 36, 2 (1999) p.237. See also map on *The Economist* which illustrates the lack of freedom in Turkey, 'A Survey of the New Geopolitics: The Road to 2050', *The Economist*, 31 July 1999, p.13. The lack of civil society and civil structure was highlighted in a tragic way during a massive earthquake on 17 August 1999 in Ismit; see *Turkish Daily News* comment, 20 August 1999 and *The Independent*, 'They Can Kill Kurds But Can't Run Soup Kitchens', 24 August 1999.

153. Metin Heper, 'Consolidating Turkish Democracy', *Journal Of Democracy*, 3, 2 (1992) pp.105–17.

154. See D.B. Sezer, 'Turkey's Security Policies', *Adelphi Paper*, 164 (spring, 1981) p.10.

155. For further study see H. Barkey, 'Why Military Regimes Fail: The Perils of Transition', *Armed Forces and Society*, 16, 2 (1990) pp.169–90.

156. See 'In The Name of The Father', *Economist*, 1 August 1998, p.75.

157. M. Heper and A. Evid (eds), *State and Democracy and the Military: Turkey in the 1980s*, (Berlin: Walter de Gruyter, 1988) pp. 158–75.

158. See James Pettifer, *The Turkish Labyrinth: Atatturk and the New Islam* (London: Penguin Books, 1998) p.61.

159. ibid., p.62.

160. ibid., pp.62–3.

161. This view has also been supported by Pettifer, 'The Turkish', p.64–5.

162. For an analysis of the Turkish rearmament programme see T. Dokos and N. Pronotarios, *The Military Security in the 1990's: Problems of South-East Europe* (Athens: Tourikis, 1994).

163. NATO policy dictated that those countries required to lose systems under the CFE Treaty, principally Germany and the US, should transfer this equipment (quite sophisticated weapon systems) to those NATO members with obsolete equipment in order to upgrade their capabilities. Since Greece and Turkey had the largest stocks of old TLEs, they were the principal recipients; see C. Tuck, 'Greece, Turkey and Arms Control', *Defence Analysis*, 12, 1 (1996) pp.26–8.

164. See Ikay Sunar, 'State, Society and Democracy in Turkey' in Mastny and R.C. Nation (eds), *Turkey Between East and West* (Colorado: Westview Press, 1996) pp.152–3.

165. For further study see Max Weber, *Economy and Society* (Berkeley: University of California Press, 1978) pp.268–9.

166. Sunar, 'State', p.151.

167. For further study see T. Stamatopoulos, *O Esoterikos Agonas*, (Athens: Kalbos, 1971) p.202.

168. The small Greek state was destined to rely upon the volition of the protector countries of Britain, France and Russia; see Karabelias, 'Civil–Military', p.73.

169. The appointment of Crown Prince Constantine (1863–1890s) as a commander of chief and inspector of the armed forces led to the division of the officer corps into major groups,

his clients and the rest. For more information about the relations between politicians and the army see V. Papacosma, *The Military in Greek Politics: The 1909 Coup d'Etat* (Kent: Ohio State University Press, 1977) pp.21–3; see also T. Veremis, *Oi Epemvasis tou Stratou stin Elliniki Politiki, 1916–1936* (Athens: Odysseas, 1977) pp.17, 25. Despite the military coup of 1909, the emergence of Venizelos on the political scene of the country led to the complete withdrawal of the army into the barracks, their eventual drastic reconstruction, and the creation of a coherent, efficient and unified armed forces; see J. Campbell and P. Sherrard, *Modern Greece* (New York: Praeger, 1968) pp.27–8. One significant development in the civil-military relations was the personal dispute of Prime Minister Venizelos and King Constantine I over Greece's stance in the First World War, which led to national schism (*ethnikos dixasmos*) and divided the officer corps into two groups: Venizelists and Monarchists; see G. Karabelias, 'Twenty Years of Civil–Military Relations in Post-dictatorship Greece, 1975–95: Step Toward the Consolidation of Democracy', *Mediterranean Quarterly*, 10, 2 (1999) p.66. The active participation of the military in the schism was the outcome of the strong clientelistic relations that had been developed between officers and politicians. As a result, from 1922 to 1936, the military officers developed a *force majeure* to be actively involved in the political developments of the country; see E. Spyropoulos, *The Greek Military (1909–1941) and the Greek Mutinies in the Middle East (1941–1944)*, Unpublished Ph.D Thesis, Columbia University (1993).

170. For further study about the civil war and the role of Britain see Tim Jones, 'The British Army, and Counter-Guerrilla Warfare in Greece, 1945–1949', *Small Wars & Insurgencies*, 8, 1 (1997) pp.88–106 and E. O'Balance, *The Greek Civil War, 1944–49* (London: Faber, 1966).

171. Karabelias, 'Twenty Years', p.76; see also Nicos Alivizatos, 'The Greek Army in the Late Forties: Toward an Institutional Autonomy', *Journal of the Hellenic Diaspora*, 5 (1978).

172. The leader of the junta G. Papadopoulos declared that he intended to consolidate and restore democracy in the true sense; see C.N. Woodhouse, '"The Revolution" in its Historical Context', in R. Glogg and G. Yiannopoulos (eds), *Greece under Military Rule* (London: Secker & Warburg, 1972) p.16. Ultimately, the junta intended to secure and preserve the autonomy of the military over the politicians, however, it proved incapable to cope with and solve the social, economic and political problems of the country. Papadopulos's attempt to install a puppet civilian government led to the 25 November 1973 coup by the hard-liner head of the Greek Secret Service D. Ioannides. The latter's effort to overthrow President Makarios and install his own puppet government in Cyprus triggered off the Turkish invasion and proved catastrophic for the junta; for more details see Solon Georgiades, *Istoria tis Diktatorias*, 1, 2, 3, 4 (Athens: Kapopoulos, 1975) C.M.Y. Woodhouse, *The Rise and the Fall of the Greek Colonels* (London: Granada, 1985); see also Clogg and Yiannopoulos, 'Greece Under Military Rule'.

173. P.N. Diamandouros, 'Politics and Culture in Greece, 1974–91: An Interpretation', in Richard Clogg (ed.), *Greece, 1981–89: The Populist Decade* (Houndmills: Macmillan Press, 1993) pp.7–8. On the 1974 Greek transition to democratic politics see Harry J. Psomiades, 'Greece: From The Colonels' Rule to Democracy', in John H. Herz (ed.) *From Dictatorship to Democracy: Coping with the Legacies of Authoritarianism and Totalitarianism* (Westport, 1982) pp.251–73. Susannah Verney and T. Couloumbis, 'State-International Systems Interaction and the Greek Transition to Democracy in the mid 1970s', in Geofrey Pridham (ed.), *Encouraging Democracy: The International Context of Regime Transition in Southern Europe* (Leicester: Leicester University Press, 1991).

174. Students of politics have been taught repeatedly both in empirical and theoretical studies that political parties are the founding pillar in the functioning of liberal parliamentary democracy. Andrew Heywood asserts 'that constitutional parties operating in a context of electoral competition tend to be portrayed as bastions of democracy ... the existence of such parties is often seen as a litmus test of a healthy democratic system', A. Heywood, *Politics* (Houndmills: Macmillan, 1997) p.233.

175. Kevin Featherstone, 'Political Parties and Democratic Consolidation in Greece', in Geoffrey Pridham (ed.), *Securing Democracy: Political Parties and Democratic Consolidation in Southern Europe* (London: Routledge, 1990) p.179.

176. A referendum took place on 8 December 1974 which decided the abolition of the monarchy; 69% voted against the King's return. Karamanlis took strictly a neutral stance and forbade his ministers to express their preferences publicly, while at the same time allowing them to free vote. By contrast, George Mavros (EK-ND, Centre Union-New Forces) and Andreas Papandreou (PASOK) both declared their party's support for a republic. The Monarchists were allowed four television broadcasts, including two by the King himself, in which he stressed the depth of his family's devotion to their country. However, the poll went in favour of a republic by a margin of two to one. For more information about the political career of Karamanlis and his vital role towards the restoration of democracy in Greece see C.M. Woodhouse, *Karamanlis: The Restorer of Greek Democracy* (Oxford: Clarendon Press, 1982).

177. On 24 February 1975 a conspiracy by officers loyal to the former military regime to stage a new military coup was uncovered by the government. The chief instigator of this coup was Maj. Gen. Dimitrios Ioannides. As a result, twenty-three officers were arrested and tried; prosecution witnesses stated that the rebels had claimed the support of defeated Royalist elements, the Primate of the Orthodox Church and former PM Stefanos Stefanopoulos. The leniency of their sentences caused some surprise; however, in less than six months, the protagonists of the 1967 coup, the leaders of the February 1975 coup, together with the major figures in the suppression of the Polytechnic uprising were brought to trial and received sentences varying from life imprisonment for the major figures to lesser sentences to others. Furthermore, one hundred officers whom the junta had forced into retirement returned to active duty in order to strengthen Karamanlis's control over the armed forces, *To Vima*, 1 March 1975. Karamanlis also declared that his own life had been in danger, 'Of all persons, I am the most exposed to the wrath of the junta'; see Neovi Karakatsanis, 'Do Attitudes Matter? Military and Democratic Consolidation in Greece', *Balkan Forum*, 5 (June 1997) p.109.

178. The enactment of exceptional powers for the President of the Republic caused political uproar among the political elites. G. Mavros said that he would campaign for true parliamentary democracy. A. Papandreou went further and he asserts that it was 'no better than the constitution of dictator Papadopoulos'. Katsoudas stresses that the new powers to the Head of State 'exceeded by far … those of the monarch under the 1952 Constitution. However, Karamanlis's Gaullist imposition over parliamentary democracy was seen as a panacea since he 'wished to avoid the fatal weaknesses of the form of government that collapsed'. See Featherstone, 'Political Parties', p.183.

179. M. Spourdalakis, 'Securing Democracy in Post-Authoritarian Greece: The Role Of Political Parties', in Geoffrey Pridham and Paul. G. Lewis (eds) *Stabilising Fragile Democracies: Comparing New Party Systems in Southern and Eastern Europe* (London: Routledge, 1996) p.169.

180. Clogg , 'A Short History', p.107.

181. For further study see N.P. Diamandouros, 'Politics and Constitutionalism in Greece: The 1975 Constitutional in Historical Perspective', in Chenabi and Stepan (eds), *Politics, Society and Democracy: Comparative Studies in Honor of Juan J. Linz*, 3 (Boulder, Colorado: Westview, 1999).

182. On 14 August 1974, Karamanlis in order to show his frustration and disappointment about NATO's lack of action against Turkey, decided to withdraw Greece from NATO command, though Greece remained a member of the alliance.

183. The main threat is not the communist threat but the actual threat from Turkey, which after its aggressive manifestation with the Cyprus invasion, started to make territorial claims in the Aegean. Woodhouse, 'Karamanlis', p.274.

184. Spourdalakis, 'Securing', p.169. Karamanlis was a great admirer of the European idea and Greece's destiny in Europe. For Karamanlis Greece was 'the Mediterranean balcony of Europe'. He also stressed that 'Europe is our own place, where Greek and Roman and Christian spirit was synthesised, and to which Greece brought the ideas of freedom, truth and beauty', Woodhouse, 'Karamanlis', pp.274–5.
185. Spourdalakis, 'Securing', p.170.
186. There have been unsubstantiated rumours which suggested that two abortive coups took place under the Papandreou government. The first attempt is said to have occurred on 31 March 1982. Of the second of the two alleged attempts, said to have taken place on 26 February 1983, reports indicated that there was wide circulation of rumours of a coup coinciding with military exercises in the Athens area scheduled for that month. Furthermore, on 10 June 1981, Nea Demokratia's Minister Of Defence, Evangellos Averoff-Tossizza, announced that an anti-governmental conspiracy by retired army officers planned for 1 June had been prevented by the rescheduling of military exercises. For further details see Neovi Karakatsanis, 'Do Attitudes Matter? The Military and Democratic Consolidation in Greece', *Armed Forces & Society*, 24, Part 2 (1997) pp.294–5. However, these reports cannot be substantiated. *Au contraire*, after a series of official and unofficial (off the record) interviews which I conducted during 1997–9 with retired and current military officers, including a top military officer (General) during the junta period, these attempted coups were considered and characterised as 'meaningless'.
187. C.M. Woodhouse, 'Karamanlis', p.225.
188. George Kremmydas, *Oi anthropoi tis Juntas meta tin Diktactoria* (Athens: Exantas, 1984) pp.27–37. The total number of dismissals and replacements was about 100,000. They included all local councillors and mayors, all the members of agricultural committees, all the directors of state legal organisations; the purge of army officers extended to all those who had played an active role in over-throwing the democracy or supporting the dictatorship. It is also worth mentioning that in later years Karamanlis spent much time in Officers Clubs and military gatherings, elsewhere, to form his own impressions of the mood of the army and to assure himself of its reliability.
189. C.P. Danopoulos, *Warriors and Politicians in Modern Greece* (Chapel Hill, 1985) p.133.
190. It has been argued by Alivizatos that although the civilian government was made responsible for formulating the country's defence policy as well as the appointment of military leadership through KYSEA, it was the military leaders who were responsible for the implementation of all decisions. In case of emergency, the military could assume direct responsibility in defence policy making. See Nikos Alivizatos, *I Sintagmatiki thesi ton Enoplon Dinameon: I Arxi tou Politikou Elenghou* (Athens: Sakoulas, 1987). Act 660/1977 was finally replaced in 1995 with Act 2292/1995.
191. Danopoulos, 'Warriors', p.140. De-juntification must not be confused with democratisation since the former strictly implies the attempt to purge and prosecute officers associated with the previous military regimes.
192. Danopulos, 'From Balkonies to Tanks: Post-Junta Civil Military Relations in Greece', *Journal of Political and Military Sociology*, 13 (1985) p.93.
193. T.A. Couloumbis, 'PASOK's Foreign Policies, 1981–89: Continuity or Change'? in R. Clogg (ed.), *Greece, 1981–89: The Populist Decade.* For more information about PASOK's relation with Turkey see Van Coufoudakis, 'PASOK and Greek–Turkish Relations', pp.167–80, in Clogg (ed.), ibid., and defence policies under PASOK's government see Thanos Veremis, 'Defence & Security Policies under PASOK', pp.181–9, in Clogg (ed.), ibid.
194. It has been reported that a complete withdrawal from the NATO alliance would be met with strong opposition from the pro-NATO Greek military personnel. See Heinz-Jurgen Axt, 'On the Way to Socialist Self-Reliance? PASOK's Government Policy in Greece', *Journal of Modern Greek Studies*, 2 (1984).
195. Karabelias, 'Civil–Military', pp.54–5.

196. All of the military officers that have been interviewed stated that the last twenty years of civilian supremacy over military is an 'indisputable fact'. Retired Admiral Engolfopoulos and Retired General Opropoulos claimed that conditions for staging a military intervention or even thinking about it did not exist in Greece from 1974 and after, *Elefherotypia*, 2 March 1983. Furthermore, the 1995 law gave the Minister of Defence the final say on military matters. Not only is the entire chain of command accountable to him, but he has now acquired his own civilian advisers on questions that cover the whole spectrum from procurement to strategy. The Chief of the Hellenic National Defence General Staff, who according to the new law will become Commander-in-Chief of the armed forces in time of war has been deprived of certain responsibilities which have been transferred to the Defence Minister. In short, the 1995 law favours centralisation of authority and on the whole enhances the government's control over the military. Government's control over the military was highlighted in the Greece–Turkish crisis in January 1996 when Admiral Lymberis was hurriedly replaced by Air Force General A. Tsoganis without being given the time stipulated by the law to brief his successor. See T. Veremis, *The Military in Greek Politics: From Independence to Democracy* (London: Hurst & Company, 1997) pp.170–83.

197. Karakatsanis, 'Do Attitudes', p.126.

198. See Dimitrios Smokovitis, 'Greece', in Charles Moskos and Frank Wood (eds), *The Military: More Than Just a Job?* (New York: Pergammon-Brassey's Publishers Ltd, 1988).

199. For further and detailed analysis about the relations of Greece with the EU and the concept of European integration see Michael J. Tsinisizelis and Dimitris N. Chryssochoou, *Between 'Disharmony' and 'Symbiosis': The Greek Political System and European Integration*, University of Reading, Research Paper, Unpublished (1997).

200. K. Karamanlis, 'The Ideal of a United Europe', in P. Drakopoulos (ed.), *Greece–EEC: Political, Economic and Cultural Aspects* (Athens, 1979) p.39. For more information about the prospect of political modernisation in Greece in the context of European integration see Andreas Moschonas, *European Integration and Prospects of Modernisation in Greece*, Research Paper, University of Reading (1997). See also P. Kazakos and P.C. Ioakimides (eds), *Greece and EC Membership Evaluated* (London: Pinter Publishers, 1994).

201. For changes in the Greek party systems between pre- and post-authoritarian periods see Kerstin Hamann and Barbara Sgouraki-Kinsey, 'Re-entering Electoral Politics: Reputation and Party System Change in Spain and Greece', *Party Politics*, 5, 1 (1999) pp.55–77. For more information about how lower class interests have been represented since the fall of the dictatorial regime in 1974 see Dimitris Kioukas, 'Interest Representation and Modernisation Policies in Greece: Lessons Learned from the Study of Labor and Farmers', *Journal of Modern Greek Studies*, 15, 2 (1997) pp.303–24.

202. N. Mouzelis, *Modern Greece: Facets of Underdevelopment* (London: Macmillan, 1978).

203. D. Sassoon, *One Hundred Years Of Socialism* (London: Fontana Press, 1996) p.628.

204. Euclid Tsakalotos, 'The Political Economy of Social Democratic Economic Policies: The PASOK Experiment in Greece', *Oxford Review of Economic Policy*, 14, 1 (1998) pp.129–30. However, the current Greek government has shown substantial progress on many fronts, and many financial analysts consider Greece's entry into the Eurozone from 1 March 2000 as certain, *see Sunday Times*, 29 August 1999, Yannos Papantoniou, 'The World Economy and Greece: Recent Economic Developments', *Thesis*, 1, 3 (1997).

205. It is very common in Greece to secure a job in the public sector with the help of politicians. As a result, the politician is not interested about the quality and the efficiency of the person who is employed, and the employees know their positions are safe because it is their 'contact' which matters, rather than their supervisors. Relationships can also facilitate customers' access to services to which they are entitled.

206. P.N. Diamandouros, 'Greek Politics & Society in the 1990s', in G. Allison and K. Nicolaidis (eds), *The Greek Paradox: Promise vs. Performance* (Massachusetts: MIT Press, 1997) p.27.

207. P. Schmitter, 'Organised Interests and Democratic Consolidation in Southern Europe', in

Gunther *et al.*, *The Politics of Democratic Consolidation: Southern Europe in Comparative Perspective* (Baltimore: Johns Hopkins University Press, 1995) p.293; see also D. Kioukias *Organising Interests in Greece: Labour, Agriculture, Local Government and Political Development During Metapolitefsi*, Ph.D Dissertation, University of Birmingham (1991).

208. The headline inflation rate is at 2.1% in July 1999, which is the lowest since the late 1960s. The budget deficit is projected to shrink this year to 1.9% of GDP, well within the 3% of GDP ceiling set by the Maastricht Treaty. The public debt will still be more than 100% of GDP, well outside the 60% of GDP target. But it is set to fall for the fourth straight year, in line with the let-out clause under the Maastricht treaty of a steady declining trend. For further study about Greece's economic performance see *www.cthesis.com*, *23 August 1999*, *To Vima*, *Anaptixi*, 22 August 1999 and 14 August 1999.

209. For more information see Francis Fukuyama, *The End Of History and the Last Man* (New York: Free Press, 1992); see also 'A Survey of the New Geopolitics', *The Economist*, 31 July 1999. The belief that Greece is adopting the neo-liberalist school of thought has been supported by Giorgos Mourtos, *Elada kai Tourkia: Stin Meta-Psixropolemiki Epoxi* (Athens: Troxalia, 1997) p.40–2.

210. This view was evident in the Foreign Office and the ELIAMEP. Evidence of the neo-liberalism school can be found in the current Greek Foreign Office, with main advocate the Greek Foreign Minister George Papandreou; see *To Vima*, Interview with the Foreign Minister, 5 September 1999. See also *Kathimerini*, 6 September 1999. The realist school in Greece has been patronised by the Panteion University, the IDIS and by most of the military officers; see A. Platias, *To Neo Diethnes Systima: Realistiki Prosegisi Diethnon Sxeseon* (Athens: Papazisis, 1995) p.32, pp.171–2 and Ioanis Loukas *Sixroni Politiki Istoria kai Pagkosmioi Polemi: Agli kai Germani Theoritiki tis Isxios* (Athens: Troxalia, 1996).

211. The main representatives of the realist school are, Thucydides, Machiavelli, Clausewitz and Kissinger. For further study see Anatol Rapoport (ed.), *Clausewitz: On War* (London: Penguin Books, 1968) pp.93–7; L.M. Johnson, *Thucydides, Hobbes and the Interpretation of Realism* (Dekalb: Northern Illinois Press, 1993); Bruce Russet, 'A Post-Thucydides post-Cold War World', *Occasional Research Papers* – Special Issue, IDIS, Athens (1996); F. Gilbert, 'Machiavelli: The Renaissance of the Art of War', in Edward Mead Earlie (ed.), *Makers of Modern Strategy*, (Princeton: Princeton University Press, 1972); C. Bell, *The Diplomacy of Détente: The Kissinger Era* (New York: St Martin's Press, 1977); W. Isaacson, 'How the World Works', *Time*, 11 April 1994, p.80.

212. The adoption of the realist school must not be interpreted as lack of democracy; however, it highlights once more the power and the dominant role of the Turkish state (etatism).

213. The belief that democracy has not been implemented in Turkey was also insinuated by Ilnur Cevik, 'to the European mind the military in Europe is under the sole authority of the civilian government and the situation in Turkey is unacceptable. Europeans feel problems like fundamentalism should be solved within the scope of a democratic parliamentary system ... [Therefore he believes] our military has to remember that the secular system can be much better protected when Turkey is truly democratic', *Turkish Daily News*, 27 October 1999. Yilmaz Oztuna also stressed 'we should adopt democracy sincerely', *Turkiye*, 7 October 1999. Ilnur Cevik stressed that 'we can not jail people for expressing their views' referring to the decision of the Court of Appeals which approved a one year prison sentence for leading human rights activist Akin Birdal on charges on sedition, *Turkish Daily News*, 28 October 1998. Fehmi Koru also stressed the problematic relationship of Turkey with democracy. He claimed that 'we have two pictures side by side. In the first, people are embracing President Clinton and his entourage, devouring what he says in speeches about democracy and human rights ... In the second picture, some important men in authority are anxious that President Clinton's visit should finish soon, that the effect of his speeches be forgotten ... Another bunch of people in the corner of the same picture are desperate to turn the tide back with the kind of acts they have been

accustomed to committing [referring to the prosecutor of the Supreme Court of Appeals which characterised the intellectuals who demand more freedoms as "Friends of the Devil"]', *Turkish Daily News*, 18 November 1999; see also *The Economist*, 23 October 1999, pp.65–6.

5

Intra-alliance Conflict Resolution: Uncharted Waters for NATO

The best way to predict the future is to create it.
(Peter F. Drucker)

The evidence looked at suggested that it is not possible to establish a pluralistic security community in the eastern Mediterranean. NATO is the key actor in the sense that it has the greatest influence on these two countries. It is necessary therefore, to assess what contribution NATO can make towards maintaining regional peace and security and increase the stability of the Greek–Turkish relationship in the absence of a structural solution to the problem of the Turkish political system. Traditional confidence-building measures have been applied to states that are potential antagonists rather than to allies. Proposing them for Greece and Turkey is therefore rather unusual. However, as this book has demonstrated Greece and Turkey form a *Hybrid Region* and therefore confidence-building measures are appropriate to their relations.

Before attempting to introduce a series of mechanisms which would facilitate the prevention of intra-alliance conflict in the eastern Mediterranean, two specific factors should be taken into consideration. First, it is certain that an intra-alliance confrontation between Greece and Turkey would cause a spill-over effect with catastrophic repercussions for the Balkan region and the NATO alliance. This view can be expressed by a simple statement such as: in case of a sub-regional conflict (such as Chechnya, or East Timor) there is **high cost** for the parties (economic, military, political, societal) involved but **low consequence** for the region or the continent itself. In the case of a military confrontation in the eastern Mediterranean it will be **high cost** (for Turkey, and Greece) and **high consequence** for the rest of the region including most of the major western organisations (EU, WEU, NATO).

Second, since most of the Aegean Sea constitutes part of the Greek national territory, a fact which is based on International Treaties,

International Law[1] and the New Convention on the Law of the Sea, the possibility of implementing a solution based on 'equitable principles' – an assertion favoured by Turkey – would *only* affect the sovereign rights of Greece[2] (Figure 3).

Developments in the eastern Mediterranean during the 1990s reveal that the chasm between Greece and Turkey appears deeper than ever. During NATO's bombardment of Yugoslavia, Greek public opinion sided strongly with the Serbs – highlighting the deep religious and cultural fault-lines running through the alliance.[3] On the other hand, Turkey, an indirect participant in NATO's air strikes, views Kosovo – home to a small Turkish community since Ottoman times – as part of its geo-political 'backyard' and one of many places where rivalry between itself and Russia is being conducted.[4] Greeks, meanwhile, condemned the west's imposition of double standards: 'going to war with Serbia while turning a blind eye to Turkey's harsh treatment of its Kurdish minority'.[5]

Elsewhere in the Balkan region, it has become obvious that association with NATO is no longer just a matter of harmless peace-keeping exercises and diplomatic rhetoric. Countries near the unstable zone of Kosovo – such as Albania, FYROM and even Bulgaria – have been alleging that NATO should prepare to give them a formal defence guarantee or a membership status.[6]

As noted in the previous chapters, NATO's main concern in the Mediterranean during the Cold War, was the presence of a

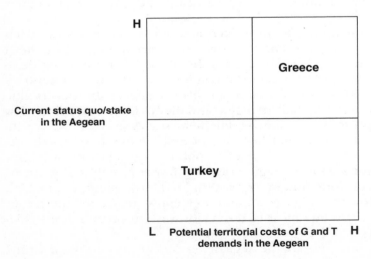

Figure 3 Aegean matrix

Soviet maritime capability developed for deployment in the region (the Sovemedron or Fifth Eskadra), the deployment of Soviet military personnel and equipment in friendly states around the littoral and the deployment of Soviet forces on the Greek–Turkish borders.[7]

The end of the Cold War and the endorsement by NATO of the New Strategic Concept of 1991 shifted the concerns of the alliance towards a series of multiple security threats. The New Strategic Concept emphasised that

> The stability and peace of the countries on the southern periphery of Europe are important for the security of the Alliance, as the 1991 Gulf War has shown. This is all the more so because of the build-up of military power and the proliferation of weapons technologies in the area, including weapons of mass destruction and ballistic missiles capable of reaching the territory of some member states of the Alliance.[8]

The Strategic Concept confirmed the alliance's commitment to safeguard the freedom and security of its members by political and military means, but it also reflects new commitments in the fields of crisis management and partnership that NATO now performs in order to enhance the security and stability of the Euro-Atlantic area.[9] With regards to the Mediterranean region, NATO has developed two main objectives: i) to survey the strategic environment and assess foreseeable security challenges and risks; ii) to cultivate peaceful relations with all the southern Mediterranean countries. However, the existence of the *Hybrid Region* in the eastern Mediterranean (see previous chapter) which has spawned an intra-alliance dispute between Greece and Turkey has hindered the development of the new alliance policy and most significantly has threatened to topple NATO's foundations.

Unequivocally, NATO is confronted with a serious challenge in formulating and implementing policy in the eastern Mediterranean. Greco-Turkish differences (over Cyprus, air space, continental shelf, maritime boundaries) have complicated NATO planning. Furthermore, US foreign policy-makers regard the stability of the eastern Mediterranean as vital for US and NATO interests in the region.[10]

The post-Cold War era has been marked by a significant re-orientation of NATO forces in the southern region. During the Cold War, geo-political realities constituted the Central Front as the focus of confrontation. The southern region, albeit critical to re-supply during the Cold War, was widely perceived as a secondary theatre. Currently, 'the Southern Region has replaced the Central Region as the cutting edge of Alliance concerns for stability'.[11]

As a result, the CFE Treaty in 1990, designed to control offensive operations in the Central Front between NATO and the Warsaw Pact allowed the reinforcement of Turkish and Greek military capabilities.[12]

Since the end of the Cold War the alliance has initiated significant changes in policy, procedure and structure while reducing and restructuring headquarters and staffs to achieve a streamlined and efficient alliance command structure. As a result, the following changes have occurred since 1991: i) defence budgets have decreased by 30 per cent; ii) armed forces have decreased in size by 28 to 40 per cent for most countries; iii) land forces are down 25 per cent, major warships by 20 per cent and combat aircraft by 30 per cent; iv) US forces in Europe are down 66 per cent from a total of 300,000 to 100,000 military personnel.[13] Moreover, after 20 months of serious deliberations, a new NATO military structure was approved on 2 December 1997.[14]

The new military structure consists of two overarching SCs, one for the Atlantic and one for Europe, with three RCs under SC Atlantic and two under SC Europe. Reporting to the RC in Europe are Component Commands and Joint Sub Regional Commands.[15]

The RC South covers approximately 1.5 million square miles which stretches from the Strait of Gibraltar to the north-eastern coast of Turkey on the Black Sea in the east and from the North African littoral in the south to the Alps and Crimea in the north.[16] Furthermore, the RC South encompasses the volatile Balkan peninsula which includes politically unsteady countries such as Albania and Yugoslavia. The long-debated NATO command structure on the one hand, managed to accommodate Greek and Spanish demands by establishing Joint Sub Regional Commanders (SouthCentre[17] and SouthWest respectively), but could not eliminate significant differences between Greece and Turkey over technical issues with regards to sub-regional commands.[18]

To return to the broader regional picture, it is critical to stress NATO's shift of attention to the strategic environment of the Mediterranean with an accompanying out-of-area focus on Middle Eastern and North African problems and challenges, including those of terrorism, radical Islamic fundamentalism and militant states with advanced weapons capabilities. However, the failure to eliminate the possibility of an intra-alliance conflict between two important NATO members questions the ability of NATO to engage in an effective role in the post-Cold War era.[19] Having witnessed the importance of NATO's south-eastern members such as the land, sea and air communications that they offered during the Gulf War and the NATO (Operation Allied Force) operation in Kosovo, establishment of allied solidarity should be high on the NATO agenda. If older NATO structures failed in meeting intra-alliance challenges and differences, the new ones must deal with them effectively and swiftly.[20] If the current eastern Mediterranean situation is providing an important test, the NATO performance so far has been unreliable, and hesitant.[21]

The post-Cold War era has witnessed the emergence of the Balkans as the most conflict-prone region in Europe and one of the world's 'powder kegs'. The establishment of a stable and peaceful environment in a region which is characterised by deep heterogeneity is a difficult task.[22] With the end of the Cold War

> a security vacuum has been created in the region – especially as far as Romania and Bulgaria are concerned – which existing western security frameworks have failed to adequately fill. In addition, the release of the various nationalistic aspirations and territorial disputes – the most prominent one being the dissolution of the former Yugoslavia, has tragically affected relations between the states of the region and hindered the development of Inter-Balkan Co-operation, as well as other forms of co-operation on a multilateral level.[23]

Currently, most of the Balkan countries are in a transition phase and they are trying vigorously to tackle social, economic and political problems.[24] In a region which is overburdened 'with historic and national stereotypes such as the one in Southeastern Europe, a certain strategic culture[25] has been created according to which the various ethno-national entities perceive one another *as a priori* aggressive and threatening.[26]

Furthermore, a certain pattern of asymmetrical relations among the states of the Balkan region in terms of social, political, economic and military power gives rise to additional concern.[27]

So why is NATO essential to the security of the new market-oriented Balkan countries? The signs witnessed so far reveal that NATO is trying to avoid the unstable and blurred landscape of the Balkans with regards to NATO expansion. In his speech for the Carnegie Report and the Balkans Today Conference in Sofia – Bulgaria (2 April 1995) Dr Zbigniev Brzezinski, former national security adviser to President Carter, elucidated NATO's approach to the Balkans: 'NATO will only come to the Balkans when it no longer has to impose security and stability in the region, but can instead secure an existing stability.'[28]

This has been a very delicate way to say that the post-communist Balkan countries have no place in the alliance for the observable future.[29]

Unfortunately, the truth of the matter is: i) that the Balkans entered the twenty-first century as a byword for instability and conflict; ii) the Balkan countries cannot reproduce security and stability by themselves:

> The Balkans traditionally reflects and amplifies all waves of instability
> generated throughout Europe. Bearing the legacy of three powerful
> empires of the past (the Ottoman, the Habsburg and the Russian
> Empire), the Balkans is the embodiment of all-European division,
> rivalries, utopian nationalist projects and ambitions. The Peninsula
> is the cultural border of Europe, the frontier, where all European
> dilemmas – ethnic, nationalist, religious and ideological – reach their
> possible extreme and absurd maximum.[30]

In such a context, two possible scenarios might resolve the Balkan
imbroglio. The first scenario presupposes the creation of ethnically
and culturally unified nation states. The second scenario requires the
development of democratic state structures, based on multicultural
principles and respect. NATO's recent involvement in Balkan
affairs through the IFOR and KFOR operations indicates clearly that
the alliance possesses the real authority to preserve and promote
peace.

As a result this chapter will evaluate the role of NATO as a conflict-
prevention mechanism. Since the spill-over effect in case of intra-
alliance conflict will unleash a chain of serious repercussions not
only for NATO and the eastern Mediterranean, but for the Balkan
region as a whole, an assessment of what role NATO can play in the
eastern Mediterranean and in the Balkans will be made separately.

CAN NATO BE A POSITIVE INFLUENCE?

At this moment of history NATO is at a crossroads. On the one hand,
NATO is adapting to the new risks and challenges of the post-Cold
War era and on the other hand, it is confronted with the prospect of
an intra-alliance conflict in the eastern Mediterranean between two
indispensable allies.[31] Another critical issue that NATO faces is the
applicability of the treaty to such a conflict:

> Would NATO countries be obliged to defend the victim against the
> aggressor? If so, how would that square with the alliance's integrated
> command structure? What would the implications be for the treaty
> signatories' commitment to solve their differences peacefully? Would
> this then set a precedent for non-negotiated conflict resolution
> between NATO allies.[32]

In such a context, it is imperative for NATO and its members to undertake a concerted effort to deal with the problems that beset the Greek–Turkish dyad or, conversely, to safeguard the interests of the alliance and attempt to contain the effects of a Greek–Turkish crisis. So what are the policy options available for the NATO alliance?

The last thirty years have been marked by continuous, concerted diplomatic efforts on both the bilateral and multilateral level to resolve Greek–Turkish differences. Although there were occasional improvements in their bilateral relations, post-Cold War Greek and Turkish security considerations are still dominated by their mutual suspicion.

Despite being NATO allies for nearly fifty years, relations between Greece and Turkey have long been characterised by mutual suspicion and a hostility and rivalry that has led them to the brink of war on more than one occasion. Former Greek Foreign Minister Theodoros Pangalos commented in 1998 that

> Our relations with Turkey have taken an added downturn since 1996, when our neighbour added direct territorial claims to its existing policy of demands, threats of war, and constant pressure in an attempt to subvert the territorial status-quo established more than seventy years ago by international law and treaties. Its attempt to back these claims by military means in January 1996 resulted in a crisis that fell short of war.[33]

A member of the main opposition ND Party described Turkey as 'Greece's main adversary'.[34] Every Greek government since 1955 has seen Turkey as its primary security threat. Similarly, Turkey also saw Greece as the main external threat of the country.[35]

In the second half of the 1990s Greek–Turkish relations deteriorated to their worst level since the Turkish invasion of Cyprus in 1974. In January 1996 the two countries came close to war during the crisis over the disputed island of Imia/Kardak. Relations reached a further low point in February 1999 when Turkey discovered that Greece had provided shelter to the Kurdish rebel leader, Abdullah Ocalan.[36] The Imia/Kardak crisis[37] convinced the Greek military that the risk of war with Turkey was a real one and therefore increased their misgivings about the relative state of the Greek–Turkish strategic balance. Turkey's population is nearly six times the size of Greece's and Turkey's GDP is twice that of Greece. Since the mid-1980s Turkey's military expenditure and weapons acquisition has consistently exceeded that of Greece.[38] In attempting to compete with this, Greece during the 1990s was forced to spend a higher proportion of its GDP on defence than any other western nation. As a result of the Turkish announcement in April 1996 of a ten-year $31 billion armament programme,[39] Greece responded in November of that year with a $14 billion programme for the next five years, 1996–2000.[40] That the risk of war between the two countries is a real one was demonstrated when Greece became a full member of the WEU. The WEU states attached a protocol to the articles of Greek accession declaring that the Article 5 defence guarantee would not apply in the event of a war between Greece and another NATO member (i.e. Turkey).[41] As the brinkmanship continues, there is an obvious need for the international community, particularly NATO, to develop a comprehensive risk reduction strategy aimed at decreasing the threat of war in the eastern Mediterranean.

MILITARY ANTAGONISM IN THE EASTERN MEDITERRANEAN

Currently Greece and Turkey are locked in seemingly intractable disputes. Notwithstanding this, both countries have been party to agreements such as the CFE Treaty, the CSCE, the Vienna Document and the UN Register on Conventional Arms Transfers.[42] The Aegean Sea is witnessing an unprecedented arms build-up which contradicts with the current orientation of most European countries.[43]

It is worth mentioning here, that independently most of the south-eastern European states have implemented a number of confidence and security building measures (CSBMs). Greece and Bulgaria signed in October 1993, in Athens, the 'Text of Improved Measures Complementary to those of the Vienna Document'.[44] Similar CSBM agreements have been signed between Bulgaria and Turkey (Sofia Document),[45] Albania and Turkey (Tirana Document),[46] the FYROM and Turkey (Skopje Document), Albania and Bulgaria, Bulgaria and Romania (Veliko Tirnovo Document)[47] and Romania and Hungary.[48]

Despite the aforementioned CSBMs in the Balkan region, 'crisis instability is clearly still a problem in the Aegean, as demonstrated in the crises that erupted in March 1987 and January 1996 between Greece and Turkey'.[49]

Although Greece and Turkey decided on 4 June 1998 to resurrect and implement two declarations that had been signed in 1988, neither country has so far entirely complied.[50] On the contrary, on 29 March 1999, the Turkish newspaper *Hurriyet* claimed that the two countries had nearly gone to war over an incident. Specifically, Turkey has alleged that Greek air defence radar systems locked on to a Turkish F-16 fighter aircraft in international air space. Turkey later sent Greece a warning stating that pilots would be instructed to destroy missile sites in the future if they were tracked by air defence radar.[51]

Currently, the Greek and Turkish arsenals have been increasing in qualitative and quantitative terms. Despite some sporadic appeals for disarmament from both sides of the Aegean,[52] new procurement plans have introduced a dangerous new level of air and naval power in the region and the stockpiling of sophisticated offensive weaponry will increase the likelihood of accidental war and makes the option of a surprise or pre-emptive attack more attractive.[53] In addition, the move towards qualitatively and quantitatively better forces was aided by NATO's Cascade Programme, under which Greece and Turkey became the principal recipients as the countries with the largest stocks of old TLEs.[54]

As mentioned previously, Greece plans to spend $24 billion over the next eight years[55] while Turkey has committed to a programme costing $31 billion over the next decade. Despite this massive military build-up the US and other NATO allies have grasped the opportunity to increase their own weapons exports. Albeit there is a serious risk of war, they are continuing to supply Greece and Turkey with advanced weaponry, on the pretext that they are trying to maintain the military balance in the region. Characteristically, the State Department asserts that US arms transfers or sales will not 'adversely affect the military balance in the region or U.S. efforts to encourage a negotiated settlement' in Cyprus.[56]

However, each sale to one state seems to accelerate the arms race, aggravating tensions and detracting from confidence-building measures.[57] Both states cite the other as an external security threat and often a justification for new arms acquisitions. For example, Turkey sought new frigates and sea helicopters following the flare-up of tensions in the Aegean in 1996.[58]

Turkey's mammoth $150 billion military programme over a period of twenty five to thirty years aims according to Turkey's National Defence Minister, Hikmet Sami Turk, 'to create small, highly capable mobile armed forces'.[59]

The bulk of the funds ($60 billion) have been allocated to the army while the main staples of the procurement plans are the purchase of 145 attack helicopters and 1,000 main battle tanks. Virtually all purchase plans require corresponding offsets by foreign investment in Turkey or a co-production arrangement with local arms manufacturers.[60]

Arms sales to Turkey have been highly politicised. Because of Ankara's poor human rights record most countries who export weapons to Turkey face domestic opposition to selling arms to Turkey. Given its role as Turkey's principal arms supplier, the US has enormous potential leverage over Turkish behaviour on critical issues such as respect for human rights and the pursuit of negotiated settlements to the fifteen year civil war with the PKK and the twenty-five-year old division of Cyprus. The State Department has acknowledged that the

> Turkish armed forces are roughly 80 percent dependent on U.S. origin equipment. Turkey received over $4.9 billion in U.S. weaponry during the first years of the Clinton administration, an average of over $800 million per year.[61]

Unfortunately, US attempts to use arms sales 'leverage' to maintain peace in the Aegean have failed to produce any drastic results. On the contrary, the US's unflagging supply to Turkey of high-tech weapons and technology, has allowed Turkey to maintain a policy of brutal repression against Kurdish opponents, and to preserve a poor human right record while at the same time offset deals directly benefit officials of the armed forces, who are heavily involved in Turkish industry via stock ownership and representation on corporate boards of directors. 'As a result, U.S. offset deals with Turkey serve to enhance the economic power of Turkey's military elite, which in turn increases their already considerable political clout.'[62]

The 25- year weapons purchasing programme has also allowed Turkey to influence export policies in the weapons manufacturing countries by simply threatening to withhold the order or to award it to another producer. The huge long-term military market has forced many countries to cast aside any concerns about Turkey's human right record and turn their efforts to secure a deal about major weapons with Ankara. The end of the Cold War has opened wide the world military market, something that Turkish military officers have realised. In a May 1999 interview, a member of the Turkish General Staff, General Batmaz Dandin, warned the US Administration that Turkey might shift its business away from the US. 'It would be quite normal for us to invest our money in other countries where we are sure that there will be no restrictions on weapon system transfers.'[63]

At the same time Greece is also trying to develop an indigenous capacity to build sophisticated weaponry, which would free it from the whims of the major exporting states. Taking advantage of the tight arms market, Greece also demands returned investment on major arms sales, often in the form of co-production deals.[64]

TESTING TIME FOR NATO: OPTIONS AND ALTERNATIVES

In 1999 Greek Foreign Minister George Papandreou said at a ceremony marking the opening of the academic year at Istanbul University, 'it is time to dare the impossible'[65] while at the same time he pointed to 'a bright future between Turkey and his country based on dialogue and the assistance of politicians who were interested in peace in the region'.[66] However, the truth is that Greek–Turkish relations are

> reminiscent of an electrocardiogram, there have been cycles of relaxation succeeded by cycles of tension occasionally reaching peaks of crisis (July-August 1974, August 1976, March 1987, January 1996 and February 1999) bordering on the threshold of warfare.[67]

Since there is no assurance that bilateral relations would not abruptly reach a point of mutual distrust and open antipathy, NATO must address the pending issue of internal conflicts institutionally. NATO to date has merely interceded between Greece and Turkey.

Currently, an inductive approach has been activated by both governments which aims at bypassing thorny issues of high politics (such as the Aegean, Cyprus, arms control) and focus on issues of low politics. This process was initiated by the Ecevit and Simitis governments, with Foreign Ministers Cem and Papandreou as the main protagonists.[68] Both sides have commenced in a climate of cautious optimism, in a dialogue on issues such as tourism, the environment, economic and commercial relations, culture, organised crime, illegal immigration, drug trafficking and terrorism.[69] Concurrently, a plethora of social, professional and business groups from both sides of the Aegean are striving for the promotion of peace between the two nations.[70] One further significant step towards elimination of mistrust and hatred was succeeded by the mutual agreement to look at one another's school textbooks. It is believed that both countries are determined to establish a joint committee of experts to examine books used in Greek and Turkish schools for chauvinistic aspects.[71]

Another significant development on the bilateral level with regards to Turkey's European vocation, is Greece's decision to shift 'from the tactic of conditional sanctions *vis-à-vis* Turkey to a strategy of conditional rewards'.[72] Greece has traditionally permitted itself to become the whipping boy in Ankara for obstructing Turkey's EU accession, despite Turkey's inability to fulfil the EU's economic criteria, and Copenhagen principles.[73] French and German reluctance to further obstruct Turkey's candidacy, coupled with a massive EU humanitarian aid package to assist Turkey's earthquake relief effort, brought Greece along the same path, and opened the door for Turkey's first positive EU development since the EU Turkey Customs Union was signed four years ago.[74] Despite the current positive developments on a bilateral level,

NATO *mutatis mutandis*, must play a proactive role in the dispute between these two countries. Although NATO has no provision for mediating in disputes between its allies, it has in the past played such a role between Greece and Turkey. It is therefore seen as the foremost institution with a stake in the peaceful resolution of problems between its southern members.[75] Taking into consideration the existence of the *Hybrid Region* in the eastern Mediterranean, it would be to everyone's advantage if the charter of the North Atlantic Treaty included an article that would provide for the peaceful resolution of disputes among allies.[76] Given the absence of a common foreign and security policy in the EU, the crucial challenge facing the world today rests on the need to establish a set of complementary and overlapping security structures in areas of actual and potential conflict.

Since the Imia/Kardak crisis, both sides have accepted a set of ideas suggested by NATO Secretary General, Javier Solana. Specifically, Greece and Turkey agreed: i) on the installation of a 'secure telephone link' between Greece and NATO, and at the same time between Turkey and NATO, which could be activated in the event of an emergency or crisis. Direct linkage is anticipated between the defence ministries of Greece and Turkey with NATO's headquarters, and more particularly with the office of NATO's Secretary General, through telephone lines which will be absolutely secure; ii) they also decided to allow NATO a role in monitoring air sorties over the Aegean. As a result, Greece and Turkey will be part of the NATO ACCS which will closely monitor the movements of their air force units and would be able therefore, to determine the aggressor.

Based on these initiatives, NATO should try to present both sides with a series of *feasible* and *workable* measures, which could on the one hand: i) prevent the possibility of an intra-alliance conflict and on the other; ii) could facilitate the development of a level of higher stability in the Aegean.[77] However, two important elements should be taken into consideration: i) Complete normalisation of bilateral relations between Greece and Turkey will be achieved *only* when civilian government takes full control over the military and therefore a complete democracy would be implemented; ii) the development of a comprehensive package of CSBMs[78] or arms control measures with regards to land and air forces is probably undesirable for Turkey, as its relations with its eastern neighbours are rather unsettled.[79] Furthermore it is not applicable to Turkey for an additional reason. The implementation of an arms control regime usually has 'three particular objectives to accomplish, namely conflict prevention, crisis stability and arms race stability'.[80]

Crisis stability refers to the ability of an adversarial military system to remain under political control, even when decision-makers take the possibility of war into account. Since this does not apply in the case of Turkey, any possible implementation will be proved unworkable and meaningless.[81] It should also be mentioned that Greek Prime Minister K. Mitsotakis's government had proposed in July 1991 the creation of an 'area free of offensive weapons', including battle tanks, attack helicopters, armoured combat vehicles, artillery and combat aircraft in the region where the Turkish, Bulgarian and Greek borders meet. Subsequently, Bulgaria also suggested the withdrawal of troops from an 80-kilometres zone from its borders with Greece and Turkey. Nevertheless, Turkey turned down both proposals almost certainly because they were incompatible with its strategic objectives.

Under these circumstances, NATO could suggest the implementation of operational[82] and structural[83] CBSMs at sea[84] since Turkey is not currently facing any serious threat at sea.[85] Some of the measures[86] that can be proposed which aim at contributing towards greater mutual confidence are:

- freezing of the number of the main naval units (submarines, destroyers, frigates, corvettes, guided-missile craft, landing ships and crafts);
- increasing the frequency of meetings between Naval Chiefs of Staff;
- exchange visits between the directors of the naval war colleges;[87]
- interchange of junior officers on short-term courses;[88]
- visits of warships to ports of the other country;
- port visits by training ships to ports of the other country;
- interchange of naval publications;
- reduction or even the withdrawal of Turkey's landing fleet from the Aegean since it does not affect Turkey's defensive military capability;[89]
- participation in bilateral exercises;[90]
- establishment of direct telephone lines between the Naval Chiefs of Staff;[91]
- regulation of activities of naval vessels by means of 'rules of the road'. These rules can include avoiding collisions: i) non-interference with manoeuvre; ii) separation of naval forces during a crisis; iii) abstaining from manoeuvres in areas of heavy traffic; iv) requiring surveillance ships to maintain a safe distance; v) providing notification three to five days in advance of activities which might present a danger to other ships or aircraft; vi) and using accepted international signals when manoeuvring in close proximity.[92]

Since both states are NATO members, the organisation is the most appropriate forum for initiating and arranging the aforementioned initiatives. Other conflict-preventing measures that can also be initiated by NATO are the following:

- NATO pressure should be brought to bear on Turkey to acknowledge the mediation role of the ICJ in the Hague. Unresolved territorial questions should be referred to the ICJ.
- The two sides should build on the agreement signed by Turkish President Suleiman Demirel and Greek Prime Minister Kostas Simitis in Madrid in July 1997. In this agreement, both sides made a commitment to respect international law and to refrain from threats of armed aggression. However, one day after the agreement Turkish F-4 aircraft violated the Athens FIR regulations on four occasions.[93] Based on this agreement NATO should urge both sides to sign a non-aggression treaty based on the understanding that the Aegean can neither be transformed into a 'Greek lake' nor subdivided so as to surround and isolate Greek territories (islands).
- NATO should demand from both sides the annulment of *casus belli* statements for reasons other than violation of sovereignty.[94]
- NATO should also obligate the cessation of bellicose and provocative statements by officials at the highest levels.[95]
- NATO should invite both sides to sign a bilateral Open Skies Treaty.[96]
- NATO should initiate problem-solving workshops, where academics and military officials would attempt to get the parties to engage in joint analysis of the problems they face.[97]
- NATO should declare that it will enforce in case of an intra-alliance warfare, *a pre-attack status.*

Since a viable and effective arms control regime or CSBMs in the eastern Mediterranean (with regards to Greece and Turkey) is a rather difficult task at the moment, NATO should also adopt measures to prevent any spill-over effect – in the event of a Greek–Turkish war – in the Balkan region.[98] The outcome of the Bosnian and Kosovo warfare provided the international community with the sharp reality that NATO through IFOR and KFOR has the real authority and power to prevent and preserve peace in the Euro-Atlantic region. A Balkan incorporation into the NATO alliance has been perceived by many political analysts and Balkan leaders as a panacea for their security concerns.[99] The repercussion of NATO's Balkan enlargement for the future development of the region will be critical. More specifically:

- The incorporation of the Balkan countries into the NATO alliance and the implementation of the NATO criteria and conditions[100] for membership will eventually create a homogeneous region which is conformed to western values and culture.
- By joining NATO the Balkan states will be forced to develop a regional security strategy based on the NATO new military structure which will strengthen their national security.[101]
- By joining NATO the Balkan states will be part of an organisation with great potential and international prestige.
- By becoming members, the Balkan states will be able to efficiently prevent the establishment of any hostile regional configurations. Most states will be focused on the promotion of common strategic interests rather than employing chauvinistic goals.[102]
- By becoming members, the region will be transformed from a region of instability to a region of stability and great economic opportunities. The establishment of a peaceful and secure environment will create the appropriate conditions for unhindered foreign financial investments. An adherence to NATO will also boost the chances of the Balkan countries achieving full membership in the EU.
- By joining NATO, the existing problem of the military imbalance which exists in the Balkan region will be under control while at the same time the probability of new armed conflicts will diminish.[103]

In contrast, a negative approach towards the Balkan countries' demand for early acceptance into the alliance would probably negatively affect the future development of the region. Most of the Balkan countries will perceive themselves as unreliable and unattractive on political and economic matters. It is highly likely that this decision would implant a feeling of lasting insecurity in the minds of the Balkan peoples, in the countries' governments, political parties, and economies. Furthermore, it is possible that this feeling of isolation might turn to one of hostility towards the alliance.[104]

Under these circumstances NATO should adopt a multi-faceted regional approach in order to prevent, promote, and secure peace and stability for the Balkan region. Some of the measures that can be initiated or advocated by NATO[105] are:

- The creation of the MPFSEE.[106] The purpose of Multinational Peace Force will be to contribute to the incorporation of the former communist south-east European states into the western security institutions such as NATO rather than as a regional body able to pursue independently a peacekeeping operation in the region. Furthermore, as the Bulgarian Defence Minister said: 'The multinational peace force is a unique achievement for this region. It is a unique attempt of collective interaction in the area of defence and security.'[107]

As a result, the force could be developed as a forum of co-operation between traditional enemies such as Greece and Turkey while at the same time combined military interaction could be beneficial in a region torn by ethnic strife. To this end, NATO should actively support joint regional initiatives that enhance security and co-operation outside the NATO structure. Moreover, interaction with NATO members such as Greece, Italy and Turkey would also help other members in the force, all of which are participants in NATO's PfP programme, adopt the alliance's military standards.

- Since suspicion, mistrust and hostility are still elements of the Balkan social and political structure, it would be useful to establish an official (but informal) consultative body called the BSC as a standing forum where any security-related topic can be discussed without being under political pressure from respective governments. The aim of this forum – which can easily be supported by NATO – could be to examine and deal with a series of issues such as the deployment of new weapons, explanation of specific foreign policy decisions, and identification and diffusion of possible crises between ethnic groups or states. With regards to inter-state conflict, existing or potential, the BSC could also operate as a communications network where information about military manoeuvres and exercises can be interchanged. This would allow the parties involved to identify the true nature of the military activities and would help to reduce mistrust that breeds tensions.[108] To achieve these objectives, the BSC should be staffed by government officials and experts in the various aspects of security policy. But most importantly, it should be focused on the attempt to produce transparent information and clarification. Since all Balkan countries desire to avoid crisis or deal with problems which might cause crises, they have a common interest in implementing such a suggestion.
- NATO's recent decision to anchor potential new member states closer to the alliance via the MAP can be seen as a positive measure towards security stability in the Balkan region. This programme provides aspiring countries with the belief that once they implement this plan, full membership will be much closer. The plan was approved at the NATO Summit of April 1999, and is designed to prepare countries for entry into the alliance by such means as acquiring defence planning and weapons interoperability with

NATO.[109] On careful examination, the MAP provides for a very specific and intrusive set of activities that will have the effect of binding the would-be members remarkably close to the alliance.[110]

The aforementioned initiatives have a complementary and preventive character with other organisations such as the OSCE with regards to the establishment of permanent stability in the Balkan region.[111] The ultimate goal of most of the Balkan countries is full NATO membership since they realise that only NATO can guarantee their territorial integrity. NATO itself has drastically evolved since 1989, by transforming itself from a classical alliance for collective defence to one with a wider mission.[112] The new strategic challenge for NATO currently lies in the Balkans, but the fear of further incorporation of the Balkan countries or active involvement with intra-alliance conflict-prevention measures lies on NATO. Time will tell if NATO will pay for its lack of commitment.

NOTES

1. According to former Turkish Minister of National Defence Zeki Yavuzturk, 'Turkey is a staunch supporter of the status quo in the Aegean, established by international treaties', *NATO's Sixteen Nations, Special Issue* (September, 1986) 31, p.63.
2. For further study about the *status quo* in the Aegean see Fotios Moustakis, 'Conflict in the Aegean', *Contemporary Review*, 274, 1596 (1999) pp.8–12; Lieutenant Colonel M.N. Schmmitt, 'The Greek–Turkish Dispute', *Naval War College Review*, XLIX, 3 (1996) pp.43–72 and Syrigos and Arvanitopoulos, *The International Legal Status of the Aegean* (Athens, 1998), *www.idis.gr/people/arvan9.html*. The Third International Conference on the Law of the Sea aimed to create a new code of rules covering all facets of the law of the sea. It concluded in 1982 and resulted in the LOSC signed at Montego Bay, Jamaica. Almost all issues pertinent to the law of the sea are regulated by the 320 Articles of the Convention. See also the Treaty of Lausanne in *www.zeus.hri.org/docs/lausanne*. The Lausanne Treaty specified the Turkish borders in the Aegean by fixing them to the insular territories being within the 3-mile zone (Article 12) from the Turkish coast plus the Imbros and Tenedos islands. Turkey renounced all its rights to islands situated outside the 3-mile zone (Article 16).
3. See *Eleftherotypia*, 27 March 1999 and *Ta Nea*, 27 March 1999 and *the Macedonian Press Agency*, 27 March 1999.
4. For further study about the arrival of the Ottoman Turks in Kosovo see the first seven chapters of Miranda Vickers in *Between Serb and Albanian: A History of Kosovo* (London: Hurst Publishers, 1998); see also Noel Malcolm, *Kosovo: A Short History* (London: Macmillan, 1998) pp.209-16.
5. 'Knights in Shining Armour, A Survey of NATO', *The Economist*, 24 April 1999, p.4. It is worth mentioning that US President Clinton argued one reason for NATO's intervention in Kosovo was the risk of war between Greece and Turkey. This danger was denied categorically from both sides of the Aegean; see Simitis, Greek Press Conference, 26 March 1999.
6. See Radio Free Europe, *Newsline*, 3, 80, 27 April 1999; *Newsline*, 3, 83, 30 April 1999; *Open Media Research Institute*, 2, 7, 18 February 1997. The Minister of Defence of Bulgaria, Georgi

Ananiev, asserted that 'Bulgaria … will go on working actively to realise the two basic foreign political priorities of the country – membership in NATO and the European Union', 'Moving Towards NATO & the EU', *Military Technology*, 22, 5 (1999) p.55. Even Romania's main objective is 'to create a military background able to grant NATO membership', Constantin Degerau, 'Romania: Five Years In Partnership For Peace', *Central European Issues: Romanian Foreign Affairs Review*, 5, 1 (1999) p.45.

7. Richard. G. Whitman, 'Securing Europe's Southern Flank? A Comparison of NATO, EU and WEU Policies and Objectives', *NATO Report* (1999) p.5.
8. The Alliance's New Strategic Concept, *www.nato.int/docu/comm/49-95/c911107a.htm*. Agreed by the Heads of State and Government participating in the meeting of the North Atlantic Council in Rome on 7–8 November 1991.
9. Anthony Cragg, 'A New Strategic Concept for a New Era', *NATO Review*, 47, 2 (1999) p.2.
10. See Asmus, Kugler and Larrabee, 'NATO Expansion', pp.25–31. Currently, US President Bill Clinton has been highly involved in the Greco-Turkish differences and the Cyprus issue. See *Hurriyet*, 28 September 1999 and to *Vima*, 26 September 1999, *Elefterotypia*, 27 September 1999. See also M. Nimetz, 'Mediterranean Security after the Cold War', *Mediterranean Quarterly*, 8 (1997) p.27 and Zalmay Khalilzad and Ian O. Lesser (eds), 'Sources of Conflict in the 21st Century: Regional Futures and US Strategy', *Rand Report* (1998) p.240. To state a simple example, a potential Greco-Turkish armed conflict would destroy all NATO and US radar installations in the eastern Mediterranean.
11. *NATO's Sixteen Nations*, 42, 1 (1997) p.57.
12. For more details see R. Aliboni, 'European Security Across the Mediterranean', *Chaillot Paper 2*, Institute for Security Studies, Western European Union, Paris (1991). For more information about the CFE see John Speight, 'CFE 1990: Achievements and Prospects', *Faraday Discussion Paper* 15, (1990); see also John E. Peters, 'CFE and Military Stability in Europe', *Rand Report* (1997). It is worth mentioning that the CFE Treaty did not alter south-eastern Europe's regional imbalances, *au contraire* it was exacerbated; see Yannis Valinakis, *Greece and the CFE Negotiations* (Ebenhause: Stiftung Wissenschafft und Politik, 1991) p.22.
13. *Fact Sheet: How NATO Has Changed In The post-Cold War Era*, prepared and compiled by the Bureau of European and Canadian Affairs, State Department, 21 March 1997, *www.mtholyoke.edu/acad/intre//natousis.htm*, pp.2–3. See also *NATO's New Force Structures*, NATO Basic Fact Sheet, 5, (January, 1996), *www.nato.int/docu/facts/nnfs.htm*.
14. General Klaus Naumann, 'NATO's New Military Structure', *NATO Review*, 46, 1 (1998) p.4. See also Robert S. Jordan, 'NATO's Structural Changes for the 1990s', in S. Victor Papacosma and Mary Ann Heiss (eds), *NATO in the Post-Cold War Era: Does it Have a Future?* (New York: St Martin Press, 1996) pp.41–69.
15. ibid., p.1.
16. Regional Commander South will see the creation of two new Joint Sub-Regional Commanders (JSRC) (SouthWest and SouthCentre, in Madrid and Larissa, respectively) and the transformation of two existing land component commanders, Commander Allied Land Forces Southern Europe in Italy and Commander Allied Land Forces South-eastern Europe in Turkey into JSRCs (South and SouthEast, respectively), along with the continued existence of separate air and naval component commanders. For more information see Thomas-Durell Young, 'Reforming NATO's Military Structures: The Long-Term Study and Its Implications for Land Forces', *Report for the Strategic Studies Institute of the US Army*, 15 May 1998.
17. The official activation of the NATO sub-headquarters at Tyrnavos near Larissa took place on 6 October 1999. Within the activation framework of the Southern NATO Wing sub-headquarters, the Airforce Operations Centre (AKE) of the Tactical Airforce Headquarters evolved into a Co-ordinated Action Operational Centre (CAOC), coming directly under the operational jurisdiction of the Southern NATO Wing Airforce Commander.

18. See Nikos Kouris, *Ellada-Tourkia, O Pentikontaetis Polemos* (Athens: Nea Sinora Livanis, 1997) pp.368–96. The Former Greek Chief of General Staff illustrates his apprehension with regards to the new NATO military structure. In contrast, Greek National Defence Minister Akis Tsohatzopoulos stressed that 'Greece will have operational responsibility for the entire national space ... in the case of every exercise, training or operation, Greece will have the right of veto at the Military Committee or the Political Committee (Council of Ministers)', *Athens, News Agency*, 3 December 1997.

19. George Tenet, the Director of Central Intelligence, in his Senate Intelligence Committee testimony on January 1998, described the possibility of armed conflict between Greece and Turkey over differences concerning the Aegean Sea, *Western Policy Center*, 5 February 1998.

20. 'If a serious crisis erupts in the Aegean, it won't be just U.S. security interests that are affected, but the broader interests of the international community ... a threat of war would transcend the local stakes of the disputants and even those of the NATO alliance', Charles Maechling Jr., 'The Aegean Sea: A Crisis Waiting to Happen', *Naval Institute Proceedings* (March, 1997) p.73. Greek Defence Minister, A. Tsohatzopoulos claims that Greece embarked on a five-year arms modernisation programme in response 'to the steady increase in Turkey's armed strength and the need to meet Turkey's quantitative superiority with superior quality'; see 'A Stabilising Factor: The Modernisation of the Greek Armed Forces', *Armed Forces Journal* (October, 1998) p.22. The aforementioned statements provide clear evidence of lack of allied solidarity.

21. Despite NATO's commitment on conflict prevention and crisis management, this does not apply in case of an intra-alliance conflict. Furthermore, a NATO study stipulates that existing members and mainly new members must meet both political and military criteria: 'i) resolve ethnic and extraterritorial disputes by peaceful means ii) establish civilian control of the military', Kori Schake, 'NATO Chronicle: New World Disorder,' *Joint Force Quarterly* (spring, 1999) p.24. The terms ensured that all new members shared the political values of the alliance; however, this is not the case in Turkey since the military control the civilian government (see previous chapter). In such a context, one might ask 'what kind of future does NATO have?'; see Papakosma (ed.), p.273.

22. The Balkans are a region that has been repeatedly 'retailored' by the great powers following every major war or collapse of empires (Austria–Hungary, the Ottoman Empire, Yugoslavia). As Umberto Eco notes, 'over the centuries the Balkans have aggregated the negative effects of the collapse of at least five empires: the Roman, the Byzantine, Ottoman, Austro-Hungarian and Russian (Soviet) empires'. In most cases, the boundaries of the Balkans countries have been drawn without giving consideration to the actual distribution of ethnic groups constituting a substantial part of the population in a given sub-region. For further study see Nansen Behar, 'Ethnic Identity and Border Disputes in the Balkans', *Review Of International Affairs*, XLIX, 15 October 1998, pp.25–32.

23. Panayiotis J. Tsakonas, 'Creating Conditions of Stability in Southeastern Europe: Prospects for an Arms Control Regime', *NATO Report* (June, 1999) p.3. During the Cold War, a limited but effective stability had been established between the Balkan states as a result of the bipolar system. The application of the bipolar system ensured limited co-operation and prevented the rise of nationalistic aspirations and territorial disputes. See Dimitris Constas, 'Future Challenges to Greek Foreign Policy', in Konstas and Nikolaos Stavrou (eds), *Greece Prepares for the Twenty First Century* (Baltimore: Johns Hopkins University Press, 1996).

24. See Janusz Bugajski, 'The Balkans: On the Brink Again', *The Washington Quarterly*, 20, 4 (April, 1997) pp.211–22.

25. For the notion of strategic culture see Ken Booth, *The Concept of Strategic Culture Affirmed*, in Carl. G. Jacobsen (ed.), *Strategic Power: USA/USSR* (London: Macmillan Press, 1990) p.121 and Klein Yitznak, 'A Theory of Strategic Culture', *Comparative Strategy*, 10, 1 (1991).

26. Tsakonas, 'Creating Conditions', p.4.

27. All formerly communist states in the Balkans are economically prostrate and strategically

weak. Greek GDP is by some measures equal to the total of the GDP of all formerly communist states in the Balkans put together, including Romania and all former Yugoslav republics. Moreover, Greece's defence spending is determined by Turkey's armament programme. See 'Greek Policy Responses to the post-Cold War Balkan Environment', in Coufoudakis, Psomiades and Gerolymatos (eds), *Greece and the New Balkans: Challenges and Opportunities* (New York: Pella, 1999) pp.215–17. See also H. Papasotiriou, 'The Dynamics of Greek–Turkish Strategic Interaction', *www.idis.gr/people/papasot.html*. For more details see *White Paper of the Hellenic Armed Forces 1996–97*, Hellenic Ministry of National Defence.

28. Valeri Ratchev, 'NATO and South-Eastern European Security Perspectives: Implications for the Evolution of National Security Institutions and the Decision-Making Process in Bulgaria', *NATO Fellowship Report* (Brussels, 1999) p.8.

29. See also Elena Zamfireskou, 'NATO and the Balkans', *Perceptions: A Journal of International Affairs*, IV, 1 (March–May, 1999), *www.mfa.gov.tr*, p.4.

30. ibid., p.9.

31. The personal adviser of Bill Clinton, S. Berger stated recently that the current military competition in the eastern Mediterranean and the lack of confidence building measures enhance the possibility of an intra-alliance conflict which would be catastrophic for the US and the NATO alliance; see *Eleftherotypia*, 11 October 1999.

32. See Lucas Cadena, 'Greek–Turkish Relations', *Princeton Journal of Foreign Affairs* (winter, 1998), *www.princeton.edu/~foreigna/winter1998/turkey.html*, p.4.

33. T. Pangalos, 'Principles of Greek Foreign Policy', *Mediterranean Quarterly*, 9, 2 (1998) pp.4–5.

34. Fanni Palli Petralia (M.P., Member Of New Democracy Foreign Affairs Committee, 'Greek Foreign Policy: Facing New Problems', *Mediterranean Quarterly*, 9, 4 (1998) p.14.

35. See *Jane's Defence Weekly – International Edition*, 30, 7 (1998) p.26 and Sukru Elekdag, '2 1/2 Strategy', *Perceptions* (March–May, 1996), *www.mfa.gov.tr/grupf/percept/I1/per1-3.htm*, p.1.

36. *Economist*, 20 February 1999, p.54.

37. See M.R. Hickok, 'The Imia/Kardak Affair, 1995–96: A Case Of Inadvertent Conflict', *European Security*, 7, 4 (1998) pp.118–36.

38. Harry Papasotiriou, 'The Dynamics of Greek–Turkish Interaction', (Athens: IIR, 1998) p.2.

39. Turkey has committed to a $31 billion expenditure over the next decade in the first stage of a massive modernisation programme expected to reach nearly $150 billion over the next 25–30 years; see *Arms Sales Monitor* (February, 1999) *www.fas.org/asmp/ASM39.html*. For a further update about the Turkish military modernisation programme, see also interview with the Turkish Chief of General Staff, H. Kivrikoglou, 'Peace in the Nation, Peace in the World', *Military Technology*, 9 (1999) pp.9–24.

40. P. Tsakonas, 'Creating Conditions of Stability in Southeastern Europe: Prospects for an Arms Control Regime', *NATO Report* (June, 1999) p.13. In November 1996, the 1996–2000 Unified Medium Term Programmes of Development and Modernisation (EMPAE) of 4 trillion drs was approved by the Government Council on Foreign Affairs and Defence, out of which 1.95 trillion drs is expected to be disbursed until 2000, immediately after the placing of orders, and the remaining according to deliveries; see *White Paper of the Hellenic Armed Forces 1996–97*, Hellenic Ministry of National Defence (1997) p.107.

41. Stearns, 'Greek Security Issues', in G. Allison and K. Nicolaidis (eds), *The Greek Paradox: Promise vs Performance* (Cambridge, Mass. and London: MIT Press, 1997) p.69; see also M. Ward, '*The Enlargement of WEU*' (Political Com.), *Rapporteur*, Document 1360, 19 April 1993, pp.5–6.

42. They are required to exchange detailed information on weapons stocks and acquisitions.

43. Most of the European states, the US and Russia have been cutting their defence budgets in an effort to benefit from the end of the Cold War. About the arms race see C. Tuck 'Greece, Turkey and Arms Control', *Defence Analysis*, 12, 1 (1996) pp.23–32. See also *Fuelling Balkan Fires: The West's Arming of Greece and Turkey*, Project on the Arms Trade, The British American Security Information Council (1993).

44. Tsakonas, 'Creating Conditions', p.10. The provisions of the text stipulates that: (a) notification of military activities will take place at a lower level than in the Vienna Document. Furthermore, the two countries will notify each other of any activity even at the level of an augmented battalion conducted in areas adjacent to their common border in a depth of 15km. (b) More intrusive verification; in addition to the quotas specified by the Vienna Document, this document grants each state one inspection and two evaluation visits per year with the zone of application of the complementary CSBMs. (c) Early notification of mobilisation activities; any activity involving increase of personnel strength by more than 1,000 reservists will be notified as soon as possible, but no later than 42 days in advance of this activity. After six years of implementation, one can argue that a climate of trust and co-operation between armed forces of the two countries has been established. There is a speculation that both countries contemplate the extension of the agreed measures to specified areas beyond the 15km zone on each side of the common borders.

45. The Sofia Document was signed in December 1991, and it was designed to establish security and confidence along the Bulgarian–Turkish border. In November 1992, the Edirne Document implemented additional confidence-building measures and it was signed by the two states' Chief of the General Staffs. See S.F. Larrabee, 'The Balkans', in Zalmay Khalilzad (ed.), '*Strategic Appraisal*', *Rand Report*, (1996) p.111.

46. The 'Tirana Document on Mutually Complementary CSBMs and Military Contacts' was signed in February 1995. The Chiefs of General Staffs agreed to establish (a) the mutual invitation of observers, at least twice a year (b) the promotion and facilitation of contacts between relevant institutions; naval visits; joint exercises. It is also worth mentioning that a bilateral military agreement was signed in Tirana, in July 1992, which stated that Turkey would modernise and train the Albanian army; see Louis Zanga, 'Albania and Turkey Forge Closer Ties', RFE/RL *Research Report*,12 March 1993, pp.30–3. This military agreement was perceived in Greece as a Turkish attempt to create a 'Muslim arc'.

47. The agreement on 'Mutually Complementary CSBMs, and Military Contacts' was signed between the Ministers of Defence of the two countries in December 1995.

48. This agreement on 'CSBMs Complementing the OSCE Vienna Document of 1994 and on the Development of Military Relations between Hungary and Romania' was signed in September 1996.

49. Athanasios Platias, 'Greek Deterrence Strategy', Institute of International Relations, *Report*, (Athens, 1999) p.13.

50. These agreements were (a) a Memorandum of Understanding on Confidence-Building Measures, signed in Athens in June 1988 (The Athens Memorandum); (b) Guidelines for the Prevention of Incidents on the High Sea and International Airspace, signed in Istanbul in September 1988. This limited set of CSBMs was initiated by NATO Secretary General Javier Solana.

51. Global Intelligence Update, 'Greco-Turkish Threatens to Deepen Fissures in NATO', 30 March 1999, *www.stratfor.com/services/giu/033099.asp*. Greece claims that the Turkish aircraft was in the FIR of Athens and the real reason of the Turkish complaint was the deployment of the Russian surface to air missiles OSA(SA-8B Gecko)AK.

52. Turkish MPs and the Greek Foreign Minister, G. Papandreou have stated that competition in defence expenses between Turkey and Greece is harming the two countries, economically and socially and destabilises the region; see *Proini*, the Greek–American newspaper, 21 October 1999 and *Avgi*, newspaper, 21 September 1999, respectively. Despite Turkey's serious economic problems it has already signed within the first half of 2002 contracts on military programmes estimated around $3 billion, see *Defence Biblos 2002–2003* (Athens: Strategiki, 2002) pp.48–9.

53. By looking at maps showing the current Greek/Turkish order of battle it is evident that Greek and Turkish forces are directed against each other. This contradicts the argument put forward by Richard Ned Lebow who argues that 'the best evidence for the existence of

a pluralistic security community is the general absence of military plans by one community member for operations against another', Lebow, 'The Long Peace', p.269.

54. The NATO Cascading Programme allowed the transfer of sophisticated weapon systems from certain countries (US, Germany) to those member states that had obsolete weapon systems such as Greece and Turkey. This programme streamlined offensive weapons in the central front but increased the offensive capabilities of those in the flanks, namely Greece and Turkey. For the military procurements in Greece and Turkey see BASIC, 29 (August, 1998) *www.basicint.org/bpaper29b.htm*. For updated and detailed information about the Greek and Turkish military modernisation programmes see *Amyntiki Biblos (Defence Bible) 1999–2000 and 2002–2003*, Special Edition published by Strategiki Athens, 1999, and *Isoropia Dinameon (Balance of Power)*, Special Edition published by Ptisi (Flight) (Athens, 1999) pp.119–78. It is also instructive to mention that Turkey was negotiating the purchase of a small aircraft carrier accompanied by 5–6 TF2000 Anti-Air Warfare frigates, see *Amyntiki Biblos 1999–2000*. For updated and detailed information about the Greek military modernisation programme see also *Military Technology*, XXIII, 10 (1999) pp.23–49. See also 'Defence and Economics in Turkey', *NATO's Sixteen Nations & Partners for Peace, Special Supplement* (1998) and the Turkish Undersecretariat for Defence Industries, *www.ssm.gov.tr*.

55. The Greek government has announced it will purchase 60–80 fourth generation Eurofighters, while at the same time it would participate in the Eurofighter's production programme. On Friday 30 April 1999 Greece also announced the purchase of 50 F-16 Block 50 Plus combat aircraft, 15 Mirage 2000s and new weapons systems for its fleet of Mirage 2000 as part of its multi-million dollar armaments programme for the Hellenic air force. The total cost of the F-16 aircraft will come to approximately $2 billion while the Mirages will cost about $700 million; see *Defence Systems Daily News* and *Eurofighter Typhoon News*, 15 February 1999, 3 May 1999, 30 April 1999.

56. 'Preserving the Military Balance in the Aegean', *Arms Sales Monitor*, published by the Federation of American Scientists Fund 39, February (1999) *www.fas.org*.

57. For example, Turkey's decision in the summer of 1999 to co-produce Popeye air-to-ground missiles with Israel prompted the US government to release a sale of similar air-to-ground missiles to Greece, see Umit Emginsoy and Ege Bekdil, 'Turkey, Israel Move Closer to Popeye 2 Accord', *Defense News*, 9 August 1999.

58. Umit Enginsoy, 'Greek Conflict Fuels Turkish Navy Upgrades', *Defense News*, 5–11 February 1996, p.4

59. Interview with Turkish National Defence Minister, Hikmet Sami Turk, *Jane's Defence Weekly*, 14 April 1999.

60. Money for this programme has been secured through a combination of the Turkish Defence Department's share of the government budget and a separate Defence Industry Support Fund. The latter gets its funding from private donations and a special tax on alcohol, gambling, tobacco, gasoline and imported goods.

61. Tamar Gabelnick, William D. Hartung and Jennifer Washburn , 'Arming Repression: U.S. Arms Sales to Turkey During the Clinton Administration', World Policy Institute and the Federation of American Scientists, *Report* (October, 1999) p.2, *www.fas.org/asmp/library/reports/turkeyrep.htm*. This detailed report elucidates US arms sales in Turkey during the Clinton administration. It also recommends that all future US arms sales to Turkey should be conditioned on concrete improvements in human rights and democratisation. The US should replace its military-orientated, 'arms for influence' policy towards Turkey with a more balanced, strategy that emphasises classic diplomacy and economic ties. Congress should also enact a uniform set of criteria for arms exports that would subject all countries to the same strict standards.

62. ibid., p.14.

63. *Weekly Defense Monitor News*, 3, 24, 24 June 1999.

64. The confirmation of the Greek participation in the Eurofighter Typhoon consortium is seen as further strengthening Greek links with the European defence and aerospace industry. It is envisaged that Greece will consequently take a stake of approximately 10% in the Eurofighter consortium, while Hellenic Aircraft Industry (HAI) will be an industrial partner, *Jane's International Defence Review*, 32, (June, 1999). For further updated information see, 'Athens' New Wings', *Military Technology*, 9 (1999) pp.77–90. For further study about Greece's participation in military programmes see *Amyntiki Biblos*, 1999–2000, 2002–2003, pp.25–97, 31–50.

65. *Reuters News Agency*, 4 October 1999.

66. *Turkish Daily News*, 5 October 1999.

67. T. Couloumbis, 'Dealing with Greek–Turkish Tension', *Athens News Agency*, 6 October 1999.

68. It is worth mentioning that Washington is maintaining a low profile that frees Papandreou and Cem to jointly build the framework that advances their countries' shared interests, see J. Stilides, *Western Policy Center*, 15 September 1999.

69. See *To Vima*, 3 October 1999, 14 October 1999, 24 October 1999 and *Athens News Agency*, 28 October 1999. The last round of talks took place in Athens on 27 October 1999. According to a joint communiqué, 'the talks were conducted in a friendly and business like atmosphere'. It was decided to establish working groups related to the aforementioned fields and aimed at further elaborating draft texts already exchanged, while conclusions will be ratified in the fourth round, tentatively scheduled to begin in December. The ultimate results will be presented to the countries' Foreign Ministers.

70. See article in *Kathimerini* by T. Veremis and Duygu Sezer, on 3 October 1999. The Greek–Turkish Business Council has decided to organise workshop groups in order to develop relations and co-operation between the two countries' business communities, *Turkish Daily News*, 14 October 1999.

71. See *Ta Nea*, main article, 26 October 1999 and *Athens News Agency*, 28 October 1999. It is instructive to mention that there is a successful precedent for this set by France and Germany in the 1950s.

72. *Athens News Agency*, 6 October 1999.

73. Membership requires that the candidate country has achieved stability of institutions guaranteeing democracy, the rule of law, human rights and respect for and protection of minorities, *European Council in Copenhagen*, Conclusions of the Presidency, 21–22 June 1993, Document 93/3/, p.6. Turkey still maintained a poor human record, its military campaign against Kurdish PKK separatists, and its continued occupation of Cyprus.

74. For more details on the Greek–Turkish relations within the EU context see Fotios Moustakis and Michael Sheehan, 'Greek Security Policy After the Cold War', *Contemporary Security Policy*, 21, 3 (2000) pp.95–115.

75. During a series of unofficial and official interviews I conducted in Greece from 1996–8, senior military officers, academics and Foreign Office officials, all endorsed the plausibility of NATO intervention between Greece and Turkish disputes, so long as the sovereign rights of the country were respected. Meanwhile, Atila Eralp, in a survey of the Turkish political elites regarding the role of NATO in the post- Cold War era, discovered that most of the Turkish political elites want NATO to be used 'as a platform to solve problems between Turkey and Greece', 'Turkish Public Perceptions of NATO', *NATO Report* 1995–1997 (Brussels, 1997) pp.43, 45.

76. Former Greek Foreign Minister Theodoros Pangalos, on numerous occasions has suggested that NATO should include an article concerning the competence of the organisation in resolving disputes among allies, see *Athens News Agency*, 19 February 1997. This proposal was linked with NATO's expansion to the east and it has managed to highlight the greater possibility of the eruption of conflict in the new post-Cold War Europe. Furthermore, he has also underlined the need for the establishment of a particular mechanism for conflict management.

77. K. Tsipis is trying to resolve whether a common security regime is in principle feasible in the Balkans. He attempts to propose institutions and procedures that will allow Bulgaria, Greece and Turkey participating in a common security regime to take advantage of technological opportunities to strengthen their military capabilities without creating the perception of threat to their companion nations participating in the regime. See Kosta Tsipis, 'New Technologies and Common Security Regimes in the Balkans', in Tsipis (ed.), pp.181–202.

78. It is important to stress the historical distinction between the use of the term 'confidence building measures' and 'confidence and security building measures'. The first arose from the negotiations leading up to the Helsinki Final Act in 1975; the second from the later negotiations which produced the Stockholm Document in 1986. Currently both acronyms CBMS and CBSMs mean the same thing. For further study about CSBMs in the Balkans see Dorinda G. Dallmeyer, 'Moderating Threat Perception: The Role of Confidence and Security Building Measures in the Balkans', in Tsipis (ed.), pp.203–32. For further study about CBSMs see Michael Krepon et al. (eds), *A Handbook of Confidence Building Measures for Regional Security* (Washington: Henry Stimson Center, 1995). For arms control and CBSMs see also Seyom Brown, *Causes and Prevention of War* (New York: St Martin Press, 1994) pp.201–27. See also Igor Scherbak, *Confidence-building Measures and International Security, The Political and Military Aspects: a Soviet Approach*, United Nations Institute for Disarmament Research, (New York, 1991).

79. It is rather paradoxical that two 'allies' have to adopt CSBMs; however, this is mainly due to the development of a *Hybrid Region* in the eastern Mediterranean. Furthermore, it is also worth mentioning that 'if military confidence is not established (i.e. if security is not assured) there is little likelihood that any overall confidence will develop between two rivals', Marie-France Desjardins, 'Rethinking Confidence-Building Measures', *Adelphi Paper*, 307 (1996) p.20. Since the military controls the political structure of the country and the civilian governments, is it possible to implement true military confidence?

80. Tsakonas, 'Creating', p.17.

81. Ilnur Cevik also asserts that 'the image of Turkey abroad is one of the country where the military is influential in the way the country is being run and that the Armed Forces is not under the control of the civilian government', *Turkish Daily News*, 27 October 1999.

82. This refers to naval activities, notifications, inspection, etc.

83. This refers to control and reduction of naval armaments, and/or capabilities.

84. CBSMs at sea are only feasible since Turkey has rejected on 1991 land CBSMs while CBSMs at air forces are perplexed by the status of the Greek FIR. On confidence-building measures in the naval domain see Barry M. Blechman et al. (eds) *Naval Arms Control: A Strategic Assessment* (New York: St Martins, 1992); Sverre Lodgaard (ed.), *Naval Arms Control* (Oslo: SIPRI, 1990); see also Pedro Fuente, 'Confidence-Building Measures in the Southern Cone: A Model for Regional Stability', *Naval War College Review*, (Winter, 1997), *www.nwc.navy.mil/press/review/1997/winter.*

85. I am taking into the account the poor operational shape of the Russian Black Sea fleet which has been affected by the current economic crisis in Russia.

86. The following suggestions are aimed at creating attitudes of co-operativeness. Their purpose is to generate a feeling of understanding, collaboration, friendship and above all familiarity. Once constant human interaction is achieved, elimination of false hostile impressions will be accomplished eventually.

87. College settings are especially suited for exchange of ideas, for exploring strategic issues and for the development of combined approaches towards bilateral problems. Frequent visits from the directors could also produce common understanding.

88. The exchange of junior naval officers would expose them to another culture at a formative age. Human interaction and cultivation of friendship would be valuable points of

contact during the early part of a naval career. An exchange officer will display his culture, education and naval skills to a group where he will be observed and appreciated. The approach the Argentine and Brazilian navies have initiated could be an ideal model for the Greek–Turkish navies.

89. Turkey maintains 'a large fleet of amphibious landing craft ominously based in Ismir, a few kilometres from Greek islands in the Eastern Aegean and a fleet of 15 submarines (six of them modern high-quality craft) which Greece takes as sure signs of aggressive intent. Both nations maintain two dozen large surface combatants and a school of small fast attack boats armed with anti-ship missiles. Given the geographic disposition of the Greek islands it is difficult to justify the existing symmetry of naval forces. Given also the numerical advantage of Turkish forces in Asia Minor it is unrealistic to worry about a Greek invasion there. Therefore there seems to be no defensive role for Turkish naval forces of the present size and complexion', Tsipis, 'New Technologies', p.193.

90. Combined exercises on search and rescue operations in undisputed waters would be a positive step. The scope of exercises could also be broadened to combined operations in which both countries face common problems such drug trafficking and illegal immigrant trafficking. Of course there is naval co-operation on the NATO level but not on the bilateral level.

91. Since the catastrophic earthquakes in Greece and Turkey, the Commander of the Greek Navy, Vice Admiral Giorgos Ioannides has developed a friendly relationship with his Turkish counterpart, Salim Devrisiglu. They have agreed to exchange mobile numbers in case a 'hot' incident occurs again in the Aegean.

92. Dallmeyer, 'Moderating', p.219.

93. *Athens News Agency*, 11 July 1997. This action raises questions as to what degree the Turkish military agree with the politicians' decisions to stabilise relations with Greece. Normalisation of relations with Greece would cast a shadow on the announcement of the mammoth Turkish military modernisation programme.

94. Since 1994 and after the endorsement of the 1982 Law of the Sea Convention, which calls for a territorial waters' width up to 12 miles, former Turkish Prime Minister, Tansu Ciller and other government officials explicitly and repeatedly stated that any Greek extension to 12 miles would be considered a *casus belli*; see for further study about Turkish threats after the Imia/Kardak incident, S. Georgoudis and S. Soltaridis, *Imia: I Anamfisbiti Elliniki Kyriarxia, I Apili Enos Neou Casus Belli* (Athens: Nea Sinora, Libanis, 1996).

95. In many cases Greek statements tend to infuriate the Turkish side while Turkish official statements such as 'half of the Aegean is ours' 'the group of islands that are situated within 50 km of the Turkish coast ... should belong to Turkey', as well indirect questioning of Greek sovereignty over the Aegean islands, have been viewed even by moderate Greeks with great alarm; Tsakonas, 'Creating', p.40. See also A. Syrigos, *Factors of Stability and Instability in the Eastern Mediterranean and the Pacific*, IDIS, Athens, pp.6–15.

96. The Treaty on Open Skies was signed on 24 March 1992 by 25 states, including Greece and Turkey. Currently only Romania and Hungary have signed an additional bilateral Open Skies accord. The treaty is designed to enhance mutual understanding and confidence and gives to all participating countries, a direct role in gathering information about military forces and activities of concern to them. The treaty is based on territorial openness, the use of airborne sensors and quotas of annual overflights that each signatory to the treaty is willing to accept. The implementation of this treaty by Greece and Turkey would be a positive step toward building confidence and security in the context of an arms control and verification process.

97. For further study see the analysis of J. Burton, *Conflict: Resolution and Prevention* (New York: St Martin Press, 1990).

98. It is widely accepted that the Balkan region is still characterised by deep heterogeneity in political, military, economic, cultural and religious terms.

99. Since the Kosovo crisis most of the Balkan analysts and Balkans leaders, including those of Greece and Turkey have repeatedly stated that it is imperative for NATO to accept Balkan states such as Bulgaria, Romania, Albania, Slovenia and FYROM. Andrew Pierre in a special report about 'De-Balkanizing the Balkans: Security and Stability in South-eastern Europe', *US Institute of Peace* (September 1999) argues that 'now is a pivotal moment. If South-eastern Europe does not advance towards integration with the Euro-Atlantic community, it risks being permanently relegated to renewed ethnic tensions and dangerous instabilities' pp.3–4.
100. Schake, 'NATO Chronicle', p.24.
101. Ratchev, 'NATO', p.9.
102. See N. Marakis, 'I Allages sta Balkania', *To Vima*, 31 October 1999.
103. See Article 5 of the NATO alliance; during the Kosovo crisis Albania, Bulgaria and FYROM all expressed fears of spill-over of the conflict on their territories. For example, the NATO presence in FYROM was seen as diminishing prospects for Albanian nationalistic aspirations to FYROM territory.
104. Albania, Bulgaria, FYROM and Romania having stood by NATO's side during the Kosovo crisis, having suffered huge economic losses, and having been promised by leaders of the other NATO member states such as British PM Blair, early acceptance into the NATO alliance, it is not surprising that the aforementioned states emerged from the war with considerable expectations regarding the future. These expectations include compensation for losses, financial assistance for the rebuilding of bridges, aid for the restructuring of foreign debt, the provision of foreign direct investment but at the top of their agenda is early accession into NATO. See an excellent analysis by Pierre, 'De-Balkanising', pp.4–17. For an elaborated report about Balkan reconstruction after the Kosovo crisis see 'Special Focus Reconstruction in Balkans, and Opinions', *www.eliamep.gr* (June, 1999).
105. In most cases these suggestions have already been activated.
106. In September 1999, the Regional Peacekeeping Force of seven nations was activated in Plovdiv, its base for the first four years. The 5,000 member force comprised of troops from Albania, Bulgaria, FYROM, Greece, Italy, Romania and Turkey, will take on regional peacekeeping or humanitarian operations under the umbrella of international bodies, including the UN, WEU, OSCE and NATO. Bulgaria, Greece, Italy and Turkey will each contribute a mechanised battalion to the 5,000-strong force, an infantry battalion will come from Romania, and Albania and FYROM will each send one infantry company, *Stratigiki*, (September, 1999) p.43.
107. *Reuters Agency News*, 10 September 1999.
108. This recommendation is based on Tsipis' suggestion about the establishment of a Common Security Council and on Tsakonas about the establishment of a Crisis Prevention Center; see Tsipis, 'New Technologies', pp.233–40; Tsakonas, 'Creating', pp.42–5.
109. 'The MAP does not replace the Partnership for Peace (PfP) programme. In fact, participation in PfP for aspiring countries is considered essential, as it provides a well-established way of developing progressive interoperability with Alliance forces ... The provisions of the MAP will complement these activities available under PfP by addressing the broader spectrum of preparations required for eventual membership', *NATO Review*, 2 (Summer, 1999) p.25. For further study about MAP see K-P Klaiber, 'The Membership Action Plan: Keeping NATO's Door Open', *NATO Review*, 2 (summer, 1999) pp.23–5.
110. For further analysis see Pierre, 'De-balkanizing', pp.18–20.
111. The OSCE has been seen as a regional security organisation which can be utilised in order to prevent local conflicts, restore stability and bring peace to war-torn areas. The OSCE has also an array of tools which it can use to attempt to resolve conflicts. The principal instrument for co-ordinating and promoting OSCE activities in the field of military aspects of security is the Forum for Security Co-operation. These include: CBSMs, a Code of Conduct on Politico-Military Aspects of Security, and regional arms control

agreements (Articles II, IV and V of the Dayton Peace Agreement). Albeit most of the Balkan countries are members of the OSCE, the OSCE has *no legal status* under international law and *all its decisions are politically but not legally binding* (emphasis is added); see *www.osceprag.cz.*

112. For NATO's latest strategic concept, see 'Slocombe's Senate Testimony on NATO's Strategic Concept', *Department of State,* 28 October 1999, *www.usembassy.org.uk/ nato91.html.*

Conclusion

During the past few years, the international community has concluded that an open Greek–Turkish conflict will be detrimental to the stability of the Balkan region and the cohesion of NATO. With the demise of a Soviet threat and the proliferation of regional crises and conflicts, especially in the Balkans, normalisation of Greek–Turkish relations is considered critical for European security. To this end, both states must be supported and assisted by NATO while Greek and Turkish leading politicians must embrace a conciliatory approach with regards to their bilateral issues. For NATO's eastern Mediterranean policy to have the greatest likelihood of success, a stable and clear policy regarding the prevention of future intra-alliance conflicts must be implemented.

Having examined the Greek–Turkish security challenges and their relationship with NATO, the following conclusions can be drawn:

- Despite current western rhetoric NATO membership does not itself create a pluralistic security community for all its members.[1]
- Greece's and Turkey's defence and foreign policy establishments have been shaped mainly by a realist world view.[2] The mutual suspicion and hostility between them has remained unaffected by the end of the Cold War. As a result, their respective role (mainly the issue of co-operation and non-co-operation) within NATO has been determined by the quality of their bilateral affairs.
- The tradition of enmity between Greeks and Turks is powerful and long-standing. Their respective security and foreign policies have suffered from traits which made positive engagement and rapprochement difficult if not impossible. These included a total lack of trust, a general state of misinformation about each other, the existence of nationalist-oriented education, populist and sensationalist media, conflation of minority issues with territorial claims, and overemphasis on rights rather than interests.

- Since 1989 the Turkish foreign policy agenda and security challenges have expanded dramatically. Today Turkish security priorities encompass the areas of the Balkans, Caucasus, Middle East and Mediterranean. The utilisation of its natural and human resources together with its geo-strategic location has placed Turkey in a unique location. For the first time in its modern history, Turkey is trying to transform itself into a regional power. This hegemonic discourse has inevitably raised distrust among the Greek political elite and has contributed to a continuation of antagonistic relations between Greece and Turkey.
- Greek mistrust over Turkey has also been generated by the Turkish decision to implement a huge military modernisation programme estimated at around $150 billion over the next twenty-five to thirty years. This modernisation project aims at: i) acquiring the capability of power projection abroad; ii) and the establishment not of a balance of power but of military superiority over all its potential adversaries except Russia.
- Greece having experienced all the pathological symptoms of nationalism, state corporatism, clientalism is currently under the Socialist government winning its gamble to break with its monolithic past. Prime Minister Simitis managed to cure Greece's economic malaise and brought the country successfully into the heart of European political and economic integration. This objective was considered by the entire Greek political spectrum as vital for the safeguarding of Greek national interests from external threats.

With reference to the question of workability of Deutsch's pluralistic security community in the eastern Mediterranean the following conclusions can be drawn:

- The eastern Mediterranean has witnessed the uneven democratic evolution in Greece and Turkey which has resulted in the development of the *Hybrid Region* within the NATO structure in the post-Cold War period.
- This is because the Turkish Kemalist establishment is an elite-driven, top-down movement which has not allowed the development of social pluralism, but has mainly focused on the creation of a modern, homogeneous and secular state.
- As a result Turkish politicians are unable to control and dominate the political scene in modern Turkey due to the ability of the military to promote itself and its principles by claiming to be the legitimate guardians of the Kemalist ideas.
- The heavy involvement of the Turkish military within the political structure of the country is detrimental to Greek–Turkish relations.

This is not because the military is by nature expansionist, but because it prevents the maturation of Turkish politics. Turkish political leaders tend to defer to populist and nationalist policies without considering the costs of their actions since they fear that the military will intervene and take over. Unless the political leadership emancipates itself from military guidance, it will remain prone to populism and thus, Turkish foreign policy will continue to be hostage to nationalism.

- Furthermore, the political control over the military has been hindered by the establishment of an independent economic power by the military. The army has succeeded in developing a number of financial groups which have given them a large stake in Turkey's corporate economy.
- The current Turkish constitution which was drafted by the military has not allowed room for the liberalisation of socio-cultural institutions and as a result it cannot accommodate diversity and respect of minority rights.
- The current Islamic and Kurdish challenges are a manifestation of the incomplete and dysfunctional nature of the Turkish political structure.

A summary of the defining characteristics of the PSC *Hybrid Region* as well as the nature of the PSC in the eastern Mediterranean in the post-Cold War era is presented as follows (Figures 4, 5).

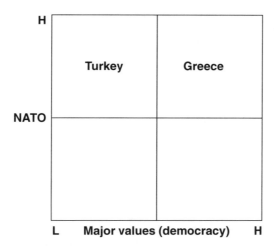

Figure 4 PSC *Hybrid Region* in the eastern Mediterranean

---

1) State building
- Lack of democratic consolidation in Turkey; democratic consolidation in Greece.
- Pre-eminence of the Kemalist establishment in the political structure of Turkey.
- Weak democratic civilian control over political and military structures in Turkey.
- Overextended military involvement in the political sphere and consequent weakened immaturity among Turkish political parties.

2) Inter-state relations
- Cultural and normative accommodation between the two countries facilitated by a series of bilateral activities and engagements in the 'low politics' sphere.
- Weak structural and institutional co-operation in the 'high politics' sphere.
- Policy interaction: promotion of CSBMs for the prevention of an intra-alliance conflict between Greece and Turkey.

Figure 5 Defining characteristics of the PSC *Hybrid Region*
in the eastern Mediterranean

This study has attempted to

- identify the reasons behind the aberrant nature of the eastern Mediterranean
- examine these reasons
- and to propose solutions.

However, further study is required to develop mechanisms that will enable Turkey to adopt and implement truly democratic principles. Ultimately, the greatest challenge Turkey faces is a transition from a republic to a true democracy. In contrast, for Greece the greatest challenge is the formulation of an approach which will facilitate and not impede rapprochement with a non-PSC bound NATO member state.

This book was aimed at identifying and analysing the reasons of non-co-operation between Greece and Turkey within NATO based on Deutsch's theory of PSC. However, it was not aimed at assessing the usefulness of the military for the Turkish political society. Nonetheless, a critical development towards the plausibility of implementing the first criteria of the PSC was raised in the EU Helsinki Summit in December 1999 where Turkey was granted EU membership status. This development will open new questions and will necessitate further research of how Turkey would be able to successfully adopt a democratic regime.

The security risks that emanate from the sub-region of the eastern Mediterranean have been persistent, consistent and detrimental to European security. The organisation that is best placed to contribute to eliminating sources of instability is NATO. Since the region is still characterised by deep heterogeneity a key prerequisite for the stabilisation and non-deterioration of political and military relations between Greece and Turkey can be achieved by the introduction of *feasible* conflict-resolution mechanisms by NATO. The elimination of military confrontation together with the establishment of a network of mutual dependencies and relationships will reduce the possibility of an open conflict. Furthermore, a possible consolidation of fundamental political change (in Turkey), co-operation and a sense of common interests among Greece and Turkey would also bring about positive repercussions to the rest of the Balkan region. NATO's proactive involvement in the Balkan region would also provide a means to manage the inherent anarchy and uncertainty in the regional system as well as within particular problematic NATO sub-systems, such as the eastern Mediterranean.

NOTES

1. For more details on this point see Fotios Moustakis and Michael Sheehan, 'Democratic Peace and European Security', *Mediterranean Quarterly*, 13, 1 (2002) pp.69–85.
2. Greek adoption of a liberal pluralistic perspective has been evident in its foreign policy only in the last five years.

References

GOVERNMENT PUBLICATIONS

Background note: Greece, released by the Bureau of European Affairs, *US Department of State*, June 1999.

Bureau of European and Canadian Affairs, *State Department*, 21 March 1997, *www.mtholyoke.edu/acad/intre//natousis.htm*, pp.2–3.

Congress, Senate, Committee on Foreign Relations, '*United States Foreign Policy Objectives and Overseas Military Installations*', 96th Congress, 1st Session, 1979, pp.62–5.

Department of State Report, U.S. Military Equipment and Human Rights Violations, (1997) pp.1–11. H.R. 3540, *www.fas.org/asmp/library/state/turkey_dos_usweapons.htm*.

Fact Sheet: How NATO Has Changed In The Post Cold War Era, prepared and compiled by the Bureau of European and Canadian Affairs, *State Department*, 21 March 1997, *www.usia.gov/topical/pol/atlcomm/natof321.htm*, p.1.

General Directorate of Press and Information of the Turkish Republic, 1978, p.29.

Greek Ministry of Foreign Affairs, 1998 *www.zeus.hri.org/MFA/foreign/bilateral/aegeen.htm*, *www.zeus.hri.org/docs/turkey* and *www.zeus.hri.org/docs/lausanne*.

Greek Press Conference, 26 March 1999.

Migdalovitz, Carol, 'Turkey: Ally in a Troubled Region', *CRS Report for Congress*, Congressional Research Center, The Library of Congress, 14 September, 1993, p.2.

Migdalowitz, C., 'Greece and Turkey: Current Foreign Aid Issues', *Congressional Research Issue Brief*, Congressional Research Issue, Washington, D.C., 5 September 1995.

Record of the Turkish Grand National Assembly, 12 (1936).

'Slocombe's Senate Testimony on NATO's Strategic Concept', *Department of State*, 28 October 1999 *www.usembassy.org.uk/nato91.html*.

'Turkey: A Country Study', *Library of Congress*, Federal Research Division, Washington, 1992.

Turkish Ministry of Foreign Affairs, *www.mfa.gov.tr/grupa/ad/ade/adeb/default.htm*.

U.S. Center for Defense Information, 3 December 1998, *www.cdi.org/issues/ europe/gree.html.*

'United States Military Installations and Objectives in the Mediterranean', Congressional Research Service, *Library of Congress*, 27 March 1977.

US Department of State, 28/5/96.

US Information Agency, 21 June 1996.

White Paper of the Hellenic Armed Forces 1996–1997, Hellenic Ministry of National Defence (1997).

TREATIES, AGREEMENTS AND COMMUNIQUÉS

European Council in Copenhagen, Conclusions of the Presidency, 21–2 June 1993, Document 93/3/, p.6.

Mediterranean Continental Shelf, 2 (1988).

National Archives and Records Administration (US), Record Group (RG) 59, 740.5 preparations for NATO meeting, 14 September 1951.

NATO Communiqué, *www.nato.int/doc/comm/c911107a.htm.*

NATO Washington Declaration signed on 23 and 24 April 1999, paragraph 3.

'The Mediterranean Region in 2020 and its Role in the European Energy Network', *Commission of the European Communities*, MEMO/95/52.

Thessaloniki Declaration on Good-Neighbourly Relations, Stability, Security and Co-operation in the Balkans, Thessaloniki, 10 June 1997.

INSTITUTE PUBLICATIONS /INTERNET SOURCES

Aliboni, R., 'European Security Across the Mediterranean', *Chaillot Paper 2*, Institute for Security Studies, Western European Union, Paris (1991).

'Alliances and Alignments in the Middle East', *Cosmos*, 2, 1 (1997), IDIS, Athens, p.2.

Arms Sales Monitor (February, 1999), *www.fas.org/asmp/ASM39.html.*

Brassey's Defence Yearbook, 1994.

British American Information Council (BASIC) Paper, 29, August 1998, *www.basicint.org/bpaper29b.htm.*

British American Information Council (BASIC), 'Diplomacy and Arms: West Send Mixed Messages to Aegean Adversaries', 29 (August, 1998) p.1, *www.basicint.org/bpaper29a.htm.*

'Cyprus: A New Strategic Role for NATO', *Cosmos*, 1, 9 (1997) IDIS, Athens, p.6.

Eisenstadt, Michael, 'Turkish–Israeli Military Co-operation: An Assessment', The Washington Institute for Near East Policy, *Policywatch*, 262, Washington, June (1997).

ETHOS, *Direct Emergency Phone Link Between NATO, Greece and Turkey*, 19-02-97, *www.tagish.co.uk/ethos/news/lit1/s2fe.htm.*

Gabelnick, Tamar; Hartung, William D. and Washburn, Jennifer, 'Arming Repression: U.S. Arms Sales to Turkey During the Clinton Administration', World Policy Institute and the Federation of American Scientists, *Report*, (October, 1999) p.2, *www.fas.org/asmp/library/reports/turkeyrep.htm.*

Global Intelligence Update, 'Greco-Turkish Threatens to Deepen Fissures in NATO', 30 March 1999, *www.stratfor.com/services/giu/033099.asp.*

'Greece and Turkey: CBMs', *Cosmos* (March–April, 1998), IDIS, Athens, p.5.

'Greece and Turkey: Current Foreign Aid Issues', Congressional Research Service (CRS) Issue Brief, 3 December 1996, *http://www. fas.org/man/crs/ 86-065.*

'Greece's Armed Forces Modernize', *Cosmos*, 2, 1 (1997), IDIS, Athens, p.4.

'Greek–Turkish Talks Slowly Underway', *Cosmos*, 2, 1 (1997) IDIS, Athens, pp.2, 6.

International Crisis Group: The State of Albania, 6 January 1999, *www.intl-crisis-grop.org/projects/sbalkan/reports/alb05rep.htm.*

'Israel and Turkey: A Popeyed Relationship', *Cosmos*, 2, 8 (1998) IDIS, Athens, pp.5–6.

Lodgaard Sverre (ed.), SIPRI (Oslo: Naval Arms Control, 1990).

Lunn, Simon, 'NATO in Evolution: The Challenges for 1994', *Brassey's Defence Yearbook* (London: Royal United Services Institute, 1995).

Papasotiriou, Harry, 'The Dynamics of Greek–Turkish Strategic Interaction', *www.idis.gr/people/papasot.html*, (1999) IDIS, Athens.

Pierre, Andrew, 'De-Balkanizing the Balkans: Security and Stability in Southeastern Europe', *US Institute of Peace* (September, 1999).

Platias, Athanasios, 'Greek Deterrence Strategy' (1999) *Report*, IDIS, Athens.

'Preserving the Military Balance in the Aegean', *Arms Sales Monitor*, Published by the Federation of American Scientists Fund 39, February (1999), *www.fas.org.*

'Problems and Opportunities for Post-Election Greece', *Cosmos*, 1, 8 (1996), IDIS, Athens.

Sharp, Jane M.O. (ed.), *Europe After An American Withdrawal: Economic and Military Issues* (Oxford: Oxford University Press, SIPRI, 1990) pp.243–73.

SIPRI Yearbook 1998: Armaments, Disarmament and International Security (Stockholm International Peace Research Institute: Oxford University Press, 1998).

SIPRI Yearbook 1999: Armaments, Disarmament and International Security (Stockholm International Peace Research Institute: Oxford University Press, 1999).

'*Special Focus Reconstruction in Balkans*' and '*Opinions*' www.eliamep.gr (June, 1999).

Stavrinos, B., *Comparative Analysis of Greece's and Turkey's Military Expenditures*, Institute of International Relations, Athens (1997).

Syrigos, A., *Factors of Stability and Instability in the eastern Mediterranean and the Pacific*, IDIS, Athens (1999) pp.6–15.

Syrigos, A. and Arvanitopoulos, K., *The International Legal Status of the Aegean*, (Athens, 1998) *www.idis.gr/people/arvan9.html.*

'The Geopolitics of Oil in Central Asia', *Cosmos*, 1, 2 (1995) p.2.

Turkey War Arsenal Grows, *Cosmos*, 1, 3 (1995) p.2.

BOOKS

Adler, E. and Barnett, M. (eds), *Security Communities* (Cambridge University Press, 1998).

Ahmed, Rashid, *The Resurgence of Central Asia: Islam or Nationalism?* (London: Zed Books, 1994).

Akcam, Taner, *Turkish National Identity and the Armenian Question* (in Turkish), (Istanbul: Iletisim, 1992).

Aliboni, R., Joffe, G. and Niblock, T. (eds), *Security Challenges in the Mediterranean* (London: Frank Cass, 1996).

Alivizatos, Nikos, *I Sintagmatiki thesi ton Enoplon Dinameon: I Arxi tou Politikou Elenghou* (Athens: Sakoulas, 1987).

Allison, Graham and Nicolaidis, Kalypso (eds), *The Greek Paradox: Promise V. Performance* (Massachusetts: MIT Press, 1997).

Anishchenko, Vasilevskaya, Kugusheva and Mramornov, *Kommissiya Govorukhina* (Moscow, 1995).

Armstrong, H.C., *Grey Wolf* (Harmondsworth: Penguin Books, 1939).

Bac, Meltem Muftuler, *Turkey's Relations With a Changing Europe* (Manchester: Manchester University Press, 1997).

Bahcheli, Tozun, *Greek–Turkish Relations Since 1955* (Boulder: Westview Press, 1990).

Balance, Edgar O., *The Greek Civil War, 1944–49* (London: Faber, 1966).

Balkir, C. and Williams, A.M. (eds), *Turkey and Europe* (London and New York: Pinter Publishers, 1993).

Barkey, Henry J. (ed.), *Reluctant Neighbour: Analysing Turkey's Role in the Middle East,* (Washington: US Institute of Peace, 1996).

Beaufro, A., *NATO and Europe* (London: Faber, 1967).

Bell, C., *The Diplomacy of Détente: The Kissinger Era* (Martin Robertson, 1977).

Bennett, V., *Crying Wolf: The Return of War to Chechnya* (London: Macmillan Press, 1998).

Betts, Richard K. (ed.), *Conflict After the Cold War, Arguments on Causes of War and Peace* (New York: Macmillan, 1994).

Blechman, Barry M., et al. (eds), *Naval Arms Control: A Strategic Assessment* (New York: St Martins, 1992).

Boulding, Kenneth, *Stable Peace* (University of Texas Press, 1979).

Bozdogan, Sibel and Kasaba, Resat (eds), *Rethinking Modernity and National Identity in Turkey* (University of Washington, 1997).

Brown, James, *Delicately Poised Allies: Greece and Turkey* (London: Brassey's, 1991).

Bugra, Aysa, *State and Business in Modern Turkey: A Comparative Study* (New York Press, State University, 1994).

Burton, John, *Conflict: Resolution and Prevention* (New York: St Martin Press, 1990).

Buzan, B., *People, States and Fear: Agenda for International Security Studies in the Post Cold War Era* (Brighton: Wheatsheaf, 1990).

Buzan, B., Waever, O. and Wilde, J. De., *Security: A New Framework for Analysis* (London: Lynne Rienner Publishers, 1998).

Calvocoressi, Peter, *World Politics Since 1945* (London: Longman, 1992).
Campbell, J. and Sherrard, P., *Modern Greece* (New York: Praeger, 1968).
Cemal, Hasan, *Tank Sesiyle Uyanmak* (Ankara: Bilgi, 1986).
Chenabi, H.E. and Stepan, A. (eds), *Politics, Society and Democracy: Comparative Studies in Honor of Juan J. Linz*, 3 (Boulder, Colorado: Westview, 1999).
Chipman, John (ed.), *NATO's Southern Allies, Internal and External Challenges* (London: Routledge, 1988).
Churchill, W.S., *The Second World War: Triumph and Tragedy* (Boston, Mass.: Houghton Miffin, 1953).
Clogg, R., *A Short History of Modern Greece* (Cambridge Press, 1979).
Clogg, Richard (ed.), *Greece, 1981–89: The Populist Decade* (Houndmills: Macmillan Press, 1993).
Cohen, Antony P., *The Symbolic Construction of Community* (New York: Tavistock, 1985).
Coloumbis, T., *The United States, Greece and Turkey the Troubled Triangle* (New York: Praeger, 1983).
Constas, Dimitris and Stavrou, Nikos (eds), *Greece Prepares for the 21st Century* (Baltimore: Woodrow Wilson Center Press, 1995).
Coufoudakis, Van et al. (eds), *Greece and the New Balkans: Challenges and Opportunities* (New York: Pella, 1999).
Couloumbis, T., *The United States, Greece, and Turkey: The Troubled Triangle* (New York: Praeger, 1983).
Couloumbis, T., *Foreign Interference in Greek Politics: An Historical Perspective* (New York: Pella, 1976).
Couloumbis, T. and Stearns, M., *Entangled Allies: U.S. Policy Toward Greece, Turkey and Cyprus* (New York: Council on Free Press, 1992).
Crawford, B. (ed.), *The Future of European Security* (Berkeley, CA: Center for German and European Studies, 1992).
Dahl, R.A., *Democracy and Its Critics* (New Haven: Yale University Press, 1989).
Danopoulos, C. and Messas, K. (eds), *Crises in the Balkans: Views From the Participants* (Boulder: Westview Press, 1997).
Danopoulos, C.P., *Warriors and Politicians in Modern Greece* (Chapel Hill, 1985).
Davies, Norman, *Europe: A History* (London: Pimlico, 1997).
Deutsch, K., *Political Community at the International Level* (United States: Archon, 1954).
Deutsch, K., *The Nerves of Government: Models of Political Communication and Control* (New York: Free Press, 1966).
Deutsch, Karl W. et al., *Political Community and the North Atlantic Area: International Organisation in the Light of Historical Experience* (Princeton, NJ: Princeton University Press, 1957).
Dodd, Clement, *The Cyprus Imbroglio* (Eothen: Huntingdon, 1998).
Dokos, Thanos and Pronotarios, Nikos, *The Military Security in the 1990's: Problems of South-East Europe* (Athens: Tourikis, 1994) (in Greek).
Drakopoulos, P. (ed.), *Greece–EEC: Political, Economic and Cultural Aspects* (Athens, 1979).
Earlie, Edward Mead (ed.), *Makers of Modern Strategy* (Princeton University Press, 1972).

Eavis, P. (ed.), *European Security: The New Agenda* (Bristol: Saferworld Report, 1990).

Eberhard, Kienle, *Contemporary Syria: Liberalisation between Cold War and Cold Peace* (London Academic Press, 1994).

Encyclopaedia Britannica (London: *Britannia Inc.* 1994).

Eren, N., *Turkey Today – And Tomorrow: An Experiment in Westernization* (New York: Praeger, 1963).

Evans, G. and Newham, J., *Penguin Dictionary of International Relations* (London: Penguin Books, 1998).

Featherstone, Kevin and Ifantis, Kostas (eds), *Greece in a Changing Europe: Between European Integration and Balkan Disintegration* (Manchester University Press, 1996).

Feroz, Ahmad, *The Turkish Experiment in Democracy, 1950–1975* (Boulder: Westview, 1997).

Forbes, N., *The Balkans: A History of Bulgaria, Serbia, Greece, Rumania, Turkey* (Oxford: Clarendon Press, 1915).

Frank, Andre Gunder, *The Centrality of Central Asia* (Amsterdam: VU University Press, 1992).

Frey, Frederick, *The Turkish Political Elite* (Cambridge: MIT, 1965).

Fukuyama, Francis, *The End Of History and the Last Man* (New York: Free Press, 1992).

Fuller, Graham E. and Lesser, Ian O., *Turkey's New Geopolitics: From the Balkans to Western China* (Boulder: Westview, 1993).

Georgiades, Solon, *Istoria tis Diktatorias*, 1, 2, 3, 4 (Athens: Kapopoulos, 1975).

Georgoudis, S. and Soltaridis, S., *Imia: I Anamfisbiti Elliniki Kyriarxia, I Apili Enos Neou Casus Belli* (Athens: Nea Sinora, Libanis, 1996).

Gleny, Misha, *The Balkans 1804–1999* (London: Granta Publications, 1999).

Glogg, R. and Yiannopoulos, G. (eds), *Greece Under Military Rule* (London: Secker & Warburg, 1972).

Gordon, P.H. (ed.), *NATO's Transformation: The Changing Shape of the Atlantic Alliance* (London: Rowman & Littlefield Publishers, 1997).

Gray, C., *Villains, Victims and Sheriffs: Strategic Studies and Security for an Inter-War Period* (Hull: University of Hull Press, 1994).

Grilli, E.R., *The Southern Policies of the EC: Keeping the Mediterranean Safe for Europe* (Cambridge: Cambridge University Press, 1993).

Gummesson, Evert, *Qualitative Methods in Management Research* (California: Sage Publications, 1991).

Gunter, Michael M., *The Kurds and the Future of Turkey* (London: Macmillan Press, 1997).

Gunther, et al., *The Politics of Democratic Consolidation: Southern Europe in Comparative Perspective* (Baltimore: Johns Hopkins University Press, 1995).

Gurkan Ihsan, *NATO, Turkey and the Southern Flank: A Mideastern Perspective* (New York: Transaction Publishers, 1980).

Hale, William, *Turkish Politics and the Military* (London: Routledge, 1994).

Hamel, J., et al., *Case Study Methods* (California: Sage Publications, 1993).

Hansen, Bent, *Egypt and Turkey* (Oxford: Oxford University Press, 1991).

Harris, G.A., *Troubled Alliance: Turkish–American Problems in Historical Perspective* (Washington and Stanford: AEI-Hoover, 1972).

Heper, Metin and Evid, Ahmed (eds), _State, Democracy and the Military: Turkey in the 1980s_ (Berlin: Walter de Gruter, 1988).

Herz, John H. (ed.), _From Dictatorship to Democracy: Coping with the Legacies of Authoritarianism and Totalitarianism_ (Westport, 1982).

Heurtley, W.A., Darby, H.C., Crawley, C.W. and Woodhouse, C.M., _A Short History of Greece: From Early Times to 1964_ (Cambridge Press, 1965).

Heyd, M., _Language Reform in Modern Turkey_ (Jerusalem, 1954).

Heywood, Andrew, _Politics_ (Houndmills: Macmillan, 1997).

Holsti, K.J., _International Politics. A Framework of Analysis_ (Englewood Cliffs, NJ: Prentice-Hall, 1983).

Howard, H.N., _Turkey, The Straits and US Policy_ (Baltimore and London: Johns Hopkins University Press, 1974).

Humphreys, R.S., _Islamic History: A Framework for Enquiry_ (NJ: Princeton, 1991).

Huntington, Samuel, _The Third Wave: Democratisation in the Late Twentieth Century_ (University of Oklahoma Press, 1991).

Inkeles, A. (eds), _On Measuring Democracy: Its Consequences and Concomitants_ (NJ: New Brunswick, Transaction Publications, 1991).

Jacob, P.E and Toscano, James, V. (eds), _The Integration of Political Communities_ (New York: J.B. Lippincot, 1964).

Jacobsen, Carl, G. (ed.), _Strategic Power: USA/USSR_ (London: Macmillan Press, 1990).

Jelavich, Barbara, _The History of the Balkans_ (Cambridge Press, 1983).

Jelavich, C. and B., _The Balkans_ (Englewood Cliffs: Prentice-Hall, 1966).

Johnson, L.M., _Thucydides, Hobbes and the Interpretation of Realism_ (Dekalb: Northern Illinois Press, 1993).

Kaplan, L.S., Clawson, R.W. and Luranghi, R., _NATO and the Mediterranean_ (Wilmington, Delaware: Scholarly Resources, 1985).

Karabellias, G., _O Rolos Ton Enoplon Dynameon Stin Politiki Zoi Tis Tourkias Kai Tis Elladas: Sigkritiki Analisis ton Metapolemikon Stratiotikon Epembaseon 1945–1980_ (Athens: 1998).

Karat, K.H., _Turkey's Politics: The Transition to a Multi-Party System_ (Princeton University Press, 1959).

Karpat, K.H. (ed.), _Turkey's Foreign Policy in Transition, 1950–1974_ (Leiden: Brill, 1975).

Kazakos, P. and Ioakimides, P.C. (eds), _Greece and EC Membership Evaluated_ (Pinter Publishers, 1994).

Keohane, R.O. and Nye, J.S., _Power and Interdependence_ (New York: Harper Collins Publishers, 1989).

Kinross, John, _Ataturk: The Rebirth of a Nation_ (London: Weidenfeld & Nicolson, 1993).

Kirisci, K. and Winrow, Gareth M., _The Kurdish Question and Turkey: An Example of a Trans-State Ethnic Conflict_ (London: Frank Cass, 1997).

Kissinger, Henry, _The Troubled Partnership_ (New York: McGraw-Hill, 1965).

Kissinger, Henry, _Years of Upheaval_ (Boston: Little, Brown, 1982).

Kolars, F. and Mitchell, W.A., _The Euphrates River and the Southeast Anatolia Development Project_ (Carbondale: Southern Illinois University Press, 1991).

Kollias, Costas, _I Politiki Ikonomia tis Aminas_ (Thessaloniki: Paratiritis, 1998).

Konstas, Dimitris and Stavrou, Nikolaos (eds), *Greece Prepares for the Twenty First Century* (Baltimore: Johns Hopkins University Press, 1996).

Kouris, Nikos, *Ellada-Tourkia, O Pentikontaetis Polemos* (Athens: Nea Sinora Livanis, 1997).

Kourvetakis, Y. and Dobratz, *A Profile of Modern Greece in Search of Identity* (Oxford: Clarendon Press, 1987).

Kousoulas, D.G., *Modern Greece: Profile of a Nation* (New York: Scribner, 1974).

Kremmydas, George, *Oi anthropoi tis Juntas meta tin Diktactoria* (Athens: Exantas, 1984).

Krepon, Michael, et al. (eds), *A Handbook of Confidence Building Measures for Regional Security* (Washington: Henry Stimson Center, 1995).

Kreyenbroek, Philip G. and Sperl, Stefan (eds), *The Kurds: A Contemporary Review* (London: Routledge, 1992).

Leffler, Melvyn P., *A Preponderance of Power* (Stanford, California: Stanford University Press, 1967).

Lehmann, D., *Democracy and Development in Latin America* (Cambridge: Polity Press, 1990).

Lenczowski, G. (ed.), *Political Elites in the Middle East* (Washington, DC: American Research Enterprises, 1975).

Lewis, Bernard, *The Middle East*, Part III (London: Phoenix Giant, 1996).

Linke, Lilo, *Allah Dethroned* (New York, 1937).

Linklater, Andrew, 'The Problem of Community in International Relations Theory', *Alternatives*, 2 (1990).

Loukas, I., *Sixroni Politiki Istoria kai Pagkosmioi Polemi: Agli kai Germani Theoritiki tis Isxios* (Athens: Troxalia, 1996).

Luttwak, Edward, *The Political Uses of Sea Power* (Baltimore: Johns Hopkins Press, 1974).

Maghroori, Ray and Ramberg, Bennet (eds), *Globalism Versus Realism: International Relations' Third Debate* (Boulder: Westview Press, 1982).

Malcolm, Noel, *Kosovo: A Short History* (London: Macmillan, 1998).

Mango, Andrew, *Turkey: The Challenge of a New Role* (London: Preager, 1994).

Manishali, Erol (ed.), *Turkey's Place in the Middle East* (Istanbul: Middle East Business and Banking Publication, 1989).

Martis, Nikos, *The Falsification of Macedonian History* (Athens: Euroekdotiki, 1984).

Mastny, Vojtech and Nation, R. Craig (eds), *Turkey Between East and West: New Challenges for a Rising Regional Power* (Colorado: Westview Press, 1996).

Mathias, Jopp, et al., *Integration and Security in Western Europe: Inside the European Pillar* (Boulder: Westview, 1991).

McDowall, David, *A Modern History of the Kurds* (London: Tauris, 1997).

McInnes, C., *Security and Strategy in the New Europe* (London: Routledge, 1992).

McInnes, C., Carr, F. and Ifantis, K. (eds), *NATO in the New European Order* (Houndmills: Macmillan Press, 1996).

McNeil, William H., *The Metamorphosis of Greece Since World War II* (Oxford: Blackwell, 1978).

Mesquite, Bueno de and Lalman, *War and Reason* (New Haven: Yale University Press, 1992).

Moskos, Charles and Wood, Frank (eds), *The Military: More Than Just a Job?* (New York: Pergamon-Brassey's Publishers, 1988).

Mourtos, Giorgos, *Elada kai Tourkia: Stin Meta-Psixropolemiki Epoxi* (Athens: Troxalia, 1997).

Mouzelis, N., *Modern Greece: Facets of Underdevelopment* (London: Macmillan, 1978).

Mozaffari, Mehdi (ed.), *Security Politics in the Commonwealth of Independent Studies: The Southern Belt* (Houndmills: Macmillan Press, 1997).

Nas, F. and Odekon, M. (eds), *Liberalisation and the Turkish Economy* (Westport, Conn: Greenwood Press, 1988).

Nester, William, *International Relations* (Harper Collins College Publishers, 1995).

North Atlantic Treaty (NATO) HandBook (Brussels: 1990).

Onis, Z. and Riedel, J., *Economic Crises and Long-Term Growth in Turkey* (Washington: The World Bank, 1993).

Ordogan, G. (ed.), *Balkans: A Mirror of the New International Order* (Conference, Marmara University, EREN, 1995).

Ozbudun, E., *Making Constitutions During the Process of Democratisation* (in Turkish), (Ankara: Bilgi Yayinevi, 1993).

Papacosma, S. Victor and Heiss, Mary Ann (eds), *NATO in the Post-Cold War Era: Does it Have a Future?* (New York: St Martin Press, 1996).

Papacosma, Victor, *The Military in Greek Politics: The 1909 Coup d'Etat* (Kent: Kent Ohio State University, 1977).

Papathemelis, Stelios, *Antepithesi* (Thessaloniki: Paratiritis, 1992).

Pelletiere, S.C., *The Kurds: An Unstable Element in the Gulf* (Boulder & London: Westview Press, 1984).

Pettifer, James, *The Turkish Labyrinth: Atatturk and the New Islam* (London: Penguin Books, 1998).

Platias, Athanassios, *To Neo Diethnes Systima: Realistiki Prosegisi Diethnon Sxeseon* (Athens: Papazisis, 1995).

Pridham, Geoffrey (ed.) *Securing Democracy: Political Parties and Democratic Consolidation in Southern Europe* (London: Routledge, 1990).

Pridham, Geofrey (ed.), *Encouraging Democracy: The International Context of Regime Transition in Southern Europe* (Leicester: Leicester University Press, 1991).

Pridham, Geoffrey and Lewis, Paul. G. (eds), *Stabilising Fragile Democracies: Comparing New Party Systems in Southern and Eastern Europe* (London: Routledge, 1996).

Psomiades, Harry and Thomadakis, S.B. (eds), *Greece, the New Europe, and the Changing International Order* (New York: Pella, 1993).

Rabinow, Paul and Sullivan, William (eds), *Interpretative Social Science: A Reader* (Berkeley: University of California Press, 1979).

Rapoport, Anatol (ed.), *Clausewitz: On War* (London: Penguin Books, 1968).

Redmond, John, *The Next Mediterranean Enlargement of the European Community: Turkey, Cyprus & Malta?* (Aldershot, England: Dartmouth Publishing Company, 1993).

Reiss, H. (ed.), *Kant's Political Philosophy* (Cambridge, 1991).

Robins, Philip, *Turkey and the Middle East* (London: Pinter Publishers, 1991).

Russett, Bruce et al., *Grasping the Democratic Peace: Principles for a Post-Cold War World* (Princeton: Princeton University Press, 1991).
Sassoon, D., *One Hundred Years Of Socialism* (London: Fontana Press, 1996).
Schick, Irvin and Tonak, Erdugul (eds), *Turkey In Transition* (London: Oxford Press, 1987).
Schumpeter, J.A., *The Sociology of Imperialism, in Imperialism and Social Classes* (New York, 1955).
Sen, Serdar, *Sihahli Kuvvetler ve Modernizm* (Istanbul: Sarmal, 1996).
Seyom, Brown, *Causes and Prevention of War* (New York: St Martin Press, 1994).
Shoup, Paul (ed.), *Problems of Balkan Security* (Washington: Wilson Centre Press, 1990).
Simitis, Kostas, *Gia Mia Ischiri Koinonia Gia Mia Ischiri Ellada* (Towards a Strong Society, Towards a Strong Greece), (Athens: Plethron, 1995).
Stamatopoulos, T., *O Esoterikos Agonas* (Athens: Kalbos, 1971).
Stavrou, N.A. (ed.), *Greece Under Socialism* (New York: Orpheous Publishing, 1988).
Stuart, Douglas T. (ed.), *Politics and Security in the Southern Region of the Atlantic Alliance* (Basingstoke: Macmillan Press, 1988).
Taylor, Charles, *Community, Anarchy, and Library* (Cambridge: Cambridge University Press, 1982).
The Military Balance, 1989–1990 (London: Brassey's, 1989).
The Military Balance 1995–1996: Arms Doctrines and Disarmament (Cyprus: Aristos Aristotelous, 1995).
The Military Balance 1995–1996 (London: Brassey's, 1995).
The Turkish Economy in June 1992: Statistics and Interpretations (Ankara: State Institute of Statistics, 1992).
Theophanous, Andreas and Coufoudakis, Van (eds), *Security and Co-operation in the Eastern Mediterranean* (Nicosia: Intercollege, 1997).
Toynbee, A.I., A Study of History, IV (London: Oxford University Press, 1940).
Trimberger, Ellen Kay, *Revolution from Above: Military Bureaucrats and Development in Egypt, Peru, Turkey, and Japan* (New Jersey: Transaction Books, 1977).
Tsipis, Kostas (ed.), *Common Security Regimes* (New York: Columbia University Press, 1996).
Valinakis, Yannis, *Greece and the CFE Negotiations* (Ebenhause: Stiftung Wissenschaftt und Politik, 1991).
Veremis, T. and Couloumbis, T., *Eliniki Exoteriki Politiki: Dilimata mias Neas Epoxis* (Athens: Sideris, 1997).
Veremis, Thanos, *Oi Epemvasis tou Stratou stin Elliniki Politiki, 1916–1936* (Athens: Odysseas, 1977).
Veremis, Thanos, *The Military in Greek Politics: From Independence to Democracy* (London: Hurst & Company, 1997).
Veremis, Thanos and Triantaphyllou, Dimitris (eds), *The Southeast European Yearbook 1997–98* (Athens: Hellenic Foundation For European & Foreign Policy, 1998).
Vickers, Miranda, *Between Serb and Albanian: A History of Kosovo* (London: Hurst Publishers, 1998).
Waever, et al., *Identity, Migration and the New Security Order in Europe* (London: Pinter, 1993).

Weber, Max, *Economy and Society* (Berkeley: University of California Press, 1978).
Wessels, W. and Engel, C. (eds), *The European Union in the 1990s Ever Closer and Larger?* (Bonn: Europa Union Verlag, 1993).
Woodhouse, C.M., *Karamanlis: The Restorer of Greek Democracy* (Oxford: Clarendon Press, 1982).
Woodhouse, C.M., *The Rise and the Fall of the Greek Colonels* (London: Granada, 1985).
World Atlas (London: Dorling Kindersley, 1997).
Yin, Robert, *Case Study Research: Design and Methods* (California: Sage Publications, 1994).
Zeiner-Gundersen, H.F., et al. (eds), *NATO's Maritime Flanks: Problems and Prospects* (London: Pergamon-Brassey's, 1987).
Zloch, C.I. (ed.), *Bulgaria in a Time of Change: Economic and Political Dimensions* (Aldershot: Avebury, 1996).

THESES, RESEARCH REPORTS, OCCASIONAL REPORTS AND MONOGRAPHS

Barjaba, Kosts, 'Albania in Transition: Elite's Role and Perspective', *NATO Report* (June, 1998).
Bright, Barry P., 'Introduction to Research Methods in Postgraduate Thesis and Dissertations', *Newland Paper*, 18 (University of Hull, 1991).
'Cyprus and The United Nations', *House of Commons, Research Paper*, 95/31 (1995).
Daci Halit, 'The Impact of Democratic Changes in the Albanian Army', *NATO Report* (June, 1999).
'Denying Human Rights and Ethnic Identity: The Greeks of Turkey', *Human Rights Watch* (1992) pp.1–25.
Dodd, Tom, 'NATO Enlargement', *Research Paper*, 97/51 (London: International Affairs and Defence Section, House of Commons, 8 May 1997).
Dodd, Tom, 'NATO's New Directions', *House of Commons Research Paper*, 98/52 (1998).
Eralp, Yakup Atila, 'Turkish Public Perceptions of NATO', *NATO Report* 1995–7 (Brussels, 1997).
Feroz, Ahmad, 'The Turkish Elections of 1983', *Merip Reports* (March/April, 1984).
Frinking, Tom, 'Draft Interim Report of the Sub-Committee on the Southern Region', *North Atlantic Assembly* (November, 1984).
Fuelling Balkan Fires: The West's Arming of Greece and Turkey, Project on the Arms Trade, The British American Security Information Council (1993).
Hall, et al., 'Case Studies in Social Science Research', *Working Paper* No.78-16 (Brussels: European Institute for Advanced Studies in Management, 1978).
Human Rights Watch Arms Project, 'Weapons Transfers and Violation of the Laws of War in Turkey', *Human Rights Watch* (1995) pp.1, 23.

Human Rights Watch Report (1999) *www.hrw.org/reports/1999/turkey/ turkey993-09.htm.*

Karabelias, G, 'Civil-Military Relations: A Comparative Analysis of the Role of the Military in the Political Transformation of Post-War Turkey and Greece: 1980–1995', *NATO Final Report* (June, 1998).

Kemal, Ahmet, 'Military Rule and the Future of Democracy in Turkey', *Merip Reports* (March/April, 1984) pp.12–15.

Kennan, George, *In the Other Balkan Wars: A 1913 Carnegie Endowment Inquiry in Retrospect with a New Introduction and Reflection on the Present* (Washington, DC: Carnegie Endowment for International Peace, 1993).

Khalilzad, Zalmay (ed.), 'Strategic Appraisal', *Rand Report* (1996).

Khalizad, Zalmay and Lesser, Ian O. (eds), 'Sources of Conflict in the 21st Century: Regional Futures and US Strategy', *Rand Report* (1998).

Kioukias, D., *Organising Interests in Greece: Labour, Agriculture, Local Government and Political Development During Metapolitefsi*, Ph.D Dissertation, University of Birmingham (1991).

Kollias, Costas and Makrydakis, Spyros, *Is There a Greek–Turkish Arms Race? Evidence from Co-integration and Causality Tests*, 60, Centre of Planning and Economic Research (CPER), Discussion Papers, Athens (1997).

Kugler, Richard L., 'NATO Military Strategy for the Post-Cold War Era: Issues and Options', *RAND Report* (1992).

Larrabee, F. Stephen (ed.), 'The Volatile Powder Keg: Balkan Security after the Cold War', *RAND Study*, American University Press, Washington (1994).

Larrabee, F. Stephen, et al., 'NATO's Mediterranean Initiative', *RAND Report* (1998).

Lawless, R. (ed.), 'Foreign Policy Issues in the Middle East', *Occasional Papers*, 28, Center for Islamic Studies, University of Durham (1985).

Lesser, Ian O., 'Mediterranean Security: New Perspectives and Implications for the U.S. Policy', *Rand Report* (1993).

Luarasi, Aleks, 'Legal and Institutional Reform in Albania after the Democratic Revolution', *NATO Report* (May, 1997).

Macintosh, James, *Confidence and Security Building Measures: A Sceptical Look, Working Paper 85* (Canberra: Peace Research Centre, 1990).

Mango, Andrew, 'Turkey: A Delicately Poised Ally', *The Washington Papers* (London: Sage Publications, 1975).

Moschonas, Andreas, *European Integration and Prospects of Modernisation in Greece, Research Paper*, University of Reading (1997).

Moya, Pedro, 'Frameworks for Co-operation in the Mediterranean', *North Atlantic Assembly* (October, 1995).

Moya, Pedro, 'NATO's Role in the Mediterranean', *North Atlantic Assembly Report*, 16 April 1997, p.6.

North Atlantic Assembly Reports (1995).

Papandreou, Vasso, 'The Role of Greece as a New Europe Takes Shape', *Occasional Research Paper – Special Issue*, Panteion University, Athens (October, 1992).

Peters, John E., 'CFE and Military Stability in Europe', *Rand Report* (1997).

Ratchev, Valeri, 'NATO and South-Eastern European Security Perspectives:

Implications for the Evolution of National Security Institutions and the Decision-Making Process in Bulgaria', *NATO Fellowship Report* (Brussels, 1999).

Rato, de Rodrigo, 'Co-operation and Security in the Mediterranean', North Atlantic Assembly, Political Committee, *Report* (October, 1995).

Rato de Rodrigo, 'NATO's Mediterranean Initiative', *North Atlantic Assembly* (October, 1995).

Report of the South Balkans Working Group, *Toward Comprehensive Peace in Southeast Europe: Conflict Prevention in the South Balkans* (Twentieth Century Fund Press, 1996).

Russet, Bruce, 'A Post-Thucydides Post-Cold War World', *Occasional Research Papers* – Special Issue, IDIS, Athens (1997).

Scherbak, Igor, *Confidence-building Measures and International Security, The Political and Military Aspects: a Soviet Approach*, United Nations Institute for Disarmament Research (New York, 1991).

Spyropoulos, E., *The Greek Military (1909-1941) and the Greek Mutinies in the Middle East (1941–1944)*. Unpublished Ph.D Thesis, Columbia University, (1993).

Stavrinos, V. and Balfoussias, A., *The Greek Military Sector and Macroeconomic Effects of Military Spending in Greece*, CPER, 51, Athens (1996).

Tsakonas, Panayiotis J., 'Creating Conditions of Stability in Southeastern Europe: Prospects for an Arms Control Regime', *NATO Report* (June, 1999).

Tsinizelis, Michael. J. and Chryssochoou, Dimitris N., *Between 'Disharmony' and 'Symbiosis': The Greek Political System and European Integration*, University of Reading, Research Paper. Unpublished (1997).

Ward, M., 'The Enlargement of WEU', (Political Com.), *Rapporteur*, Document 1360, 19 April 1993, pp.5–6.

Ward, M., 'The Enlargement of WEU', Political Committee, *Report*, 19 April 1993, *www.fumet.fi/pub/doc/world/AWEU/documents/enlargement-weu*.

Ware, R., '*The End of Yugoslavia*', House of Commons Background Papers, 290, 91/42 (1992).

Whitman, Richard. G., 'Securing Europe's Southern Flank? *A Comparison of NATO, EU and WEU Policies and Objectives*', *NATO Report* (1999).

Young, Thomas-Durell, 'Reforming NATO's Military Structures: The Long-Term Study and Its Implications for Land Forces', *Report for the Strategic Studies Institute of the US Army*, 15 May 1998.

Zanga, Louis, 'Albania and Turkey Forge Closer Ties', RFE/RL *Research Report*, 12 March 1993, pp.30–33.

CONFERENCE AND WORKSHOP PAPERS

Bolles, D., Coufoudakis, V., Kozyris, J., Kuniholm, B., Philon, A., Rossides, E.T. and Rudolph, N., '*United States Foreign Policy Regarding Greece, Turkey & Cyprus: The Rule of Law and American Interests*', *AHI Conference Proceedings* (1988).

Conference on The Transfer of Caspian Oil to the Western Markets: The

Role of Turkey, *Anadolu Agency*, 13-04-99, *www.hri.org/news/turkey/anadolu/1999/99-04-13.anadolu.html*.

Dimitracopoulos, A., *Military Doctrine; The Greek Perspective*, Seminar on Security and Democracy in the New Europe, Athens 23–8 May 1994.

Joint Press Conference by C. Stefanopoulos, President of the Hellenic Republic and Bulgarian President, Petar Stoyanov, on June 1999, *The Insider*, 9, 5/6 (1999) p.29.

Kavakas, Dimitrios, *The Implications of Greece's Policies and Attitudes Towards the Issue of Macedonia, on its role in the CFSP*, BISA Conference Leeds, 15–17 December 1997.

Keyder, Caglar, 'Democracy and the Demise of National Developmentalism: Turkey in Perspective', *IEA Conference*, 113 (1995).

Pickering, T.R., Remarks at Symposium on *Atlantic Partnership: NATO's Focus for the New Millenium*, Old Dominion University, Norfolk, Virginia, 30 October 1998, *www.usia.gov/topical/pol/atlcomm/pick30.htm*.

Rossides, E.T., '*American Foreign Policy and the Rule of Law – The Aegean and Cyprus*', in *United States Foreign Policy Regarding Greece, Turkey & Cyprus: The Rule of Law and American Interests*, AHI Conference Proceeding (Washington: American Hellenic Institute, 1988) pp.99–102.

Security Communities in Comparative Perspective, Merill House Conference, 1–2 December 1995, p.1, *www.cceia.org/security.htm*.

Simic, Pedrag, 'NATO and the Balkans', *Conference Paper*, Corfu (1997).

The Rule of Law and Conditions on Foreign Aid to Turkey, Legislative Conference (Washington: American Hellenic Institute, 1990).

Tsoxatzopoulos, Akis, *I Geopolitiki tis Eurasias kai tis Anatolikis Mesogiou sto Neo Diethnes Sistima*, International Workshop organised by Greek Ministry of Defence, Athens, June (1999).

Vukadinovic, R., 'South-Eastern Europe: Instabilities and Linking Strategies', *Conference Paper*, Corfu (1997).

Walden, S. Axel, *The Balkans, Europe and Greece*, talk presented at the Centre for European Policy Studies (CEPS) on 19 February 1997, Brussels.

ARTICLES IN JOURNALS, NEWSPAPERS AND MAGAZINES AND NEWS AGENCIES

Adler, Emanuel, et al., 'Governing Anarchy: A Research Agenda for the Study of Security Communities', *Ethics & International Affairs*, 10 (1996) pp.63–98.

Alford, Jonathan (ed.), 'The Future of Arms Control, Part 3: Confidence Building Measures', *Adelphi Paper*, 149 (1978).

Alivizatos, Nicos, 'The Greek Army in the Late Forties: Toward an Institutional Autonomy', *Journal of the Hellenic Diaspora*, 5 (1978).

— 'An Ill-Judged Amnesty', *The Economist*, 4 September 1999, p.48.

Anastasi, P., 'Greece Links EMU with Turkish Threat', *The European*, 27 June, 1996, p.19.

'Arab League: Turkish–Israel Military Agreement Contradicts Peace Process', *Turkish Daily News*, 07-5-99.

Arvanitopoulos, Kostas, 'The Politics of US Aid to Greece and Turkey', *Mediterranean Quarterly*, 7, 2 (1996).

Asmus, R., Kugler, R.L. and Larrabee F.S., 'NATO Expansion: The Next Steps', *Survival*, 37, 1 (1995) pp.7–33.

Asmus, R.D., Larrabee, F. Stephen and Lesser, I.O., 'Mediterranean Security: New Challenges, New Tasks', *NATO Review*, 44, 3 (1996).

Aspin, Les, 'New Europe, New NATO', *NATO Review*, 42 (February, 1994) p.12.

— 'Athens' New Wings', *Military Technology*, 9 (1999) pp.77–90.

Atiyas, N.B., 'The Kurdish Conflict in Turkey: Issues, Parties and Prospectus', *Security Dialogue*, 28, Part 4 (1997) pp.439–52.

Axt, Heinz-Jurgen, 'On the Way to Socialist Self-Reliance? PASOK's Government Policy in Greece', *Journal of Modern Greek Studies*, 2 (1984).

Aybet, G., 'Turkey's in its Geo-Strategic Environment', *Rusi and Brassey's Defence Yearbook* (1992) p.92.

Bal, Idris, 'The Turkish Model and the Turkish Republics', *Perceptions*, 3, 3, Center for Strategic Research, Ankara, Turkey (1998) p.1.

Barkey, H., 'Why Military Regimes Fail: The Perils of Transition', *Armed Forces and Society*, 16, 2 (1990) pp.169–190.

Barkey, Henri, 'Turkey's Kurdish Dilemma', *Survival*, 35, 4 (1993) pp.51–70.

Barkey, H.J. and Fuller, Graham E., 'Turkey's Kurdish Question: Critical Turning Points and Missed Opportunities', *The Middle East Journal*, 51, 1 (1997) pp.59–79.

Bayar, Ali H., 'The Developmenal State and Economic Policy in Turkey', *Third World Quarterly*, 17, 4 (1996) p.781.

Bayazit, V., 'Black Sea and Mediterranean Challenges for the Turkish Navy', *NATO's Sixteen Nations*, 1 (1994) pp.67–73.

Behar, Nansen, 'Ethnic Identity and Border Disputes in the Balkans', *Review Of International Affairs*, XLIX, 15 October 1998, pp.25–32.

Belle, Douglas A.Van, 'Press Freedom and the Democratic Peace', *Journal Of Peace Research*, 34, 4 (1997).

Bentick, M., 'NATO's Out of Area Problem', *Adelphi Paper, 211* (1986).

Bilman, L., 'The Regional Co-operation Initiatives in Southeast Europe and the Turkish Foreign Policy', *Perceptions*, III, 3 (1998), Center for Strategic Research, Ankara, pp.1–14.

Blagoev, B., 'Two Models for Stabilisation of the Balkans and South-Eastern Europe', *Balkan Forum*, 2, 5 (1997) pp.49–63.

Blandy, C., 'Chechen Caravan Trails', *Conflict Studies Research Centre* (April, 1996).

Blandy, C.W., 'The Caspian: A Sea of Troubles', *Conflict Studies*, 31 September 1997.

Blandy, C.W., 'The Caucasus Region and Caspian Basin: "Change, Complication and Challenge"', *Conflict Studies*, UK Minister of Defence (April, 1998) p.1.

Blandy, C.W., 'Rebirth of the Great Silk Road: Myth or Substance?' *Conflict Studies* (February, 1999).

Blank, Stephen, 'Russia and Europe in the Caucasus', *European Security*, 4, 4 (1995).

Blanton, S.L., 'Instruments of Security or Tools of Repression: Arms Imports and Human Rights Conditions in Developing Countries', *Journal of Peace Research*, 36, 2 (1999).

Blumenwitz, D., 'Cyprus: Political and Legal Realities', *Perceptions: Journal of International Affairs*, www.mfa.gov.tr/grupa/percept/IV-3/blumenwitz.htm.

Bolukbasi, Suha, 'Ankara's Baku-Centered Transcaucasia Policy: Has it Failed?' *The Middle East Journal*, 51, 1 (1997) pp.80–94.

Booth, K., 'Security and Anarchy: Utopian Realism in Theory and Practice', *International Affairs*, 67, 3 (1991) pp.527–45.

Bozzo, L. and Ragionieri, R., 'Regional Security in the Balkans and the Role of Turkey', *The Southern European Yearbook 1992* (Athens: Eliamep, 1993) p.21.

Brown, N., 'Climate, Ecology and International Security', *Survival*, 31, 6 (1989) pp.519–32.

Bugajski, Janusz, 'The Balkans: On the Brink Again', *The Washington Quarterly*, 20, 4 (April, 1997) pp.211–22.

Cadena, Lucas, 'Greek–Turkish Relations', *Princeton Journal of Foreign Affairs* (Winter, 1998), www.princeton.edu/~foreigna/winter1998/turkey.html.

Cakar, N., 'Turkey's Security Challenges', *Perceptions Journal of International Affairs*, June–August (1996), p.1, www.mfa.gov.tr/grupf/percept/I2/I2-2.htm.

Cakar, Nezihi, 'A Strategic Overview of Turkey', *Perceptions*, 3, 2, June–August (1996) p.5, www.mfa.gov.tr/grupf/percept/III-2/cakar.htm.

Chipman, John, 'The Future of Strategic Studies: Beyond Grand Strategy', *Survival*, 34, 1 (1992) pp.109–31.

Clifton, T.C. and Campbell S., 'Domestic Structure, Decisional Constraints and War', *Journal of Conflict Resolution*, 35, 1 (1991) pp.187–211.

Constantinides, Stephanos, 'Greek Foreign Policy: Theoretical Orientations and Praxis', *Hellenic Studies*, 4, 1 (1996).

Cooper, Malcolm, 'The Legacy of Ataturk', *International Affairs*, 78, 1 (2002) pp.115–28.

Cornish, Paul, 'European Security: the End of Architecture and the New NATO', *International Affairs*, 74, 4 (1996) pp.751–70.

Cottey, A., 'Western Interests in the Balkan Wars', *Brassey's Defence Yearbook* (London: Royal United Services Institute, 1994).

Coufoudakis, Van, 'Greek–Turkish Relations 1972–1983', *International Security*, 9, 4 (1985).

Coufoudakis, Van, 'Greek Foreign Policy in the Post-Cold War: Issues and Challenges', *Mediterranean Quarterly*, 7, 3 (1996).

Couloumbis, Theodoros, 'Strategic Consensus in Greek Domestic and Foreign Policy Since 1974', *Thesis: A Journal of Foreign Policy Issues* (winter, 1998), www.hri.org/MFA/thesis/winter98/consensus.html.

Couloumbis, Theodoros, 'Dealing with Greek–Turkish Tension', *Athens News Agency*, 6 October 1999.

Cowell, Alan, 'Greece Finds Itself Obsessed by Unmentionable Neighbour', *The New York Times*, 21 January 1994.

Cragg, Anthony, 'A New Strategic Concept for a New Era', *NATO Review*, 47, 2 (1999).

Crawford, N., 'Once and Future Security Studies', *Security Studies*, 1, 2 (1991) pp.283–316.
'Crisis Diffused, Ankara Urges Greece to Negotiate', *Turkish Daily News*, 1-02-96, *zeus.hri.org/news/agencies/trkn/96-02-01.trkn.html.*
Danopulos, C., 'From Balkonies to Tanks: Post-Junta Civil Military Relations in Greece', *Journal of Political and Military Sociology*, 13 (1985).
— 'Defence and Economics in Turkey', *NATO's Sixteen Nations & Partners for Peace*, Special Supplement (1998).
Degerau, Constantin, 'Romania: Five Years In Partnership For Peace', *Central European Issues: Romanian Foreign Affairs Review*, 5, 1 (1999).
Delors, J., 'European Integration and Security', *Survival*, Mar–Apr 1997, pp.99–110.
Demirel, S., 'Demirel Warns Greece, and There is Absolutely no Resemblance Between What is Going on in Kosovo and the Southeast Turkey', *Anadolu Agency*, 29 April 1999.
Demirel, Suleyman, 'The Need For Dialogue: Turkey, Greece & the Possibility of Reconciliation', *Harvard International Review*, 21, Part 1 (winter, 1998/1999) p.24.
Denktash, Raoul, 'The Crux of the Cyprus Problem', *Perceptions: Journal of International Affairs*, IV, 3 (1999) *www.mfa.gov.tr/grupa/percept/IV-3/denktas.htm.*
Desjardins, Marie-France, 'Rethinking Confidence-Building Measures', *Adelphi Paper*, 307 (1996).
Dixon, W., 'Democracy and the Peaceful Settlement Of International Conflict', *American Political Science Review*, 88, 4 (1994) pp.14–32.
— 'Down but far from Out', *The Economist*, 1 August 1998, pp.44–5.
Doyle, M., 'Kant, Liberal Legacies and Foreign Affairs', Part I, *Philosophy and Public Affairs*, 12, 3 (1983) pp.205–35.
Doyle, M., 'Liberalism and World Politics', *American Political Science Review*, 80, 4 (1986) pp.1151, 69.
Doyle, M., 'Liberalism and World Politics', *American Political Science Review*, 80, 4 (1989) pp.1151–70.
Dyke, Jon M. Van, 'The Aegean Sea Dispute: Options and Avenues', *Marine Policy*, 20, 5 (1996).
Elekdag, Sukru, '2 1/2 Strategy', *Perceptions* (March–May, 1996), *www.mfa.gov.tr/grupf/percept/I1/per1-3.htm.*
Elekdag, Sukru, 'War Strategy', *Perceptions* (March–May, 1996) pp.1–11, *www.mfa.gov.tr/grupf/percept/I1/per1-3.htm.*
Enginsoy, Umit and Bekdil, Ege, 'Turkey, Israel Move Closer to Popeye 2 Accord', *Defense News*, 9 August 1999.
Enginsoy, Umit, 'Greek Conflict Fuels Turkish Navy Upgrades', *Defense News*, 5–11 February 1996, p.4.
Evriviades, Marios. L., 'Turkey's Role in United States Strategy', *Mediterranean Quarterly*, 9, 2 (1998) pp.30–51.
Eyal, J., *Europe and Yugoslavia: Lessons from a Failure* (London: Whitehall Papers, RUSI, 1993).
Forsythe, Rosemarie, 'The Politics of Oil and the Caucasus and Central Asia', *Adelphi Paper*, 300, International Institute of Strategic Studies (1996).

Frey, Frederick, 'The Army in Turkish Politics', *Land Reborn* (1966) pp.7–8.

Fuente, Pedro, 'Confidence-Building Measures in the Southern Cone: A Model for Regional Stability', *Naval War College Review* (winter, 1997) *www.nwc.navy.mil/press/review/1997/winter.*

— 'FYROM Coalition Partners Back Closer Relations with Greece', *Athens News Agency*, Interview, 22-10-98, *zeus.hri.org/news/greek/ana/1998/98-10-22.ana.html.*

Gabelnick, Tamar, 'In Focus: Turkey: Arms and Human Rights', *Foreign Policy in Focus*, 4, 16 (May, 1999).

Gleditsch, Nils Petter, 'Democracy and Peace', *Journal Of Peace Research*, 29, 4 (1992).

Goetz, Roland, 'Political Spheres of Interest in the Southern Caucasus and in Central Asia', *Aussenpolitik*, 48, 3 (1997) p.263.

— 'Going Wolfish', *The Economist*, 12 June 1999, p.55.

— 'Gov't Opts for "Patriot" Long Range Missiles, French and Russian Short-Range Systems', *Athens News Agency*, 10-10-98, *zeus.hri.org/news/greek/ana/1998/98-10-10.ana.html.*

— 'Greece: Rocky Start', *The Economist*, 22 June 1996, 339, p.50.

— 'Greece and Albania Bury Hatchet', *Financial Times*, 31 March 1996.

— 'Greece–EMU Bound Despite Rise in Inflation', *Reuters Agency*, 12 November 1999.

— Greek Premier's speech to Parliament, *Journal of Parliamentary Debates*, Period D, Session B, 23 January 1987, p.2912.

Gresh, Alian, 'Turkish–Israeli–Syrian Relations and their Impacts on the Middle East', *The Middle East Journal*, 52, 2 (1998) pp.189–90.

Gruen, G., 'Ambivalence in the Alliance: U.S. Interests in the Middle East and the Evolution of Turkish Foreign Policy', *Orbis*, 24, 2 (1980).

Guerdilek, R., 'View From Ankara', *NATO Sixteen Nations*, 38, 5/6 (1993) p.14.

Gunter, Michael, Interview with Ocalan, *Middle East Quarterly* 5, 2 (1998) pp.79–85.

Guttman, R.J., 'Greek Foreign Policy', *Europe*, Commission of the European Communities (October, 1997).

Haas, E.B., 'The Study of Regional Integration: Reflections on the Joy and Anguish of Pretheorizing', *International Organisation*, 24, 4 (1970).

Haas, R., 'Alliance Problems in the Eastern Mediterranean – Greece, Turkey and Cyprus', *Adelphi Paper*, 231 (1988).

Haftendon, H., 'The Security Puzzle: Theory-Building and Discipline-Building in International Security', *International Studies Quarterly*, 35, 1 (1991) pp.3–17.

Hamann, Kerstin and Sgouraki-Kinsey, Barbara, 'Re-entering Electoral Politics: Reputation and Party System Change in Spain and Greece', *Party Politics*, 5, 1 (1999) pp.55–77.

Hami, K., 'The Past, Present and Future of Turkish Industry', *Turkish Review*, 3, 15 (1997).

Harris, George, 'The Causes of the 1960 Revolution in Turkey', *Middle East Journal*, 24 (1970).

Harris, George, 'The View from Ankara', *The Wilson Quarterly*, 6, 5 (Special Issue), (1982) p.132.

Henderson, C.W., 'Conditions Affecting the Use of Political Repression', *Journal of Conflict Resolution*, 35, 1 (March, 1991) pp.120–42.

Henze, Paul, 'Russia & the Caucasus', *Studies in Conflict and Terrorism*, 19, 4 (1996).

Heper, Metin and Keyman, E. Fuat, 'Double-Faced State: Political Patronage and the Consolidation of Democracy in Turkey', *Middle Eastern Studies*, 34, 4 (1998) pp.259–76.

Herman, Margaret and Kegley, Charles, 'Rethinking Democracy and International Peace: Perspectives form Political Psychology', *International Studies Quarterly*, 39, 4 (1995).

Hickok, M.R., 'The Imia/Kardak Affair, 1995–96: A Case Of Inadvertent Conflict', *European Security*, 7, 4 (1998) pp.118–36.

Hill, Fiona, 'Pipeline Politics, Russo-Turkish Competition & Geopolitics in the Eastern Mediterranean', *Cyprus Review*, 8 (1996) p.98.

Hillery, G.A., 'Definitions of Community: Areas of Agreement', *Rural Sociology*, 20 (1995).

Hope, Kerin, 'Oil Pipeline Boost for Balkans', *Financial Times*, 30 September 1994, p.5.

Howe, Jonathan T., 'Link or Barrier – Defense of the Mediterranean', *NATO's Sixteen Nations* (April, 1990).

Huntington, Samuel, 'The Clash of Civilisations', *Foreign Affairs*, 72, 3 (1993) pp.22–49.

Iordanides, C., 'Greece and European Security', *Kathimerini*, 13 November 1991.

Isaacson, W., 'Wow the World Works', *Time*, 11 April 1994, p.80.

Ismet, Ismet G., 'Wiping out the PKK Again … Again,' *Turkish Probe*, 6 July 1993, pp.4–7.

— 'In The Name of The Father', *Economist*, 1 August 1998, p.75.

Jones, Tim, 'The British Army, and Counter-Guerrilla Warfare in Greece, 1945–1949', *Small Wars & Insurgencies*, 8, 1 (1997) pp.88–106.

Kaizer, Karl, 'Reforming NATO', *Foreign Policy*, 103 (1996) pp.129–43.

Kalandarov, K., 'No Kaspi stolknulis' interesty mirovykh derzhav – Zapad stremitsa vytesnit' Rossiyu iz etogo regiona [There is a Clash of Interests of the World Powers – The West is trying to put Russia out of the Region]', *Nezavisimaya Gazeta*, 110 (1426), 4 June 1997, p.5.

Kamm, Henry, 'For Greeks, it is More Than a Name', *The New York Times*, 23 April 1993.

Karabelias, G., 'Twenty Years of Civil–Military Relations in Post-dictatorship Greece, 1975–95: Step Toward the Consolidation of Democracy', *Mediterranean Quarterly*, 10, 2 (1999).

Karakatsanis, Neovi, 'Do Attitudes Matter? Military and Democratic Consolidation in Greece', *Balkan Forum*, 5 (June, 1997).

Karakatsanis, Neovi, 'Do Attitudes Matter? The Military and Democratic Consolidation in Greece', *Armed Forces & Society*, 24, Part 2 (1997).

Karapasan, Omer, 'Turkey's Armaments Industries', *Middle East Report*, 144 (Jan–Feb, 1987) pp.29–30.

Karpat, Kemal, 'The Military and Politics in Turkey 1960–64: A Socio-Cultural Analysis of a Revolution', *American Historical Review*, 75 (1970).

Kazamias, Andreas, 'The Quest for Modernization in Greek Foreign Policy and its Limitations', *Mediterranean Politics*, 2, 2 (1997).

Kili, S., 'Kemalism in Contemporary Turkey', *International Political Science Review*, 1 (1980) pp.387–92.

Kioukas, Dimitris, 'Interest Representation and Modernisation Policies in Greece: Lessons Learned from the Study of Labor and Farmers', *Journal of Modern Greek Studies*, 15, 2 (1997) pp.303–24.

Kivrikoglou, H., 'Peace in the Nation, Peace in the World', *Military Technology*, 9 (1999) pp.9–24.

Klaiber, K-P, 'The Membership Action Plan: Keeping NATO's Door Open', *NATO Review*, 2 (summer, 1999) pp.23–5.

— 'Knights in Shining Armour, A Survey of NATO', *The Economist*, 24 April 1999, p.4.

Koker, Levent, 'Local Politics and Democracy in Turkey: An Appraisal', *The Annals of the American Academy of Political And Social Science*, 540 (July, 1995).

Kollias, Costas, 'The Greek–Turkish Conflict and Greek Military Expenditure 1960-92', *Journal of Peace Research*, 33, 2 (1996).

Kourvetaris, G., 'Survey Essay on the Cyprus Question', *Journal of Political and Military Sociology* (1976).

Kourvetaris, G., 'Attilas 1974: Human, Economic and Political Consequences of the Turkish Invasion of Cyprus', *Journal of the Hellenic Diaspora* (1977).

Kranidiotis, Yannos, 'Greece and Co-operation Among South-East European Developments', *Thesis: A Journal of Foreign Policy Issues*, 1, 3 (1997).

Lagaras, E., 'Sea Control of the Eastern Mediterranean: The Role of the Greek Islands', *NATO Sixteen Nations*, 1 (1992).

Lebow, R.N., 'The Long Peace, the End of the Cold War, and the Future of Realism', *International Organisation*, 48, 2 (1994).

Lemnitzer, L., 'The Strategic Problems of NATO's Northern and Southern Flanks', *Orbis*, XIII, 1 (1969), pp.101–6.

Lewis, Bernard, 'Why Turkey is the Only Muslim Democracy', *Middle Eastern Quarterly*, 1, 1 (1994) pp.41–9.

Liland, Frode, 'Keeping NATO Out of Trouble: NATO's Non-Policy on Out-Of-Area Issue during the Cold War', *Forsvarsstudier* (4/1999), pp.36–9.

Lochery, N., 'Israel & Turkey: Deepening Ties & Strategic Implications 1995–98', *Israel Affairs*, 5, 1 (1998), pp.45–62.

Lopez, T., 'AFSOUTH – Focus on the Southern Europe', *NATO Sixteen Nations*, 1 (1997) p.57.

Loyd, John, 'Moscow Claims Caspian Energy Deals Veto', *Financial Times*, 9 November 1994, p.3.

Loyd, John and LeVine Steve, 'Russia Demands Veto Over Caspian Oil Deals', *Financial Times*, 31 May 1994, p.2.

MacDonald, Ronald, 'Alliance Problems in the Eastern Mediterranean – Greece, Turkey and Cyprus': Part II, *Adelphi Paper* 229 (1988).

MacMillan, John, 'Democracies don't Fight: A Case of the Wrong Agenda', *Review of International Studies*, 22, 3 (1996), pp.278–9.

Maechling, Charles Jr., 'The Aegean Sea: A Crisis Waiting to Happen', *Naval Institute Proceedings* (March, 1997).

Malaj, A. and Goga, H., 'How and Why Albania Touched Chaos', *Balkan Review*, Balkan Press Centre, Thessaloniki (1997) pp.63–70.

Mango, Andrew, 'The Turkish Model', *Middle Eastern Studies*, XXIX, 4 (October, 1993) p.726.

Maoz, Ze'ev and Abdolali Nasrin, 'Regime and International Conflict 1816–1976', *Journal of Conflict Resolution*, 33, 1 (1991), pp.3–35.

Marakis, Nikos, 'I Allages sta Balkania', *To Vima*, 31 October 1999.

Mardin, S., 'Power, Civil Society and Culture in the Ottoman Empire', *Comparative Studies in Society and History*, 12 (1969).

Markovsky, Alan, 'Turkey's Nationalist Moment', *Policywatch*, 384, 20 April 1999.

— 'Mea Culpa Kai Therma Logia', *To Vima*, 21 November 1999.

Melvin, Small and Stinger, J.D., 'The War-Proneness of Democratic Regimes, 1816–1965', *Jerusalem Journal Of International Relations*, 1 (Summer, 1976), pp.50–69.

Metin, Heper, 'Consolidating Turkish Democracy', *Journal Of Democracy*, 3, 2 (1992) pp.105–17.

Moustakis, Fotios, 'Turkey's Entry into the EU: Asset or Liability', *Contemporary Review*, 273, 1592 (September, 1998) pp.128–35.

Moustakis, Fotios, 'Conflict in the Aegean', *Contemporary Review*, 274, 1596 (1999) pp.5–12.

Moustakis, Fotios and Sheehan, Michael, 'Greek Security Policy after the Cold War' *Contemporary Security Policy*, 21, 3 (2000) pp.95–115.

Moustakis, Fotios and Sheehan, Michael, 'Democratic Peace and the European Security Community: The Paradox of Greece and Turkey', *Mediterranean Quarterly*, 13, 1 (2002) pp.69–85.

— 'Moving Towards NATO & the EU', *Military Technology*, 22, 5 (1999) p.55.

Nachmani, Amikam, 'The Remarkable Turkish–Israeli Tie', *Middle East Quarterly*, 5, 2 (1998) pp.19–29.

— 'Nation and Tribe the Winners', *The Economist*, 24 April 1999, p.57.

Naumann, K., 'NATO's New Military Command Structure', *NATO Review*, 46, 1 (1998) pp.10–14.

Newman, Barry, 'Oil, Water and Politics Make a Volatile Mix in Crowded Bosporus', *Wall Street Journal*, 24 August 1994, p.1.

Nimetz, Matthew, 'Mediterranean Security After the Cold War', *Mediterranean Quarterly*, 8, 2 (1997).

Noam, Chomsky, 'The Current Bombings: Behind the Rhetoric', *www.ibbs.org/current_bombings.htm*, p.3 (April, 1999).

— 'Not Really their Business at All', *Current Affairs*, (1992) pp.9–11.

Nye, J.S. and Lynn-Jones, S.M., 'International Security Studies', *International Security*, 12, 4 (1988) pp.5–27.

'Ocalan and the Taboo', *The Guardian*, 23 June 1999.

— 'Oil Pipeline Deal Bypasses Russia', *The Independent*, 18 November 1999.

Olgun, E., 'Cyprus: A New and Realistic Approach', *Perceptions: Journal of International Relations*, IV, 3 (1999), *www.mfa.gov.tr/grupa/percept/IV-3/olgun.htm*.

Olson, R., 'The Kurdish Question Four Years On: The Policies of Turkey, Syria, Iran and Iraq', *Middle East Policy*, 3, 3 (1994) pp.36–44.

Olson, R., 'The Kurdish Question and Geopolitic and Geostrategic Changes in the Middle East after the Gulf War', *Journal of South Asian and Middle Eastern Studies*, XVII, 4 (1994) pp.49–67.

Olson, R., 'The Kurdish Question & Chechnya; Turkey versus Russia since the Gulf War', *Middle East Policy*, 4, 3 (1996) pp.106–18.

Onis, Ziya, 'Turkey in the Post-Cold War Era: In Search of Identity', *Middle East Journal*, 49, Part 1 (1995).

Owen, John, 'How Liberalism Produces Democratic Peace', *International Security*, 19 (fall, 1994) pp.87–125.

Ozbudum, Ergun, 'Turkey: How Far from Consolidation', *Journal of Democracy*, 7, 3 (1996) pp.123–38.

Palmer, J. and Whitley, A.G., 'The Balance of Forces in Southern Europe: Between Uncertainty and Opportunity', *The International Spectator*, XXIII, 1 (1988).

Pangalos, Theodoros, 'Basic Principles of Greek Foreign Policy', *Thesis* (spring, 1997), *www.hri.org/MFA/thesis/spring97/principles.html*.

Pangalos, Theodoros, 'Principles of Greek Foreign Policy', *Mediterranean Quarterly*, 9, 2 (1998).

Papandreou, George, 'Greece and the Day After in the Balkans', *Thesis: A Journal of Foreign Policy Issues* (spring, 1990) *www.mfa.gr/thesis/spring99/dayafter.html*, p.2.

Papantoniou, Yannos, 'The World Economy and Greece: Recent Economic Developments', *Thesis*, 1, 3 (1997).

Petralia, Fanni Palli, 'Greek Foreign Policy: Facing New Problems', *Mediterranean Quarterly*, 9, 4 (1998).

Pettifer, James, 'Albania's Way Out of The Shadows', *The World Today*, (April, 1991), Royal Institute of International Affairs, London, pp.55–7.

— 'Points to EMU accession as Key for Greece's Stability', *Athens News Agency*, 15-10-98, *www.zeus.hri.org/news/greek/ana/1998/98-10-15.ana.html*.

Poulton, Hugh, 'The Struggle for Hegemony in Turkey: Turkish Nationalism as a Contemporary Force', *Journal of Southern Europe and the Balkans*, 1, 1 (1999) pp.15–19.

Robins, Philip, 'The Overlord State: Turkish Policy and the Kurdish Issue', *International Affairs*, 69, 4 (1993) pp.657–71.

Rohle, Michael, 'Taking Another Look at NATO's Role in European Security', *NATO Review*, 46, 4 (1998) pp.20–3.

Roos, John, 'Allies: Misstep by Greece or Turkey Could Trigger War over Cyprus', *Armed Forces Journal International* (1997) p.44.

Rummel, R.J., 'Libertarianism and International Violence', *Journal of Conflict Resolution*, 27, 1 (1983) pp.27–71.

Rupert, James, 'Dateline Tashkent: Post-Soviet Central Asia', *Foreign Policy* (1992) p.172.

Russett, Layne, Spiro and Doyle, 'Correspondence: The Democratic Peace', *International Security*, 19, 4 (1995) pp.164–84.

Sanguineti, Vittorio, 'Turkey and the European Union: Dreaming West but Moving East', *Mediterranean Quarterly*, 8, 1 (1997) pp.11–26.

Santis, Nicola de, 'The Future of NATO's Mediterranean Initiative', *NATO Review*, 1 (1998) p.32.

Sariibrahimoglu, L., 'Arming for Peace', *Jane's Defence Weekly – International Edition*, 30, Part 7, 19 August 1998, p.26.

Sarno, Niccolo, 'Rights-Europe: Ocalan's Sentence Drives Turkey away from EU', *World News, Internet Press Service*, 30 June 1999, *www.oneworld.org.*

Sazanidis, C., 'The Greco-Turkish Dispute Over the Aegean Airspace', *Hellenic Review of International Relations* (1980).

Schake, Kori, 'NATO Chronicle: New World Disorder', *Joint Force Quarterly* (spring, 1999).

Schmmitt, M.N., 'The Greek–Turkish Dispute', *Naval War College Review*, XLIX, 3 (1996).

Schweller, R.L.,' Domestic Structure and Preventive War. Are Democracies More Pacific', *World Politics*, 44, 2 (1992) pp.235–69.

Sergeyev, I., 'We Are Not Adversaries, We Are Partners', *NATO Review*, 46, 1 (1998).

Sezer, D.B., 'Turkey's Security Policies', *Adelphi Paper*, 164 (spring, 1981).

Simitis, Kostas, 'Greece in the Emerging System of International Relations', *Review of International Affairs*, Belgrade, 15 August 1996.

Soguk, Nevsat, 'A Study of the Historico-Cultural Reasons for Turkey's Inconclusive Democracy', *New Political Science*, 26 (1993) pp.89–116.

Solana, Javier, 'NATO – A Reliable Alliance for Dynamism and Leadership', *NATO's Sixteen Nations*, 42, 1 (1997) pp.7–10.

Solana, Javier, 'The Washington Summit: NATO Steps Boldly into the 21st Century', *NATO Review*, 47, 1 (1998) pp.3–6.

— 'Special Issue on the Future of NATO', *Journal of Strategic Studies*, 17 (1994).

Sorenson, D.S. 'National Security and Political Succession in Syria', *Mediterranean Quarterly*, 9, 2 (1998) pp.69–92.

Speight, John, 'CFE 1990: Achievements and Prospects', *Faraday Discussion Paper*, 15 (1990).

Stagas, H.N., 'The Hellenic Navy's Role in Mediterranean Security', *NATO's Sixteen Nations*, 1 (1994) pp.32–4.

Starr, Harvey, 'Democracy and War: Choice, Learning and Security Communities', *Journal Of Peace Research*, 29, 2 (1992).

Starr, Harvey, 'Democracy and Integration: Why Democracies Don't Fight Each Other', *Journal Of Peace Research*, 34, 2 (1997).

Stathakis, George M., 'Approaches to the Early Post-War Greek Economy: A Survey', *Journal of Modern Hellenism*, 7, 2 (1999).

Stephen, Michael, 'Cyprus and the Rule of Law', *Perceptions: Journal of International Relations*, IV, 3 (1999) *www.mfa.gov.tr/grpa/percept/IV-3/stephen.htm.*

Storey, David, 'US Still Unhappy Over Greek Security Efforts', *Reuters Agency*, 10 November 1999.

—'The Chill Descending on Turkey', *The Economist*, 24 January 1998, pp.51–2.

—'The Future of NATO: A New Kind of Alliance', *The Economist*, 1 June 1996, pp.21–3.

—The Kurds: An Ancient Tragedy, *The Economist*, 20 February 1999, p.58.

—'The New Geopolitics', *Economist*, 31 July 1999, p.10.

—'The Reception of Foreign Law in Turkey', *International Social Science Bulletin*, 9, 1 (1957) pp.7–81.

— 'They Can Kill Kurds But Can't Run Soup Kitchens', *The Independent*, 24 August 1999.

Tinaz, J., 'Maritime Security in a New Environment: The Role of the Turkish Navy', *NATO's Sixteen Nations*, 1 (1992) pp.65–8.

Tirman, John, *Understanding Turkish Nationalism and its Contribution to the War against the Kurds* (January, 1998) p.1, *www.wf.org/turknational.htm*.

Triantaphyllou, Dimitirs, 'The Greek Approach to the Balkans', *The South-east Yearbook 1997–98*, Hellenic Foundation For European and Foreign Policy, Athens (1998).

Tsakalotos, Euclid, 'The Political Economy of Social Democratic Economic Policies: The PASOK Experiment in Greece', *Oxford Review of Economic Policy*, 14, 1 (1998) pp.129–30.

Tuck, Christopher, 'Greece, Turkey and Arms Control', *Defence Analysis*, 12, 1 (1996) pp.23–32.

— 'Turkey Seeks US-Style Legislation to Stop Russian Tankers in Straits', *Turkish Daily News*, 23-05-96, *www.gri.org/news/agencies/trkn/96-05-23.trkn.html*.

Ullman, R., 'Redefining Security', *International Security*, 8, 1 (1983) pp.129–53.

Veremis, Thanos, 'Greek Security: Issues and Politics', *Adelphi Paper*, 179 (1982).

Veremis, Thanos, 'Greece and NATO', *Yearbook 1988*, The Hellenic Foundation for Defence and Foreign policy, Athens (1989).

Veremis, Thanos, 'The Ongoing Aegean Crisis', *Thesis* (spring, 1997), *www.zeus.hri.org/MGA/thesis/spring 97*.

— 'View from Athens', *NATO's Fifteen Nations* (February–March 1980).

Vorohkov, Lev, 'The Challenges of NATO Enlargement', *Balkan Forum*, 2, 5 (1997) pp.5–39.

Wallerstein, I, 'The Concept of National Development, 1917–1989: Elegy and Requiem', *American Behavioural Scientist*, 35, 3-4 (1992) pp.517–29.

Walt, S.M., 'The Renaissance of Security Studies', *International Studies Quarterly*, 35, 2 (1991) pp.211–39.

Wanterbury, J., 'Export-Led Growth and the Center-Right Coalition in Turkey', *Comparative Politics*, (January, 1992) pp.127–42.

Whetten, Lawrence L., 'Turkey's Role in the Atlantic Alliance', *Atlantic Quarterly*, (autumn, 1984) p.262.

— 'Who Runs Your Country: Greece', *The Economist*, 28 September 1996, p.60.

Wilson, Andrew, 'The Aegean Dispute', *Adelphi Paper*, 155 (1980).

Windsor, Philip, 'NATO and the Cyprus Crisis', *Adelphi Paper*, 14 (1964).

'Yilmaz-Denktash-Occupied Areas', *Cyprus News Agency*, 03-11-98, *www.zeus.hri.org/news/cyprus/cna/1998/98-11-03.cna.html*.

Yitznak, Klein, 'A Theory of Strategic Culture', *Comparative Strategy*, 10, 1 (1991).

Zamfireskou, Elena, 'NATO and the Balkans', *Perceptions: A Journal of International Affairs*, IV, 1 (March–May, 1999) *www.mfa.gov.tr*.

Zelikow, Philip, 'The Masque of Institutions', *Survival*, 38, 1 (1996) pp.6–18.

NEWSPAPER/INTERNET SOURCES

Agence France-Presse, 10 June 1999.
Aksam, 6 October 1999.
Amyntiki Biblos (Defence Bible) 1998–1999, pp.25–7.
Amyntiki Biblos (Defence Bible) 2002–2003.
Anadolu Agency, 20-05-99.
Armed Forces Journal, October 1998.
Associated Press, 7 August 1999, 4 September 1999.
Athens New Agency, 24-11-98 and 3-01-99, *www.zeus.hri.org/news/greek/apeen/*
    1998/98-11-24.apeen.html and *www.zeus.hri.org/news/greek/apeen/1999/*
    99-01-13.apeen.html.
Athens News Agency, 11 July 1997.
Athens News Agency, 3 December 1997.
Athens News Agency, 12 May 1998.
Athens News Agency, 28 October 1999.
Athens News Agency, 6 October 1999.
Athens News Agency, 28 October 1999.
Athens News Agency, 11 November 1999, *www.zeus.hri.org/news/greek ana/*
    1999/99-11-09.ana.html.
Avgi, Newspaper, 21 September 1999.
BBC Cold War Documents Series, Episode 1 (1999).
BBC News, 23 July 1999.
Cosmos, 1, 6 (February–March 1996), IDIS, Athens.
Cumhuriet, 19 January 1989.
Daily Telegraph, 19 July 1999.
Defence Systems Daily News, 15 February 1999, 30 April 1999 and 3 May 1999.
— *Discovery Turkey, BBC World Service*, 1995.
Elefherotypia, 2 March 1983.
Eleftherotypia, 27 March 1999.
Elefterotypia, 27 September 1999.
Eleftherotypia, 11 October 1999.
Eurofighter Typhoon News, 15 February 1999, 3 May 1999, 30 April 1999.
European, 11 April 1996.
— *www.usembassy.org.uk/nato85.html.*
— *www.burn.ucsd.edu/archives.*
— *www.hri.org/docs/fyrom/95-27866.html.*
— *www.enet.gr/on-line/politika.htm, 21-04-98.*
— *www.nato.int/docu/comm/49-95/c911107a.htm.*
— *www.zeus.hri.org/MFA/foreign/bilateral/aegeen.htm.*
— *www.cthesis.com, 23 August 1999.*
— *www.library.cornell.edu/collde/mideast/kurd.htm.*
— *www.osceprag.cz.*
— *www.seas/gwu.edu/student/stratos/hol/crisis1.html.*
— *www.ssm.gov.tr.*
— *www.zeus.hri.org/news/greek/ana/1999/99-05-10.ana.html.*
Hurriyet, 28 September 1999.

Jane's Defence Weekly, Interview, 30, 2, 15 July 1998, *www.janes.com/defence/ interviews/980715.html.*
Jane's International Defense Review, 32 (June 1999).
Jane's Defence Weekly – International Edition, 30, 7 (1998).
Kathimerini, 6 September 1999.
Kathimerini, 3 October 1999.
Macedonian Press Agency, 27 March 1999.
Military Technology, XXIII, 10 (1999) pp.23–49.
Milliyet, 5 April 1993.
— Morris, Chris, *BBC,* 6 September 1999.
NATO Review, May 1995/January 1996.
NATO Review, March 1996.
NATO Sixteen Nations, 1 (1992).
NATO Sixteen Nations, 1 (1997) pp.57, 58.
NATO Sixteen Nations, Special Issue (September, 1986), 31.
— *NATO's New Force Structures,* NATO Basic Fact Sheet, 5 (January, 1996) *www.nato.int/docu/facts/nnfs.htm.*
NATO's Sixteen Nations, Special Edition (1992), pp.14–24.
NATO's Sixteen Nations, Special Supplement (1998).
Newsline, 3, 83, 30 April 1999.
Open Media Research Institute, 2, 7, 18 February 1997.
Newsweek, European Edition, 9 May 1994.
Proini, Greek–American Newspaper, 21 October 1999.
Ptisi (Flight) (Athens, 1999) pp.119–78.
Radio Free Europe, *Newsline,* 3, 80, 27 April 1999.
Reuters Agency News, 10 September 1999.
Reuters News Agency, 4 October 1999.
Reuters Agency, 4 November 1999.
Reuters Agency, 21 November 1999.
— *Reuters Agency,* 18 November 1998, *www.diaspora-net.org/Turkey/ US_Frigates_to_Turkey.html.*
— *www.erols.com/mqmq/solana.htm.*
— *www.eliamep.gr*
Strategiki, Athens, 1999.
Stratigiki, September 1999.
Sunday Times, 29 August 1999.
Ta Nea, 27 March 1999.
Ta Nea, main article, 26 October 1999.
The Turkish Press, 1925–31, Athens, 1931.
The Economist, 22 June 1996.
The Economist, 28 September 1996.
The Economist, 7 February 1998, p.56.
The Economist, 1 August 1998, pp.45–6.
The Economist, 20 February 1999, p.57.
The Economist, 'A Survey of the New Geopolitics', 31 July 1999.
The Economist, 31 July 1999, p.13.
The Economist, 7 August 1999, p.46.
The Economist, 14 August 1999, p.41.

The Economist, 28 August 1999, pp.39–40.
The Economist, 23 October 1999, pp.65–6.
The Economist, 20 July 2002.
The Economist, 10 August 2002, pp.35–6.
The Economist Intelligence Unit, Country Reports, Greece 2000, Greece 2001.
The Financial Times, 21 February 1992.
The Guardian, 10 January 1992.
The Guardian, 16 November 1999, p.16.
The Observer, 26 March 1995.
The Times 8 April 1994.
To Vima, 1 March 1975.
To Vima, 6 July, 30 March 1997, 13 April 1997.
To Vima, Anaptixi, 22 August 1999, 14 August 1999.
To Vima, 29 August, 5 September 1999, 3 October 1999, 10 October 1999, 14 October 1999, 24 October 1999, 21 November 1999.
To Vima, 26 September 1999.
Turkish Daily News, 5 and 31 March 1993.
Turkish Daily News, 24 March 1994.
Turkish Daily News, 14 March 1995, 10 June 1995.
Turkish Daily News, 11 May 1997.
Turkish Daily News, 28 October 1998.
Turkish Daily News, Comment, 20 August 1999.
Turkish Daily News, 5 October 1999.
Turkish Daily News, 14 October 1999.
Turkish Daily News, 27 October 1999.
Turkish Daily News, 18 November 1999.
Turkish Official Gazzette, 177708, 29 May 1982.
Turkish Press Review, 10 September 1999, p.9.
Turkiye, 7 October 1999.
Washington Post, 21 July 1974, p. A6.
Washington Post, 16 October 1982 and 1 November 1982.
Weekly Defense Monitor News, 3, 24, 24 June 1999.
— *Weekly Defense Monitor*, 3, 24, 24 June 1999, *www.cdi.org/weekly/1999/issue24.html*.
Western Policy Center, 5 February 1998.
Western Policy Center, 15 September 1999.
Yeni Yuzul, Turkish newspaper, 17 October 1995.

INTERVIEWS

Channel 4, Main News, 31 July 1996.
Interview of Greek Foreign Minister T. Pangalos, Athens, 21-01-98, *www.hri.org/MFA/foreign/bilateral/aegeen.htm*.
Interview with N. Chomsky, in WBUR Boston's NPR News Station, 12 April 1999.
Interview with P. Simic, Corfu (1997).

Interview with Turkish National Defence Minister, Hikmet Sami Turk, *Jane's Defence Weekly*, 14 April 1999.

Milliyet Interviews PKK Leader Ocalan, Part II, *Foreign Broadcast Information Service – West Europe*, 27 March 1992.

Index